Wired to th

BEST WISHES
TO
JOHN GILLESPIE 2006.

i

WINTER GARDENS

Phone 8 MORECAMBE Car Park

 TWICE NIGHTLY 8-30
6-0 FOR A SEASON

FRANK RANDLE PRODUCTIONS *present*

The Personal Appearance of the Famous
Stage, Screen, Radio & Television
Star Comedian

FRANK RANDLE

in his Spectacular Summer Season Show

"RANDLE'S SUMMER SCANDALS"

HAL **SWAIN**	JON **BODEN**	SONNY ★ ROY	KAY **SOTHERN**	JIMMY **CLITHEROE**
RITA **SHEARER**	FOUR **GRAHAM** BROS	DON CARLOS James Edgar Raymond Walter Bob Hulme, Ernie Dale	GUS **AUBREY**	IRENE **MANSEL**
KERRY PIPERS BAND AND DANCERS		A.J. POWELL with JOHNNY PETERS		Florence Whiteley's - 16 -
HAL MACK		THE SWING SISTERS THE DANCING DEMONS		ZIO ANGELS

ARTHUR CANNON	THE EXOTIC	STAN STAFFORD
WINNIE SILVER		FATIMA WAZZAN
KITTY PEMBERTON	**KARINA**	BOBBY COLLINS
DORIS POWELL		PAT WILLIAMS
BILLY DIXON WOOD	*with* VADIO & HERTZ	NINA RATHBONE

WAZZAN TUNISIANIS TROUPE

Wired to the Moon

❧

**Philip Martin Williams
& David L. Williams**

❧

History on Your Doorstep

Published in Great Britain in 2006
by History on Your Doorstep
15 Welbeck House
Welbeck Street South
Ashton-under-Lyne
Lancs. OL6 7TB
Tel: 0161 308 3013
email: historyonyourdoorstep@btinternet.com

ISBN 0 9518012 5 2

FIRST EDITION

Acknowledgements:

After writing this book the task of writing the acknowledgements should have been a fairly straight forward one. Unfortunately for us this was not to be the case as due to a computer malfunction many of our files were lost. Thankfully the main part of the book was backed-up but many names of people who had given any sort of help, information or photographs were gone. We have therefore had to search out letters, documents, note books, scraps of paper and wrack our brains to discover as many names as possible.

Many of those listed have also supplied photos and in using these we have tried to trace present copyright holders. Apologies are made in advance for any unintentional omission. We will be happy to insert an appropriate acknowledgement to companies or individuals in any subsequent editions of this book. Specific photographic acknowledgement is made to Popperfoto for use of the photograph on page 105, Garth Dawson (Accrington Hippodrome photo), Blakeley Films, and the BBC.

We know we will have failed to come up with everyone so please accept our apologies if you are not listed. You know who you are and we thank you all the same.

Mrs M. Dearman, Ronnè Coyles, Joe Lee, Sadie Corré, Leslie Oates, Mrs Doris Boden, Ms Diane Speakman, Gerry George, Geoffrey Lord, Brian Russell, Laura Beaumont, Brenda Burthom, Arthur Goulding, Winnie Flemming, Barry Band, Mike Craig, Bob Monkhouse, C. P. Lee, Mike Blakeley, Julio Morales Shearer, Mrs Helen Taylor, Arthur Cannon (jnr), Michael Pointon, Paul Sullivan. Peter Green – Bolton Hospital Saturday. Tony Sharkey – Blackpool Central Library, The British Library, Leeds Central Library, Sheffield Library, Bradford Library, Manchester Central Library, Tameside Local Studies Unit, Rochdale Library, Oldham Library, Accrington Library, Westminster Central Library, Colindale Newspaper Library. Special thanks to the late Jeff Nuttall for all his help, to Ryan M Williams who diligently read and re-read our manuscript and made corrections where necessary, to Jack Douglas for supplying the Foreword.

Foreword
by Jack Douglas

I think that after sixty years in showbusiness there are so many wonderful things that have happened to me and so many honours that come with the job. But one that is particularly close to my heart is writing the Foreword for this wonderful book on Frank Randle.

I was just a youth when I first met the great man. I was working for my father, Producer John D. Robertson, at the Blackpool office he shared with fellow producer Jack Taylor. It was through them that I really got to know him, I saw him perform many times and I learnt so much from him. He was so wise, so clever, a fine comedian and a brilliant character man and most of all a perfectionist at his job. It was amazing when he got into character to see how he transformed himself to actually become the character. Although I was only a trainee director back then, I remember Frank saying to me, 'you're going to be an actor one day'. Had he spotted something? It was years later and entirely a fluke how I became an actor. However, he had said to me, 'you're going to become an actor and when you do, remember one thing, always wear the cloths and shoes to suit the character'. Many years later when I was to play the part of a 70 years old man I thought, 'how can I get that walk'. Then the words Frank had spoken came back to me. I bought an old pair of shoes from a junk shop which, as he had recommended, were a half size too small. These gave me the very walk I was seeking. Everyone commented on my performance, but the praise belonged to Randle. I couldn't take the credit. Likewise, with my creation of Alf Ippititimus, it was the clothes that helped with the character – thanks Frank.

There have been many people who simply did not like Randle, on stage or off. Others seemed just to jump on the bandwagon in putting him down. However, there were just as many who believed that on stage he was the greatest of all character performers; even off stage they would not have a word said against Randle. I am proud to say that for many years Frank and I became great, great friends.

Although it must have been extremely difficult for them, the Williams' brothers with their book have tried to separate truth from fiction regarding the many aspects of Randle's life. As they point out, he was a deeply complex man whose life seemed overflowing with problems – some of course of his own making. No matter if you loved or despised Frank Randle you do have to admire his strength and courage and after reading this excellent account of his life and career you may have a different understanding of the man. Whatever your opinion, if you can reach one, you will agree that the book is a fascinating insight into a chapter of theatre sadly no longer with us. Frank Randle was a man who perfected his craft and made audiences laugh, not just 'oop north', in his part of the country, but throughout Britain. Oh how I wish we had him with us today – I'd be the first in the queue for a ticket.

Frank has of course left us happy memories and glimpses of his genius with his one gramophone recording and his knockabout films and now, thanks to Philip and David, we have this wonderful book. And 'It's a hot un', so thanks guys.

Jack Douglas, Isle of White, 2006

Introduction.

June 2007 will be the 50th anniversary of Frank Randle's death and to mark this occasion we present this book. Other significant tributes to the great comic will include the unveiling of a Blue Plaque in Randle's adoptive town of Blackpool and scene of his many triumphs and also a BBC radio repeat of Trevor Hoyle's play 'Randle's Scandals'.

Two of the major factors Frank Randle will be remembered for are first and rightly his 'Randle's Scandals' touring shows which became a phenomenon of the variety theatres for over ten years. Secondly his off stage antics which so often hit the headlines and unfortunately could also carry the tag 'Scandals'. On stage Randle wasn't a comedian in the sense of the stand-up variety he didn't tell jokes per se - the small collection in his repertoire were to last him his whole career. His act consisted mainly of sketches or routines in which he played differing character creations. Three of these characters were to become almost as famous as the man himself 'The Boatman', 'Grandpa' and his classic 'The Old Hiker'. Like other comedians he did have his catchphrases, which included 'Gerrof mi foot', I've supped some ale toneet' and 'She's a hot 'un' (the last being a Randle-ism for a young shapely female). So often it has been said that southern audiences didn't take to Randle like those 'up north'. While it may be true that he was more at home playing to Lancashire and Yorkshire audiences it is a fact that the southern working classes also lapped up his brand of humour – though it should be said that here he toned down his Lancashire accent. Randle also had a successful film career between 1940 and 1953 starring in ten low budget offerings mostly for the Mancunian Film Corporation. These cheap productions were by no means classics; however they all made money and were box office winners at many provincial cinemas often taking in more money than the Hollywood hits of the time.

Unfortunately Randle, who couldn't perform without a dressing room stocked with Guinness and an intake of sixty Woodbine cigarettes a day, was his own worst enemy and with his temper and excessive drinking often pressed his own self-destruct button. Here was a man who at the height of his career could go missing from his own show leaving his colleagues to explain to a wondering audience why there was no star performance and yet return the next day as if nothing had happened. His stooge or feed for sixteen years had been the drag artiste Gus Aubrey but dint of service didn't stop Randle sacking him on a regular basis – then taking him back almost as quickly. Not for nothing had Randle been dubbed the 'stormy petrel of showbusiness'. His distaste for people in authority were illuminated on many occasions including throwing food at mayoral portraits, verbally assaulting the police and destroying dressing rooms of pompous theatre managers. The comedian Jimmy James when arriving at Morecambe for a week's booking was informed that he would have to have the number two dressing room as Frank Randle had destroyed number one the previous week. Over the years he also amassed a quantity of firearms of varying descriptions and on occasions used them quite threateningly - he once chased Jimmy Clitheroe around a film studio swearing loudly and firing his pistol. Yet despite all this Frank Randle was a comedian who was adored and loved by the people. If Randle failed to turn up for a particular show his fans would simply get their money back and go see his next performance. What was it about the man that so endeared audiences to him? For the main part they identified with him. His audiences were in the main made up of the working classes, people who worked hard and enjoyed their simple pleasures, football and sport, beer and cigarettes. These were people with no pretensions, if something annoyed them they swore, if beer gave them wind they belched. Other bodily functions weren't hidden either in fact couldn't be hidden as most had to share communal lavatories. This was their world and was the world inhabited by Randle's characters. Who else could stand on stage take out his false teeth and throw them into the audience or while drinking real beer continually belch with a loud 'boyee'. *"I think I'll have a sup - aye. All slops... aye, aye...boyee... he hee... By gum you'll have t'excuse me-oyee. It's sharp stuff is this ale I'll tell you. It's all legs and arms there's no body... boyerp... body in it you know. I said t' landlord o't pub when I got this... I said, 'it's a bit thin mister'. Aye he said, 'you'd be thin if you'd come up same pipes as this ale has'. Aye... 'He said, 'I'll bet you've never tasted owt better'. I said, 'No. but I've paddled about in it'...boyee.* Those who criticised him artistically thought him to be extremely rude, crude or downright filthy. He himself said, *"I'm after belly laughs, I'm vulgar but not filthy. "It's just honest to goodness vulgarity. We've all burped after a bottle of beer".* Much of Randle's humour was based on him playing a drunkard, a lecher, an aggressive character of unruly behaviour or more often than not all of these rolled into one. *"Hey there's a young tart bathing in the river theer... I was just goo-in past... she was doing the breast stroke. I said na then theer... she looked up at me an she sez... he hee... she sez 'how owd are you?' I sez I'm 82 blast it... he hee aye... she sez 'well come in'... I sez get away I'll stab you with my pickle tooth... he hee".* To some people, fans and colleagues, Randle was more than a first rate comedian he was a man who was kind hearted, generous, charitable and a thoroughly well-mannered gentleman. To others he was devious, aggressive, foulmouthed, drunken or quite plainly mad. Certainly his life was at times troubled and he seemed to have been a man burdened with many inner complexities. In writing this book almost fifty years after his death it has been extremely difficult to discover what made the man tick – Indeed even during his lifetime it appears that no one truly got to know him. Perhaps he was so complicated that he didn't even really know himself. Nonetheless we hope the following chapters will give more of an insight into the life of undoubtedly one of Britain's greatest ever character comedians.

Chapter One:

Wigan Pier to Blackpool Pier.

The industrial Lancashire township of Aspull in the parish of Wigan was in 1901, like most of the country, mourning the death of Queen Victoria who died on January 22nd. Amidst the cotton mills and coalmines Aspull's 8,000 residents lived mostly in overcrowded, simple terraced housing. In one such cramped household, eight days after the passing of the Queen, a family anxiously awaited the delivery of a new born child. On January 30th at her family home at 50 Wigan Road, New Springs, Aspull, 21-year-old Rhoda Hughes gave birth to an illegitimate son, whom she named Arthur after her own father.

Fifty-eight-year-old Arthur Hughes, a hardworking moulder at the local iron works, had since the death of his wife, seen to the upbringing of his youngest daughters. They were 11-year-old Elizabeth who was still receiving her education and 14-year-old Sarah, who, having left school the previous year, was now working as a cotton weaver. There were other providers in the household as Arthur Hughes had fathered three other daughters; 17-year-old Norah and 19-year-old Janette were both also toiling at local cotton mills, while Florrie the eldest had already left home.

The unmarried Rhoda, prior to her pregnancy, had been employed as a domestic servant working as a housekeeper. Today there is no disgrace in illegitimacy, indeed with the use of more suitable terms like 'unmarried mother' or 'one parent family', the modern mother and baby are readily accepted without embarrassment into the community. However, at the beginning of the 20th century illegitimacy was still a severe burden which could bring shame on a household. With a newborn baby and no father on the scene, Rhoda and her family were no doubt suffering the familiar stigma and may well have been a prime target for the gossip mongers. With her youngest sister at school and the rest of the family in work it was obvious to Rhoda that she would have to look at means of supporting herself and her child. Seen as the most suitable solution, Rhoda placed the infant Arthur in the care of her older married sister Florence and her husband Thomas, who lived at 13 Cale Lane, Aspull. Florence, or Florrie as she was known, also had a young infant, a two year old daughter whom she had named Rhoda after her sister.

Florrie and Thomas relieved some of the pressure from the family by taking in Arthur while his mother left the area in search of work. Rhoda did eventually find suitable employment and accommodation in Blackpool, but it was decided that despite this, Arthur was to remain living with his Aunt - though Rhoda visited whenever possible. However, by the time young Arthur was of an age to start his schooling, Florrie could no longer look after the lad and a more permanent home had to be found. Consequently, Rhoda took him to live with a family named Heath who resided at 6 New Square, Wigan.

Annie and Thomas Heath had just the one child of their own, a girl named Lily who was eleven years Arthur's senior. The Heath's home was just a brief walk from St. George's School, which Arthur would shortly be attending and only a stone's throw from where George Formby lived. In 1936 when George Formby and Frank Randle appeared together in a Blackpool show, Randle wrote that he and Formby were boyhood friends. However, a number of discrepancies within the article throw this statement into doubt and also by the age of seven, George had been sent away from Wigan to train as a jockey.

A two-year-old Arthur

The time spent growing up within the bosom of the Heath family home was not an unhappy experience for Arthur and throughout his childhood days Annie Heath was in most respects his 'mother' and always had his welfare at heart. 'Mamma Heath' as he called her was a caring and loving person and one who had an anxious time when, whilst only six years old, Arthur needed nursing through pneumonia. Outside the confines of the home though, things were quite different. Any illegitimate child at this time was looked upon by many as being less than worthless, without any equals. Arthur too, quickly learned this truth, through phrases such as 'dirty little bastard', which were often harshly thrown his way. While living with the Heath's and in an attempt to avoid embarrassment, Arthur Hughes became Arthur Heath but there were those that knew this was a fabrication. This in all probability would have played on the young lad's mind, and to have thoughts of being 'inferior' and 'dirty', together with not knowing who your father was or even his name; and not even being allowed to use your own name, must surely have left lasting scars. Of course, all this was coupled with the fact that he saw his mother only infrequently. So it was that the stigma of illegitimacy was implemented in the young

2

boy's mind and it was sadly, something he never seemed to overcome even in to his adulthood. Indeed, much of the later Randle temperament can be put down to his troubled mind on the subject. While living with the Heath's his Aunts and real Grandfather were all still in close proximity and he often visited them, which in effect must have increased the turmoil in his mind. Arthur's few childhood friends were those that didn't know his background or happily chose to ignore it. One of these friends was Tom Hall who on many occasions would travel with him to Blackpool when visiting his mother. Together the two youngsters would perform a dance routine on the beach, which they had invented while playing and dressing-up at the back of their Wigan homes. It has been said that on one occasion the pair had to walk back to Wigan having spent their return fare from Blackpool. They had hoped that their 'sand dance' performance would have given them sufficient money for the return journey. Unfortunately, their rewards were poor and they failed in their bid to buy train tickets. This situation does seem somewhat implausible for a number of reasons. After all return tickets were readily available and of course were the cheaper way to travel. Being youngsters they may have naively thought buying two single tickets from Wigan would initially give them more money to spend in Blackpool and with their beach antics would be able to make good the shortfall. But would they really have taken that chance? They could have had a return ticket in their pockets and still raised money to spend. It seems unrealistic to assume that two young boys, not yet in their teens, would have walked over 35-miles at night time, while two sets of worried families frantically awaited their return. Even if this had been the case, the simplest solution would have been to ask Rhoda for the fare - even risking a telling off, for the boys would have surely had one at the other end in Wigan.

On 7th May 1913 three months after Arthur's twelfth birthday, his mother Rhoda married Richard McEvoy at Blackpool Parish Church. A mechanic by trade, Richard McEvoy had been a member of the armed forces and though he was four years younger than Rhoda, it appears she may not have admitted this to Richard as on their wedding certificate she gives her age as thirty. Up to the time of their marriage the couple had been living as neighbours in Highfield Road, South Shore, Blackpool. Unfortunately, by this time Rhoda's father had died and it is not known if any other family members or any of the Heath's attended the wedding. It is safe to assume though, that young Arthur could well have been in attendance. On the whole, the Hughes family had remained close and Arthur had always kept in contact with his Aunties and his Grandfather up to his death. Even though Rhoda had now married, Arthur remained with the Heath's until completing his education at thirteen years of age.

After leaving school in 1914 finding suitable work for the young Arthur wasn't an easy task. The lad had already tasted it with several evening and Saturday jobs, one at a Chorley market greengrocery stall where he could be heard shouting, *'finest oranges i' Wiggin'.* With the laughing shoppers answering him back with, *'Aye, but tha in Chorley nah lad'.* Like many other locals he tried his hand in the cotton mills only to be dismissed almost immediately for sleeping on the cotton bales. Putting the unpleasant thoughts of work behind him he once more set forth on the road to Blackpool to visit his mother. At the height of the summer season, Arthur and pal Tommy again tried out their usual 'sand dance' routine this time with Arthur impersonating Charlie Chaplin. Once more they failed to impress their beach audience and this is another occasion when the two lads are supposed to have walked back to Wigan. Before the summer had ended Arthur had left Wigan and Mamma Heath to move in permanently with his mother. His beach based solo Chaplin routines continued while the late summer months remained. Arthur, like many people had become a great Chaplin fan having seen the comic's first films released in Britain that same year, 1914. In 1936 Randle recalled his Chaplin impressions and explained how he had dressed in baggy trousers, funny moustache and bowler hat. As a child he thought it a very good imitation - the opinions of the holidaymakers were however, to the contrary, and he continued blissfully unaware of their scorn until they ultimately chased him off the beach. *"It was a great blow to the small boy - or, in other words to me. "More trouble followed when I got home. "Having darkened my hair for the 'part' with soot, it produced disturbing results on my pillow, - well, what my mother said and did is still a painful recollection".*

Now living permanently with his mother and step-father at Heald Street, Blackpool, Arthur again underwent a name change becoming Arthur McEvoy. Still under the age of twenty-one this was a decision obviously agreeable to all concerned. There was no such thing as legal adoption before 1927 and any arrangements carried out enabling Arthur to take his step-father's name were informal only - yet nonetheless an acceptable practice. For the rest of his life Arthur would quite legitimately be Arthur McEvoy.

His first ever stage appearance came in January 1916 when he appeared in a touring show of *'Charlie Chaplin Mad'* when it stopped off at the Palace Theatre, Blackpool. In this show he simply appeared on stage as one of the supernumeraries. In a newspaper article, Randle once recalled that he would have been 13-years-old when in this show however, the play date for *'Charlie Chaplin Mad'* confirms that he would have been just weeks away from his 15th birthday. Although by no means a leap into entertainment, he no doubt enjoyed the experience and the feel for show business. Arthur had always been a physically fit and active young man with a keen interest in boxing and to further this pursuit soon joined a local gym run by Harold Gregory. Over the next six or seven years he had a succession of jobs ranging from shop assistant to odd-jobbing for a printing firm and even a programme seller at the resort's Winter Gardens. Apparently, work didn't seem to agree with Arthur - *"As fast as I went into a job my employers had me out"*, Randle once admitted. *"About five weeks in each was about my limit. I was not in fact what one would call a steady worker."* The situation was soon to change however, when the acrobatic and gymnastic skills acquired under Harold Gregory began to bring show business opportunities Arthur's way. One such, came in 1918 when he joined the trampoline and tumbling act 'The Three Ernestos' at the Tower Circus – unfortunately this season was marred by the untimely death of his stepfather Richard who died in August. Heartbroken, Rhoda was to never marry again. However, after his stint at the Tower Circus, Arthur was finding his niche and steady employment followed with spells in several similar acts and at least one summer season at a tent circus in Cleveleys. He appeared here in the summer of 1922 before embarking on his first ever theatre tour. The Cleveleys circus was held every summer on the site of the old pleasure beach on the Promenade close to Beach Road and was operated by Johnnie Watson who also appeared with his team of performing dogs. Arthur took on the guise of Nobby the clown giving a combined performance of tomfoolery and trampolining. These early steps into show business all took place within the vicinity of his Blackpool home and where Rhoda could still keep a watchful eye on the yet youthful Arthur. However, for Arthur to pursue any ambition of making a mark in entertainment he would have to broaden his horizons. Once again his destiny was given a helping hand courtesy of Gregory's Gym. Both Gregory and his gym were well-known especially among circus and theatrical performers, many of whom paid regular visits when in the resort. Consequently, when Fred and Harry Retter realised they needed another person while deciding to put an act together, they found themselves one Saturday afternoon in the packed Gregory gymnasium. Their visit was not to find a replacement, contrary to certain reports, but to acquire an original third member for their new act. In 1979 Fred Retter actually recalled how they had decided to form the act and spoke of their visit to the gym and of first seeing

Arthur McEvoy, a tough aggressive fighter in the boxing ring. Having impressed the pair with his capabilities, the Retters' invited him to join them. Arthur's agreement saw the introduction of the act 'The Roy Brothers & Mac', where McEvoy was obviously the 'Mac'. Their debut came at the Queens, Farnworth, after which the trio toured the country performing at the smallest of venues for the smallest of wages. Inexperienced in the world of show business Fred Retter naively thought they would be well paid for their new act but his monetary aspirations were soon brought down with a bump. Randle once recalled, *"We played every valley in South Wales, and once topped the Workmen's Hall, Tredegar, for £3.00 a week. "But we were living from hand to mouth and spent half our time waiting for telegrams".* This too for performing two shows a day, six days a week - not a great deal of money and life was obviously a struggle. On one occasion Arthur McEvoy had to turn to his mother for help. She duly sent him twenty-five shillings to pay for their lodgings which often would see them sleeping three in a bed tossing a coin to see who would sleep in the middle.

The show which the 'Roy Brothers & Mac' joined at Bolton was *'Wild Oats'* produced by Jack Taylor and T. Elder Hearn. This would be the first time that the path of McEvoy would cross with Taylor. In line with the agricultural theme of the title, the show was advertised as a fascinating medley of Revue, Drama and Comedy in 16 crops. The cast included Tommy Mostel, T. Elder Hearn and Ray Zack, with the Roy Brothers & Mac way down the bill. Frank Randle in 1936 looked back to this time and recalled, *"We set forth to play our first variety date in a theatre near Bolton".* There was of course the big thrill of seeing our first press notice... and there it was: 'Roy Brothers & Mac closed the bill'".* Of his own personal performance Randle said, *"On the opening night I did so many wrong things that I wonder the stage didn't collapse in sheer horror. I fell off the horizontal bars for one thing, and for another missed my cue to go on the stage through being absorbed in light conversation with a pretty little soubrette in the wings. On the stage was one of my partners, balancing about a ton of things on his forehead. He had a table, lampshades and all sorts of things, everything bar the kitchen range. My job was to come on stage and hand him a set of Indian clubs with which he was to complete the trick. He waited, the mass of things towering above him, for the clubs. Half a minute later he was still waiting. "Clubs," he hissed, "Clubs you fool". But I was still very much occupied in the wings. It was a case of hearts with me that evening not clubs, and at last he had to lower the mass of things he was balancing without completing the trick".* The late Jeff Nuttall author of the Randle biography 'King Twist' was of the opinion that the soubrette in question was Genevieve Delaney. Though this is quite possible, it seems more likely that they would meet around five years later when they would then embark on an amorous relationship.

Like most theatricals, the 'Roy Brothers & Mac' eventually arranged for publicity photographs to be taken. One which has survived, shows Fred, Harry and Arthur together in costume accompanied by the original printed caption announcing *'Roy Brothers & Mac - youthful comedy gymnasts and jugglers'.* These photographs would not have been produced if McEvoy had only been a temporary stand-in. They are added testimony that the 'Roy Brothers & Mac' were indeed a totally new act.

ROY BROTHERS & MAC,
Youthful Comedy Gymnasts and Jugglers.

The original caption says it all

7

For the next few, years travelling from town to town, show to show, 'The Roy Brothers & Mac' were gaining a good deal of experience from their lowly positions on the bills, while providing audiences with reasonable entertainment. Whereas the Retters' would throughout their lives remain as highly respected and accomplished jugglers never wanting for work, Arthur visualised more for himself.

From his early forays into showbiz with his clownish circus antics combined with his athletic bodily skills, he had enjoyed making people laugh. Working with the Retters' had given him stage presence and confidence but he was now looking at ways of breaking away. Fred Retter could see his determination, "*He was always scheming, scheming how to become a comic*". Arthur wasn't contented to carry on playing a secondary role to the Retters' and so he sought a solo career, or, if he was to have partners, then as the American's would say, he was going to be Top Banana. McEvoy now took on the stage persona of Arthur Twist presenting an act which again combined his talents into a comedy routine set on the trampoline and parallel bars. In due course, travelling in revues throughout the country more comedy came to the fore and Arthur Twist would transform into a Chaplinesque looking principal comedian.

Arthur Twist

In 1926 Arthur Twist was appearing in *'On Leave'* a show which also included Genevieve Delaney. Genevieve, or Eva as she was known, was a talented tap dancer and performed with her sister Mona, as 'Delaney and Lee'. The two sisters were following the showbusiness tradition set by their father who under the name of Billy Willis had trod the boards for many years as a comedian. Along with a third sister Ronnie (Veronica), they had for a time also presented a three-handed act billed as 'The Willis Sisters'. Eva Delaney although unmarried at this time was already mother to an illegitimate son Danny, who was taken care of by Eva's mother Honoria Delaney, while she toured. As the tour of *'On Leave'* progressed, Arthur McEvoy took a liking to the good looking Eva and the pair soon became quite close. So much so that it was not long before a full scale sexual relationship developed. This relationship progressed at such a rate that by March of the following year, Eva had fallen pregnant again and ultimately, gave birth to yet another illegitimate son on December 9th 1927. In the weeks leading up to the birth, Arthur McEvoy had been appearing in a show called *'Better Still'* which had opened at Wigan in September 1927. Also appearing in this show was May Douglas a young female vocalist who performed as Victoria May. Although her name over the years has been misinterpreted as Connie May, her full name was in actuality, May Annie Victoria Douglas - though she was informally known to everyone as 'Queenie'. For Arthur and Queenie, it was to be love at first sight. Indeed, if ever there had been a serious relationship between McEvoy and Delaney, the beautiful young Londoner certainly ended it.

The absence of a father's name on any birth certificate was a certain sign of an illegitimate birth as was the case with Eva's son. However, the names Arthur McEvoy do appear on the boy's certificate as they were given to the child as his forenames. Eventually Eva did marry and had two more sons Chris and Peter with husband Chris Burgon.

In 1928 Leeds impresario Monty Marks - then known as Mark Ginsberg, was presenting a touring revue called *'And You'* in which McEvoy as Arthur Twist was appearing. However, when the show played Shrewsbury, an important date forced him to miss the last performances on Saturday 5th May. For on this day, Arthur McEvoy and Queenie were married at the Church of the Assumption at Greenwich, London. Coming from a staunch and typically large Catholic family - she was one of seven children - all of whom held strong religious beliefs. The Church of the Assumption was the family church and the priest, Father James Mahoney, was also an invited guest at a party held at the home of Queenie's parents Alfred and Beatrice

A right royal do – Queenie and Arthur's wedding day 1928

Douglas at Batavia Road, New Cross, London. With the house being of the typical working-class, small back to back terrace variety, the house-party in reality transformed itself into a street party which Londoners in those days didn't need an excuse to hold.

It also appears that *'And You'* was the last show in which McEvoy used the stage name of Arthur Twist. From January 1929 he began performing in sketches as Frank Randle as well as appearing with partner Billy Sibley in the act 'The Bouncing Randles'. This latter act was in similar vein to the then famous 'Bouncing Dillons' who in 1931 would replace the 'Bouncing Randles' on the bill of *'The Happy Party'.* Coming in on that show as they did has lead some people today to believe that both the Bouncing 'Randles' and 'Dillons' were one and the same. Whereas they were indeed two separate entities with the latter already being firmly established when Randle formed his act. Although now known as Frank Randle, the final incarnation of his various stage names, there would over the next few years be noticeable alterations to his act. For his appearances on the trampoline with Billy Sibley (also known as Billy Sibb) he would dress in similar garb to a circus clown, baggy trousers, colourful braces, oversized check jacket, check cap and

10

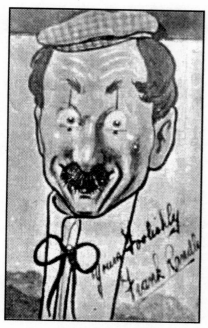

Yours foolishly, so signs a young Frank Randle in check cap and bright red wig

bright red wig - And he was of course getting laughs, for as he went in one direction his trousers went in the other.

In 1929 both Randle and his wife 'Queenie' appeared together along with Randle's old friends and one time working partners Fred and Harry Retter in Harry Berresfield's *'The Mile-A-Minute Review'*. Randle once said of his wife, *"Her stage name was Victoria May and I remember that as a joke in one town we billed her particular act as 'Victoria May Sing'. We abandoned humour of this sort for the future however, when some caustic soul wrote under this 'Victoria May Not'"*. *'The Mile-A-Minute Review'* consisted of around thirty artistes with the Victor Duprez Manhattan Band topping the bill. As well as appearing as *'The Bouncing Randles - The Springing Fools'*, Frank was also performing as the principal comedian in several sketches - some of which he would still be using much later in his career. The sketches that were to stand the test of time were 'The Medical Board', one which centred on a boxing match, and a supposed drama 'Set a Thief to Catch a Thief'. The story to this drama concerned Flash Joe (Billy Pardoe) who, having stolen a wallet, returned home to his wife (played by Randle's wife Victoria May). While he was explaining events to his spouse a Police Inspector McGuinness (Billy Sibb) arrived to arrest him. Throughout the 'acting' there was one audience member who continually interrupted their performances - this was of course Frank Randle. He would in 1952 re-present this as a 'new' drama. One reviewer who saw the show in Rochdale and noting Frank Randle taking the lead in the humorous episodes said, *"...he was a very natural comedian"*.

On occasions Queenie and Frank had to spend time away from each other as they were appearing in different shows. This was not an ideal situation and while it may have been a necessity, the longer it continued the more Randle disliked it. It wasn't just the feeling of being away from a loved one that was getting to him, the situation was bringing out another side of his nature, that being a great sense of jealousy. Whenever Queenie was away he was always thinking that someone may take her from him. To ensure this would never happen he demanded that if she wished to continue performing then it had to be in the same show as him. Alternatively she could stop performing but still travel along with him on his shows, which she eventually agreed to do.

Over the next few years while still being booked as 'The Bouncing Randles' he started to introduce more comic sketches. He played in various shows and revues including *The Happy Party* and *Yorkshire Relish*. It was during this latter show that Randle was asked by the show's star Reg Bolton to step in as a front cloth comic to cover for a scene change; this was to be in addition to his 'Bouncing Randles' act. This it seems is where Randle first introduced to the theatre-going public his character 'The Old Boatman' in his 'Anymore for Sailing' routine.

The Bouncing Randles propping up the bill

Randle's portrayal of the Boatman was based on similar characters he had seen countless times while growing up in Blackpool. Simply, he was an old sea dog trying to entice the public onto his old boat for a brief trip on the Irish Sea – though without much success.

1:   Enny moor for sailin... Is there enny moor for sailin... Enny Moor... Not a blinkin sossige... If there's anybody fer ere... This is it.... By gum... It's a 'ell of a busy place is this... I've seen livelier mortuaries than this 'ole... I have 'onest... I've only seen one Seagull awl't time I've bin 'ere... and that couldn't fly... Enny moor fer going... we're 'avin our illuminations next week... they're goin' to light the other lamp.

12

2:      We're salin' right away, if we're lucky... You can tell what sort of place this is... Mind yer... A chap dropped dead out side o't' Post Office last Monday morning... they didn't find him 'till Friday neet... We did 'ave a bit of excitement a day or two back... mind yer... Landlord's wife from t'pub cum swankin past wi' one of these new low backed bathing costumes on... It was a low backed 'un too... I'll tell yer... Only damn foo' had it on back to front...Eeee... I felt 'shamed for her... I did honest... I couldn't look her in't face... Only my eyesight's not been so grand lately.

3:      Enny moor fer sailin... Room fer two more... Yer know there must be a whist drive on someweer... Yer know it gets that quiet at times round 'ere I can 'ears mi 'air grow... I feel sorry fer't landlord o't' "Glue Pot" 'ere... Hif it wasn't fer me... he'd have to close up... It's a grand little pub... is "Glue Pot"... I get stuck in theer very often... I went in for a pint t'other day and had to come out to git meself some 'bacca'... landlord says ... hey don't leave yer ale on't counter there... some one might come in and sup it... Si I wrote on a piece of paper... I have spit in this ale... when I went back... me ale was still there... somebody had written underneath... so have I... but I supped it just same... I tell ye.

4:      Enny moor fer gooin... No waitin'... You know I'll be getting pinched fer talkin' to meself... I've had one lousy customer in three weeks... and he was a hescaped lunatic... I didn't find that out until we'd got half a mile on't sea... and he says...We'll git out here...Aye... Then he stands up in't boat... grabs hold o' me round neck... and says... you are Wilfred Pickles... I ses aye and thi're Professor Joad... I ses by gum it's a good job I can swim... I'll tell yer... I would't have cared but they took both of us back to find out which was barmy.

5:      Enny moor fer sailin - back in time fer tea... Well... There's only my old woman and a nanny goat at home yonder... An if things don't buck up... I shall have to get shut of one of them... An I'm very fond o't' nanny goat... I'll tell ye... It's a wonderful hanimile... when I first got it... I ses we'll keep in in't bedroom... missus says aye... but what about the smell... I ses, Oh... It'll have to put up wi' that.

6:      Enny moor fer gooin... Come and be sick fer a shilling... Oh... It's a waste of time... Ye know... I've often wondered what t'other end of this anchor looks like... But there's one thing... It's a very healthy place mind yer... aye... It's a grand place for rheumatics... I got mine 'ere any rode... But there's one thing... We've only had one wreck here in ninety-odd years... aye... one wreck, this is it... But she's not bin a

13

Randle's first character creation 'The Old Boatman'... Any more for sailing?

*bad old tub... Talk about yer racing yachts... we can pass 'em all... pass
'em all... providing they're not goin' same way... mind yer... aye... aye...I
wouldn't part wi' her for all't money there is in Christendom... Tho'*

there's lots of folks bin after her... mind yer... aye... This 'ere racing fellow Malcolm Campbell... he took a great fancy to her last summer... aye... he called me on one side and whispered... if you ever you feel like selling it... I wish you luck... Oh... I've had several offers... what the 'ells the good of a yo-yo to me.

7:    Enny moor fer gooin... If we goo... Anybody want to buy a boat... By gum... It's cumin a bit dark... I notice... I don't think there'll be much more doin' to-day... well... I've been on this beach fifty odd years or more... aye... fifty odd years... and they say I'm getting' too old fer me job... Well... We all git too old sooner or later... I suppose... (Scratch) ... There's a 'ell of a lot of sand fleas knicking about 'ere... I'll tell ye.

MONOLOGUE

Well... Sarah old girl... I've had yer fer years
And me father he had you before
Youv'e sin days of gladness... Youv'e also sin tears
But maybe ye'll not see menny more
Youv'e ridden the ocean as proud as a queen
I've quided your oath many miles (I've guided your oars many miles)
When herrings were plentiful... oh how I'd sing
And I'd praise you with blessings and smiles
It seems to me lass... we're not wanted now
It seems that we're getting too slow
We haven't the comfort to please 'em somehow
We haven't the dash and the go
But neer mond old lass... you've well earned your keep
But you're going to pieces like me
And I only hope when I take me long sleep
That they bury us both out at sea
And if me spirit comes back to the "Glue Pot"
Where the price charged for ale is so sinful
I hope they sell it like sossiges for tuppence a heck of a skinful.

By the mid-thirties 'The Bouncing Randles' had fallen by the wayside as Frank Randle solo comedian was climbing the bills. Ex-colleague Billy Sibley's showbusiness career was to continue as under his real name of Grant he teamed up with a new partner in the act 'Reading and Grant'. This acrobatic partnership proved to be very successful and even made an appearance in the 1941 film 'Old Mother Riley's Circus'. Several years later both Billy and his wife returned to work for Randle not just as performers but also in a back stage capacity on a number of 'Scandals' shows.

The audience reaction to the 'Old Boatman' had made it clear to Randle that he was right to pursue a solo career. With more work starting to come his way he soon began to build a good reputation and later introduced further routines including 'The Old Hiker' and 'Grandpa's Birthday'

Around this same time a show business friend of Randle's from Blackpool was also experiencing a similar change in his show business career. Like Randle he was an acrobat, who had teamed up with his brothers to form an act. Now just as Randle was doing, he also settled on a solo career as a comic. The person in question would eventually find fame as Scottish born comedian Alex Munro. Another similarity between the two friends was their name changes, for Alex Munro was born Alexander Neilson Horsburgh. He started out in show business as part of the 'Star Trio' along with his brother Archie and sister, June. Later with another brother, Tommy they became 'The Horsburgh Brothers and Agnes' acrobats. They eventually turned their hand to comedy after working with Florrie Forde and taking advice from Bud Flannigan. After a while the brothers worked out a crazy comedy routine with which they toured under the name of 'The Horsburgh Brothers'. Alex chose Munro as his stage name after deciding to go solo and this name would in time, legitimately become his surname. On September 28th 1934 his wife Phyllis gave birth to their daughter Janet Neilson Horsburgh, sadly Phyllis died when the child was eight years old. Alex would eventually marry three times and father further children; all of whom were given the surname Munro at birth. His second wife Lilias not only became Janet's stepmother but also her big sister and her best friend and guiding light. Janet Neilson Horsburgh whom Frank Randle was Godfather to, would later find fame as actress Janet Munro starring in several feature films including Disney's *Darby O'Gill and the Little People*.

Three months after Janet's birth in Blackpool Frank Randle was appearing at the resort's Palace Theatre in a bill headed by Macari and his Dutch Serenaders. As if to prove his 'Bouncing Randles' days were truly behind him he was now being billed as 'The New Star Comedian' with the local newspaper reviewer noting, "...*he is an artist of whom more should be heard in the future*". In July of 1935 he was back again at the Palace being billed second to Roy Fox and his band with the reviewer on this occasion saying, "*Frank Randle gave a couple of brilliant items, the hiker and the boatman and he captured the house.*

Frank Randle in 1935

The originality of his work was refreshing". Randle's progress had not gone unnoticed by Jack Taylor who on several occasions in the past had booked Randle for his touring revues. Taylor was now a big time producer based in Blackpool where, from offices in Birley Street, he worked alongside fellow producer John D. Robertson. For a period the two worked jointly on various productions. Since Randle had first encountered Taylor the producer had gained a reputation for staging quality programmes which often incorporated innovative lighting that he himself had designed. After obtaining the contract to provide the summer spectacles at the Central Pier Theatre his business prospered. He was also providing touring revues for the country's major number one theatres. Now he was working for 'The Blackpool Tower Company' and producing summer shows at their Opera House Theatre. After the 1935 Blackpool season in which he starred Albert Burden and Randolph

17

Sutton in *'Shout for Joy'*, he decided to continue its success by touring it around the country. However, due to other commitments, the original stars were unavailable for the tour and consequently Taylor needed to find replacements. As a result a contract was given to Frank Randle and Billy Russell with the show once again proving successful during the latter part of 1935 and early 1936.

After this tour Randle teamed up with comedian Jimmy James and Randolph Sutton for Taylor's *'The Show that Jack Built'*. It was in this production that Frank Randle made his London West End debut opening on March 18th 1936 at the Alhambra Theatre and playing until May 1st. While some said the show lacked polish and finesse, one reviewer wrote, *"Another principal who calls for warm praise is Frank Randle, a very funny comedian whose quiet method is well suited in an item about an ancient hiker and in a laughable sketch 'Nearly All-in Wrestling'. His 'Threading the Needle' business with Mr Sutton also causes great fun."* Theatre magnate Sir Oswald Stoll had decided on a plan of twice nightly variety shows for his

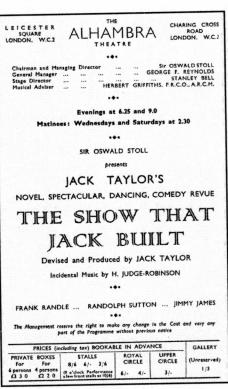

Frank Randle's West End debut

Alhambra venue and the reviewer stated that this policy was *"successfully continued with The Show that Jack Built"*. He also noted that to bring it into the West End much had been added in its staging and it was now an elaborate production and a gorgeous spectacle. Amongst other venues the show played were the Holborn Empire, the Finsbury Park Empire, the Brighton Hippodrome and the Portsmouth Hippodrome.

Being eminently satisfied with Randle's performances in these touring productions Taylor felt justified in offering him a summer season. Not as star though, but a worthy position nonetheless, as second comic to George Formby in the 1936 Opera House spectacular 'King Fun'.

The show billed as a 'Grand Season Spectacular Ballet Revue' and featuring a cast of one hundred had cost Taylor in excess of £20,000 to produce. Quite a lot of this expenditure had gone into the lavish sets, costumes and lighting. Many of the scenes allowed Taylor's artistic and lighting creativity to shine through with quite stunning effect. Along with several other dance-orientated scenes it is understandable why Taylor billed the show as he did. Even without Formby and Randle he would have had a show to please most audiences - their inclusion however, gave it added dimension and obviously more of a family 'holiday show' appeal. On the subject of 'family', George Formby's wife Beryl also featured in the show; as did Jack Taylor's daughters, Vashti and Pansy. When Pansy married it was to Tony Legate, who like her father was a producer of theatrical shows and who would be responsible for staging the first of the 'Scandals' type of shows with Frank Randle. 'King Fun' opened on Friday June 26th and ran until October 17th 1936.

By this time Formby had already made his breakthrough and was a firm favourite in the public's eye. His rise to such status irked Randle who couldn't understand why he was not in the same position. For here they were two natives of Wigan, both comics — though he believed himself the funnier. So why was he not rated as highly as Formby? The answer as far as he was concerned was the fact that Formby had a father and a father who had been in show business. The more Randle dwelt on this the more neurotic he became. As things turned out though, that summer of 1936 proved to be somewhat difficult for Formby as with the thousands of visitors to the theatre, he witnessed the elevation of Randle to that same star category. From the opening night Randle won over the public and the critics. For performance after performance, if the audience reaction was anything to go by, he repeatedly outshone Formby. Reports in the local press acclaimed his arrival as a top line entertainer with glowing reports notably in respect of his 'Old Hiker'. The buzz around Blackpool that summer was how Formby was being upstaged by Randle and how he was thriving on it. Beryl Formby, the driving force behind George, disliked intensely the attention being stolen from her husband. Beryl was the one whom people had to negotiate with for George's services and with her husband's business interests in mind, she always drove a hard bargain. When the BBC planned on broadcasting excerpts from the show Beryl had no objections in principal; but insisted that if they wanted George they would have to forget Randle. As with most negotiations Beryl had her way – the BBC scrapped any ideas of including segments of Randle's performances. Making his entrance on stage the following evening Randle approached the footlights to address the audience. He informed them that the BBC in their infinite wisdom had decided to broadcast parts of this wonderful show. However, it appears that they believe Formby to be the only star, therefore Ladies and Gentlemen that being the case Formby can entertain you all now. At which point he simply walked off stage giving the audience a wave as he left them feeling somewhat bemused.

The rivalry continued throughout the summer, both on and off stage, as both stars tried to outshine each other. At one point Randle and Formby came up with an idea that would test their endurance as both wanted to be top man. To do this it was decided that each in turn would climb up Blackpool tower. As the news of their plan spread amongst the show's company, many expressed their concern. For, whilst it was generally thought neither of them would actually attempt such a foolhardy stunt, both had the courage and nerve to do so. There were others who were making bets on whether they would carry out their quest and on who would win. It is thought that Jack Taylor placed five pounds on the outcome. In due course however, Randle was talked out of the idea and Formby's film company stopped his attempt because of insurance risks. With much boasting and bravado, Randle - as if to prove he was the more capable - began citing past achievements and was quoted as saying, "Anyway I once finished the Manchester to Blackpool walk. Did it in 10¼ hours, got a medal, the 27th out of 150". That particular sporting event had also been significant for Randle's career. Also taking part in the walk had been a very elderly gentleman who, wearing his Lancashire wooden clogs, had managed to come first in the veterans section and remained fixed in Randle's memory. So much so, that his famous 'Old Hiker' character was actually based upon him. Later, in order to help perfect this characterisation, Randle took the quite impulsive decision to have all his teeth extracted – not that he ever regretted the deed. Coming as it did from Randle himself, this has been the accepted story of how he created the 'Hiker' character. However, Arthur Goulding, who joined Randle for his 1939/40 winter tour and worked by his side as Arthur Wilton for a number of years, dismisses this story. Arthur informed us, *"Randle once said to me... to me directly, I didn't hear it from anyone else, he said, 'Arthur, the Old Hiker is from Will Fyfe', he'd copied Will Fyfe"*.

In reviewing 'King Fun' the local press commented that Randle's 'Old Hiker' was a comedy gem. The Hiker as caricatured by Randle was an aged octogenarian supposedly out on a countryside ramble - galumphing on stage to the musical strains of 'I'm Happy When I'm Hiking' he would come to rest and declare, *"So this is Blackpool is it?"* (or of course the name of whichever town the theatre was in). He would then regale his audience with tales of the people he had met or the events that had occurred whilst out and about. Dressed hilariously in khaki jacket and baggy shorts, which like his boots - worn on the wrong feet - were grossly oversized. Over his shoulder a bugle dangled ready for use. In one hand he had his walking staff, a large roughly broken tree branch, while in the other was firmly gripped his bottle of beer - real beer of course. His head seemed to be fastened to his body by the scarf tied around his scrawny neck. The aged features of his face were punctuated by popping eyes that peered through wire glasses perched precariously on the end of his nose. Time, it would appear, had taken its toll on this now toothless old man and what remained of his hair stood up in tufts as in fear. Yet, as the audience was to find out, looks were deceiving as there was still plenty of life in this old timer.

There's a cheeky kid up there. He just spotted me. He comes running to his mother. Come here mother. There's a monkey up a stick. Aye... Well... I've walked through Europe. Ear-up. Ire-up. Shutup. Wallop. Jollop. My feet are red-hot. Hikers? Hikers? I've picked them off bushes. Aye, I'm the daddy of all hikers. I'll be eighty-two in a few more days. Eighty-two and I'm as full of vim as a butcher's dog. I'm as lively as a cricket. I'll tell ye why. I'll take anybody on at my age and weight. Dead or alive, and I'll run them, walk them, jump them, fight them. Aye and I'll play them dominoes. Just look at these for a pair of legs. I tossed a sparrow for these and lost. By gum. There's another hair coming here, see not a vein on 'em. There's an old pal o' mine whose legs are covered with blue veins, he once went to a fancy dress ball as a road map, there was an old girl there trying all night to find the Great North Road. (Drinks out of bottle) Boyeee, eeh I had a narrow squeak a while back, I was goin across a field with a bull in it, it wasn't Barney's bull either, it was a fierce un'. It had a couple of prongs on it as long as this stick. Only they were a damn sight sharper than this. I'll tell you. Aye. It come tupping away. I thought it was apologising the way it was bowing and scraping away. Aye. Aye. I shooed it away with my handkerchief. Oh. It's a red one. Aye. It made it a damn sight worse. By gum. But did I pick them up? I fairly sizzled I catched up to a rabbit. I'd have passed it only it got between my legs. I said to it. I said Hey come on, hurry up or else get out of the road. I said Let somebody run as can.

21

'The Old Hiker' Randle's most famous creation

I popped in a chemists shop the other day for some cornflakes or corn plasters or whatever you call 'em. *There was a fellow came in like this* (walks with legs bents) *He said 'I want some talcum powder please', the chemist said 'certainly sir, walk this way'.* *The customer said, 'If I could walk that way I wouldn't want the talcum powder'.* (Drinks out of bottle) *Boyee.* *I once sent a bottle of beer away like this here to be* analysed. *They must have got mixed up at the other end. They sent me a postcard saying. 'Dear Sir your horse is unfit for work'. There's a draught coming from somewhere. I don't know where it's coming from but I know wheres it's going to... Boyeee... Eeh... I think it was that rabbit I had for my dinner, it wasn't quite dead.* (Looking at backcloth – which is of woodland scene and country lane) *I wouldn't like to go down there on a motor coach, nor a bicycle either.*

These are handy things aren't they (looks at bugle and holds it up - trumpet blows from orchestra) *that's the fist time I've heard one of these blow by itself. That must have been in there a hell of a long time. Do you know, it was only the other day I found out the proper name for a Dandelion. I was passing a gateway to a field about seven o'clock t'other morning, when I saw a little old postman being chased by a bull. This old postman flew across the field, he jumped over the gate scattering all his letters. I helped him to pick them up and said, by gum, that bull nearly caught you this morning. He said, 'ehh lad, he nearly catches me every blurry morning'. Only the other day I went to a funeral. I wasn't invited; I just went for the ride. As I was leaving the churchyard, the warden asked me how old I was. I said I'm 82. He said 'I don't think it's much use thee goin' home at all'. But still you are just as old as you feel. A man's not old if his hair turns grey. A man's not old if his teeth decay. But it's time he was booked for his long last sleep, when his mind makes appointments his body can't keep.*

I've never been the same fellow since my old missus passed away. Twenty-two stone she weighed - a fine figure of a woman she was. I had her cremated. I went round a day or two later for the ashes. The fellow said to me, we've no ashes for you, but there's four buckets of dripping you can have'. A was talking to an old woman down the road, eeh she were cheeky. I said I think you look like a blue nosed monkey. She said, 'well we all come from monkeys, and it wouldn't worry me if my grandfather was a great big hairy ape with a tail that long (indicating length of tail). *So I said, 'No, but it would worry your grandmother'. Well it's time I was goin', I've enjoyed my chat to you and I'll be seeing you again.*

That reminds me, a young woman called round to see me the other day I said 'now then young woman what do you want'? She said 'I've come collecting for the Lord'. I said, 'well you'd better give the box to me I'll be seeing him before thee'.

Well cheerio, I'll be seeing you all again. (Exits to music of "I'm Happy When I'm Hiking").

Without a doubt the summer of 1936 saw Randle's years of honing his act bring him his just rewards. Although he had previously topped bills he had never been regarded as a true star - that summer a star was born.

Due to the impact made by Randle, Jack Taylor had no hesitation in placing the comedian top of the bill on his touring version of '*King Fun*', which went on the road after its stint in Blackpool and didn't conclude until the spring of 1937.

Randle's impressive rise now saw him engaged as headliner or joint bill-topper which also placed him in the higher earnings bracket. He appeared on the same bills with other greats, one of the first being a July appearance with American's Ben Lyon and Bebe Daniels. In August Randle would receive an accolade which was to remain one of his most treasured memories. This came about in Blackpool, while being introduced to a packed Grand Theatre, August Bank Holiday audience by Gracie Fields with the words, *"Frank Randle is the best comic actor I have ever seen".* A top of the bill appearance by Randle in Blackburn also held happy memories for Mr P. G. Dea. The show at the Grand Theatre included two child acts, in the form of 'The Seven Dancing Girls' and the all boy 'Ten Tin Can Fusiliers' of which Mr Dea was a member. The children's ages ranged from 17 to 20 years for the girls and 10 and 13 years for the boys. *"We played those tins cans for the full week - two shows a night for which we were paid ten shillings. "Frank Randle was very kind to the boys and girls and enjoyed playing on stage with them. I would have loved to have gone on tour with him but being of school age I wasn't allowed. "Of course he told some rather naughty stories and one in particular sticks in my mind".* As Mr Dea's memory has it, Randle's 'Old Hiker' is telling the audience how while out in the countryside he approached a small footbridge that crossed a stream. As he began to traverse the bridge he noticed a young woman already upon it. Randle says to the audience 'I didn't know whether to block her passage or toss myself off'. *"I can still hear that audience responding to his act with shouts of 'more, more",* Said Mr Dea. Another significant event during 1937 had been the assembling of his own team of artistes to work with him in the sketches of his touring variety shows. This company would eventually evolve into his regular 'Scandals' team and remain with him for over fifteen years.

Certainly 1937 had been a successful year and was drawn to a close in likewise manner with a starring role for Randle in Francis Laidler's lavish pantomime 'Aladdin' at the Theatre Royal, Leeds. Laidler was a well-known and much respected producer of pantomimes with his productions having appeared in towns and major cities throughout the country. Randle's rise since his appearance with Formby had not gone unnoticed in the Laidler camp and they had moved swiftly to secure his services before rival producers made approaches.

The show opened up to a packed house on Thursday December 23rd 1937 and also to acclaimed reviews, *"This should prove one of Mr Laidler's 'Milestone' pantomimes"*. Remaining true to the well-known story of 'Aladdin and his Wonderful Lamp' it was a lavish production with all participants portraying their Chinese characters with the usual pseudo oriental accents. That is, all with the exception of Frank Randle as pointed out by the Yorkshire Evening News; *"Frank Randle totters around in his best ancient hiker style as 'The Old Vizier', and enlivens Peking with an uncompromising Yorkshire accent"*. However, the appearance in China of this old chap with his northern twang, so much enjoyed by the watching Yorkshire audience was satisfactorily explained in the script. He had been shipwrecked off the coast of China and later became invaluable to the Emperor. The reviewer added of Randle, *"For a young man in his thirties, this is a fine character study. "After he has played the old man most of the evening it must come as a surprise to many folk to see the wizard Abanazer transform him into a youngster"*. The Yorkshire Evening Post also praised the show highly and of Randle explained how *"with complete assurance"* he kept the audience at a high pitch of hilarity, *"Those who know him in his music hall guise will know what he can do, those who do not, have something to learn"*, it added. 'Aladdin' ran successfully for over twelve weeks and always to packed audiences ending on Saturday 19th March 1938.

During the spring Randle's reputation continued to spread throughout the country as he topped the bills everywhere. Although a week's work at the Chiswick Empire from Monday 25th April 1938 saw him playing second fiddle to the great George Robey. Randle however, didn't mind at all as he thought it a privilege to be on the same stage as 'The Prime Minister of Mirth' who at 69 years of age was still one of the country's best loved comics. The programme for the show said of Randle, *"Since he created that irresistibly comic character of the weather beaten longshoreman Frank Randle's rise to star status has been swift and certain"*.

Sharing the bill with Florrie Forde in November 1938

Nowadays many artistes achieving success soon surround themselves with all the trappings associated with it and Randle was no exception. He had always liked good quality clothes and being impeccably dressed, and his success would ensure this would always remain so. More extravagantly it enabled him over the years to own several fast cars including a Chevrolet, a sky blue Mercedes and his favourite, a Lagonda. Then there was the yacht and caravan that he and Queenie used to stay in when travelling the country with his shows – for he wanted her close at hand at all times. The monetary success which came Randle's way didn't see them instantly moving into larger property – though over the years there would be several of these. Since leaving the small basic terraced house at 16 Heald Street they moved to 38 Ellesmere Road. This was a slightly larger two-up and two-down terraced property consisting of a small front facing bay windowed lounge with a large kitchen to the rear. Two bedrooms, one small, one large occupied the upper floor along with the small bathroom. The property also boasted a medium sized rear garden and smaller walled front garden. Frank, Queenie and Rhoda were to remain at Ellesmere Road for several years before somewhat strangely they returned, in 1935 to Heald Street moving next door to their old house where they remained for three more years. What came next was a move to the first of their larger houses at 32 Forest Gate. Situated at the end of a block of five the house 'Minoru' was the only double fronted property in the row. It was certainly an imposing house especially in comparison to Randle's previous dwellings. The house featured two large lounges, a large hallway and staircase, a dining room and a large kitchen, below this during the early years of the Second World War an air raid shelter was installed. Upstairs consisted of four bedrooms, two large (one with en suite bathroom) and two slightly smaller. One excellent characteristic of this property was the elaborate decorative walling and ceilings.

Top: *Queenie and Arthur*

Bottom: *32 Forest Gate, Blackpool*

27

Randle's character and disposition had always been changeable. However, as he became more well-known, so too did his erratic behaviour. This was not just the usual forms of artistic temperament to which many a star could be prone. For with Randle it seemed that at times his whole personality and character could change. According to many people he could become a totally different person, one far removed from the Randle they thought they had known. More and more people were beginning to see two sides of the comedian and the difference was like chalk and cheese. On one side there was a mild mannered kind hearted gentleman; while on the other was a jealous, whisky drinking, devious, arrogant and bad tempered man.

Lawrence Wright had been producing his annual *'On with the Show'* summer extravaganzas at the Blackpool North Pier since 1926 - though occasionally this is incorrectly cited as 1924 - and since the retirement of comic Fred Walmsley he had been looking to find another great Lancashire comedian as replacement. For the summer of 1938 he announced, *"I am now able to present the greatest of them all - Frank Randle".* Wright had staged these shows initially to promote his music. He was a songwriter who during his career had written over five hundred songs, many with partners, his biggest hit being 'Among my Souvenirs'. Along with Joe Gilbert he was also responsible for the tribute song to aviatrix Amy Johnson, 'Amy, Wonderful Amy'. In 1962 Wright received an Ivor Novello award for outstanding services to British popular music. He was without doubt a leading pioneer in UK music; he was also a music publisher under his own name and wrote songs under the pseudonym Horatio Nicholls. Having moved from his hometown of Leicester to London in his twenties he was one of the first publishers to set up business in Denmark Street, which would soon become known as 'Tin Pan Alley'. In 1926 he founded the popular music journal 'Melody Maker' which is still going strong today. He died in 1964 after which his music changed hands several times and for a time was owned by U.S. pop mega star Michael Jackson. Lawrence Wright's *'On with the Show'* ran each summer until the mid-1950s. Publicity for the 1938 version of his show stated, *"Lawrence Wright... invites you to see his 14th year of 'On with the Show' the greatest pier entertainment in the world".* However, in actuality this was his thirteenth Blackpool show but it is well known that the theatre world is steeped in superstitions. Actors dare not whistle back stage - if they do they must immediately turn around three times. Macbeth cannot be mentioned by name being referred to instead as 'the Scottish play' and of course it is not done to wish fellow performers good luck - instead one tells them to 'break a leg'. So it was then that to ward off any misfortune associated with a thirteenth show the 1938 production was promoted as the fourteenth.

Randle who was now enjoying life in the resort saw his involvement as a real prestige event and on being booked by Wright he said, *"I always wanted to be in the best show in the country"*. The production featured a large cast and several glitzy Hollywood style scenes - Alongside Randle was the Welsh bundle of fun Tessie O'Shea, another firm favourite with Blackpool's holidaymakers. Much media hype accompanied the show's opening night of June 3rd, for in attendance was the Ranee of Sarawak. There can hardly have been many Blackpool summer shows, which opened with a Royal Performance. It doesn't seem likely that many of the working class audiences would have known just who the Royal visitor

On with the Show – Blackpool - 1938

was. The Ranee was the wife to the reigning Rajah of Sarawak - today Sarawak is the largest state in Malaysia. Lawrence Wright may have thought that by saying this was his fourteenth show he was ensuring the Gods would be with him and the fates would be thwarted. However, he dismissed their powers far too lightly and they were not to be deceived by Mr Wright's trickery. For shortly after the show's opening night disaster was to strike - the theatre burned down with countless pieces of scenery, props and curtains going up in smoke. Mr Wright managed to overcome the loss thanks in part to the resort's other theatre owners and impresarios, who gave freely of scenery and props, and in transferring the show to the smaller North Pier 'Arcade'. However, the Gods had not yet finished with Wright and further mishaps were to follow as the company strived to come to terms with their new venue and limited resources. The catalogue of events included a couple of sprained wrists, first for wardrobe mistress Mrs E. Ferry and then later for Tessie O'Shea who as a result was unable to play her ukulele. Robert Naylor described at the time as being the

29

greatest of all British tenors and featuring in two spots in the show lost his voice and for several performances was unable to perform. Peggy Desmond, who accompanied Mr Naylor on the piano, as well as having her own solo spot, came down with gastric troubles, an ailment also suffered by one of the Five Sherry Brothers' - Harry being the unfortunate one to miss several shows. Miss Desmond was absent for a whole week. Dorrano, one half of innovative dancers 'Alexis and Dorrano'- their speciality was an Apache Dance - was told to take a complete rest from the show. Two more dancers, Betty Day and Jane Arrol from the 'Health & Beauty Troupe' both sprained their ankles. Yet another dancer from the 'Viennese Romancers' hurt her leg when she stumbled on the stairs and was forced to miss several shows. If all these mishaps were not enough problems for one show to endure, Mr Walter M. Morris who produced the shows under the direction of Mr Wright - and also acted as his manager - collapsed after feeling unwell and was hospitalised for a short spell for observation. Lawrence Wright no doubt would have been glad to see the season come to its end when he then could truly focus on the genuine fourteenth show - that of 1939. If Mr Wright had learned anything from this experience then it was that the Gods could count.

Although the show in many ways had to be condensed to adjust to the confines of the smaller 'Arcade' it still proved a success. Randle was naturally suited to playing in the smaller environment as his performances didn't need elaborate staging - simple backdrops sufficed for his 'Any More For Sailing' and 'The Old Hiker' which he played to perfection. Indeed very few props were needed even for his 'At the Bar' sketch - the sketch could have been performed almost anywhere. 'At the Bar' was a short but very popular part of Randle's repertoire. The sketch was set inside a public house where a barmaid was standing behind the bar talking to a customer.

Customer to Barmaid: *"I'll have a double brandy".*
Randle enters stage with a drinking pal. Both are rather drunk and are singing out of tune.... *"...and when I die".* They stagger to the bar.
Randle: *"Two ales - two caraway seeds".*
Customer to Barmaid: *"Yes, of course you know my father was a baron".*
Randle (interrupting): *"Eee - a pity his mother wasn't.* - *"Two pints of blacking".*
Customer: (continuing his conversation with barmaid): *"Then of course there were my forefathers".*
Randle: *"Eh, there's a bloke here with four fathers - a thought he was a well built fella. "Give him a blood transfusion".*

Customer: *"Yes my Mater and Pater were closely connected with Royalty".*

Randle: *"His mother must have been stung by a Queen Bee. "Two ales and a quarter of liver".*

Customer: *"Oh yes we have a very extensive estate in the country reputed to have a ghost".*

Barmaid: *"Really".*

Customer: *"Yes the figure of a naked woman walks through the long grass".*

Randle: *"Two grass cutters please".*

Customer: *"Oh yes, I have a very fine countryseat".*

Randle: *"Oh aye. "Two ales - I'll get thee a drink".*

He staggers over to the other side of the bar and does business of looking at painting (on backcloth). *"What you having"?*

Barmaid: *"Oh go away".*

Randle goes back to the front of the bar and falls against customer. *"Two Bile Beans".*

Customer: *"Oh really Sir, - Go away - the four ale bar's the place for you"!*

Randle: *"Yes Sir - Very well, once a gentleman always a gentleman - good day Sir".*

Randle then bursts into song and exits the stage.

On this occasion the part of the Barmaid was performed by Marietta with the customer played by Jim Sherry. Harry Sherry as Randle's pal was visual support, as he had no lines to speak. Like several of Randle's routines this sketch could vary from performance to performance both in content and number of participants. Even beset with all its problems *'On with the Show'* for 1938 which ran until October 1st was a winner with the public and a triumph for Frank Randle.

The winning formula of the1937/38 Christmas pantomime at Leeds, along with the variety tours and the successful *'On with the Show'* at Blackpool had given Frank Randle a sense of fulfilment. He was getting a great deal of satisfaction and enjoyment from life and was reaping financial benefits as well as public acclaim.

It was through the close working relationship in 1938 of Frank Randle and Lawrence Wright that the comedian came to make his famous 78rpm recording. Wright had certainly seen the potential for success with such a recording and so, with his own influence within the music and recording world plans were soon taking place to set Randle's 'Old Hiker' sketch down on record. Engineers from the Regal-Zonophone record label were setting up their cumbersome recording equipment in the North Pier Theatre to capture the live recording during the week 23rd to 30th July. This coincided with the Wakes week for the Accrington area, which included Oswaldtwistle and consequently why Randle opens the record with the lines *"So this is Oswaldtwistle is it?"* Like most northern towns the residents of Oswaldtwistle would have been in Blackpool en masse with many actually in the audience - and consequently on the recording itself. Back home one could imagine people saying 'listen, that's me laughing there'. It was no coincidence that the record was to be released by Regal-Zonophone for, as Wright knew only too well the prospective purchasers would be the working classes and Regal-Zonophone was the budget label of the day for EMI's Columbia records. Both George Formby and Gracie Fields had released

records on the same label and indeed Gracie had insisted on the cheap label for this very reason. Randle too wanted his record to be affordable by the working classes. Whether the record was available to buy at the theatre on its release during the summer season is unknown but it was certainly well publicised in the programme and would without doubt have been easily obtainable at Blackpool's countless music

shops. There are no production credits on the record label but it does carry the legend *'From Lawrence Wright's 'On with the Show'.* Intriguingly the mention in the show's programme declares, *"...soon you will be able to buy Frank Randle's records".* The use of the plural word 'records' is interesting. Could this indicate that more than one sketch was recorded or did it simply mean the one record in great numbers. Randle did of course have other sketches suitable for laying down on record none more so than 'Any more for Sailing' which like the 'Old Hiker' was a solo performance. Perhaps more of his act had actually been recorded but unfortunately never released.

If the previous twelve months or so had been good to Randle then the next would be almost identical. Both Francis Laidler and Lawrence Wright had quickly secured his services for repeat performances of their respective shows.

So it was then that Frank Randle appeared again in Francis Laidler's *'Aladdin'* this time at his prestigious Alhambra Theatre, Bradford where the show opened on December 22nd 1938. Like the previous show this pantomime was to receive enthusiastic reviews with many acclaiming Randle highly as its star. *"One looks to merriment as the main feature of a modern pantomime and it is given in overflowing measure"*, wrote one reviewer. *"Frank Randle, as the Old Vizier, is the principal fun maker, and his humour never savours of the pantomime joke book; it is all refreshingly new"* The pantomime was reported as being the best ever seen at the theatre and Randle's performance helped to earn an extension to its original play dates. The show eventually ran for a period of ten and a half weeks - a record for The Alhambra at that time.

From the pantomime's closing performance of March 4th 1939 to the commencement of the year's summer season, Randle enjoyed his newly acquired star status. He was support act to several International stars including 'The Mills Brothers' while headlining other shows. For the summer he returned to Blackpool for Lawrence Wright's 1939 version of his *'On with the Show"* where again he proved to be the crowd puller for the North Pier theatre.

Alhambra Theatre. Bradford. 1938

After the troubled summer of the previous year Lawrence Wright was hoping for a good season. As perhaps one would expect, Randle featured frequently throughout the show and had four key spots. The first where he played a builder alongside comedy double act 'Wheeler & Wilson', who in a topical sketch referring to the building of the pier's New Pavilion Theatre, get involved in an

33

argument with Sutherland Felce. Randle performed with Felce again in 'The Prodigal's Return' billed as the 'oldest sketch in history' and indeed was one which Randle had been performing for many years. Anita Martell played Randle's wife in the sketch 'The Flower Show', in which Lance Fairfax sang 'The Floral Dance' and duetted with Tessa Deane on 'In Harvest Time'. Randle's personal finale was another rendition of 'Anymore for Sailing'. He did make other appearances on stage many unscheduled, taking his fellow artistes by surprise. A feature of this 1939 show was the inclusion of the song and dance craze 'Boomps-a-Daisy' which at the time was emerging as a huge hit in Britain and the USA. In Blackpool the audience was invited on stage to join in the dance alongside cast members - including Frank Randle - as Tessa Deane sang. The show, which opened on Friday June 23rd, played to full houses and whilst writing of Randle, Lawrence Wright said, *"The North Pier is his natural home of humour. "Lancashire has always been famous for her comedians but it is very doubtful if she ever produced a greater one than Frank Randle, the funniest character comedian in Great Britain today".*

The Blackpool summer season for Randle and indeed for all of the country's theatrical artistes was abruptly halted with the declaration of war on September 3rd 1939. The Home Secretary not wanting to put large numbers of the public at risk from air raids decided to close all places of entertainment including cinemas and theatres. A few days later on September 21st soldiers were marching along Blackpool's promenade heading for their new home at the Squires Gate camp. They were followed a few yards behind by a somewhat awkwardly out of step group of performers led by Frank Randle, George Formby and Jack Rose; who were all set to provide the resort's first forces entertainment show. Randle also performed for the British Expeditionary Force in October prior to their departure to France. That same month the Government realised that the public needed more than the entertainment provided by BBC radio. Morale would be better served if the public could enjoy an evening at the 'pictures' or theatre especially for those in need of diversion from long working hours. With air attacks not materialising the rules were relaxed and it was left to local authorities to decide whether theatres should reopen. Of course, the entertainment industry lost many of its artistes to the armed forces. However, ready for such an emergency both the performers union Equity and the Variety Artistes Federation had prepared a register of artistes that were not required for active duty. Randle was one of these people and having been turned down for active service on medical grounds, he became for a brief period a member of the Blackpool Home Guard.

Chapter Two:

Barnes! A Pain in the Arse.

When it was realised that theatres would soon be up and running again Jack Taylor signed-up Frank Randle for the forthcoming 1940 Blackpool summer season at the resort's Opera House. Before the summer show commenced however, Randle would be out and about at the country's theatres in Tony Legate's road show *'Home Service Scandals'.*

The North Pier Theatre hadn't been the only Blackpool theatre destroyed by fire in 1938 as the resort's Opera House also suffered a similar fate. The owners however, 'The Blackpool Tower Company', wasted no time in having their theatre rebuilt and 'The New Opera House' opened in July 1939. This was now the newest and biggest theatre in the country, seating around 3,000 people. Jack Taylor resumed his role in booking the shows and was also instrumental in firmly establishing the 'New Opera House' as the resort's premier theatre. Having already signed Randle to appear in the 1940 'New Opera House' summer season show he decided some time later to bring in the popular radio show 'Bandwagon'. Consequently, he approached the stars of the BBC programme, Arthur Askey and Richard Murdoch. His intention was to hopefully call the show 'Blackpool's own Bandwagon' and he was soon in discussions with Jack Hylton, owner of the stage rights. Taylor fully intended to honour Randle's contract and planned to offer him a part in the show alongside Askey and Murdoch. Askey wrote in his autobiography, *"Hylton had a confidential chat with me and said, 'you'll find Jack Taylor a most amusing and genial fellow, until you work for him'. He also said that he had heard that Taylor had booked Frank Randle for the proposed summer show. He added, 'if he's in the show you won't live with him, he'll wipe the floor with you on his own ground".* Taylor eventually invited Askey to a meeting, during which the comedian came straight to the point and asked if Frank Randle had indeed been booked. With *"yes"* as Taylor's answer, Askey declined the offer repeating what he had been told by Hylton. Taylor was adamant that he wanted Askey and told him not to worry about Randle as he could either place him in his own South Pier show or in a touring revue. Askey agreed to this. Unfortunately, the proposed solution suggested by Taylor proved more difficult to implement than anticipated. The new and prestigious Opera House was a venue in which Randle eagerly wanted to perform, especially as he had been booked as the star. Consequently, he made it clear that he had a contract with 'The Blackpool Tower Company' and that he wanted that contract honoured.

While the conflict with Taylor was ongoing, Randle had been touring the country with a show produced by Taylor's son-in-law Tony Legate. Staged in association with Frank Randle the two had put together a morale boosting show *'Home Service Follies'* which opened at the Theatre Royal, Rochdale on Monday October 2nd 1939. However, it wasn't long into the tour before the show underwent a slight name change becoming instead *'Home Service Scandals'.*

Whilst Randle had been appearing in his 1939 Blackpool summer season, Legate, who lived in the resort, was planning the format for this new venture. With this in mind he made the short journey to the neighbouring resort of Cleveleys. Here at the seafront Arena, every summer a concert party would put on a show for the holiday makers. It was a visit well worth making for Legate as in the concert party's line-up were Ernie Dale, Charlie Parsons, The Wilton Brothers and Gus Aubrey; all of whom he signed to appear in *'Home Service Scandals'.* This show brought together for the first time many artistes who would become regular performers in Randle's company. None more so than Gus Aubrey who was to develop a special relationship with Randle. Although their friendship throughout Randle's life was to be a mixture of all emotions, on stage their performances were perfection.

Gus Aubrey was born Edward Brown on July 12th 1905 in Pendleton, Salford. His parents Rosina and John both had theatrical backgrounds and Edward, the ninth of their ten children, followed suit at an early age. 'Teddy' as he was known to the family was as a nine year old juvenile one of Clare Coverdale's 'Nine Dainty Dots' appearing with Jimmy James in *'Ten to One'* at Manchester's Tivoli Theatre. He also appeared as a boy soprano and female impersonator with his parent's revue Jack and Rose Hulme's Merry Mites. He continued in showbusiness making his mark in pantomime playing the dame, his first being Mrs Tinbad. Performing under the name Gus Aubrey, an alias bestowed upon him by his father, he knew his destiny was to be in the theatre. Percy Broadhead of the Manchester based Broadhead Theatre Circuit said he was the youngest dame they had ever had - others described him as being the best dressed. Quite a compliment for a sixteen year old making his way in the business and considering the competition. Still aged sixteen he became the youngest member of the drag revue *'Splinters'.* Originating as a First World War variety show

36

with comedian Hal Jones and female impersonator Reg Stone, its popularity continued up to World War II. With plenty of songs, comedy and 'soldiers in skirts', Aubrey fitted in well with the show and for three and a half years he toured the country with it including an appearance in London's West End. He also appeared in the 1929 film version of *'Splinters'* which starred Jones and Stone along with Sidney Howard. After leaving *'Splinters'* Gus became well established as a leading 'lady' in Phil Hanson's *'Tally Ho'* revue and worked with top pantomime producers Levi & Cardwell. His appearances as a dame were apparently inspired by Nellie Wallace whom he admired enormously. Over the years before teaming up with Randle he toured the country as a comedian and female impersonator in variety, summer shows, pantomime and even a spell in a Pierrot show. Also, for a while he performed as part of a double act with his sister Rene – stage name Rene Sinclair. The appearance together of Frank Randle and Gus Aubrey in *'Home Service Scandals'* may not however, have been their first meeting. For when Rene married it was to Billy Sibley, Randle's one-time partner in 'The Bouncing Randle's'. There exists a group photograph which includes Frank Randle and Billy Sibley which Billy inscribed and sent to Rene. This photo proves that Randle was on the scene at the time Billy was with Rene. Therefore it is quite possible that through Rene, Gus and Frank could easily have met.

The picture sent from Billy to Rene

37

Gus Aubrey stood a good six feet tall and with a slender body and bony features was quite a good looking man. He also had the tell-tale persona of a homosexual, including a very feminine manner which obviously helped him in playing the female roles. His sex life was very active and he had a number of encounters before settling down with his long-time friend and dress designer, Arthur Cragges Forster. To his family and many friends his lifestyle was an open book, incidentally Leah another sister was also gay. Gus found that life at times could be extremely difficult as he was often the target for fun and ridicule both off and on stage. *'Home Service Scandals'* was to be the start of a sixteen year relationship between Aubrey and Randle.

Randle and Legate had worked hard to put together a format for *'Home Service Scandals'* which was topical and morale boosting. A tag line for the show read 'The show that is doing national service by making the country laugh'. It was however, solely reliant on the laughter makers which included Charlie Parsons, Gus Aubrey and Randle himself. There was something for everyone from vocalist, instrumentalist, dancers, and for the male population, a striptease artiste. The show opened with the scene of a village hall decorated with Union flags, male cast members wore service uniforms while the females were attired as Red Cross nurses and

'Home Service Follies' soon to become 'Scandals' - 1939

the musical director dressed as a military bandmaster. Even the presentation of striptease artiste La Vadonis was kept to the military theme, introduced by two officers involved in an argument about Mademoiselle of Armentieres. As the acts went into their routines, the audience was supposedly watching a typical English village - a community which was not going to feel depressed by what was happening in the world - one which was rallying round keeping up their spirits in troubled times and sticking two fingers up at the enemy. Randle excelled in all this leading his company with gusto and the laughter and applause the show received proved he and Legate had hit on the right formula. Randle's biggest contribution to the show was his presentation of the 'Old Hiker' sketch. By April, having already played Blackpool, Doncaster, Birmingham and several London dates including Chelsea, Brixton and Walthamstow, the show was back on home territory with two shows in Manchester. The first of these was at the New Hippodrome from April 1st followed by a week at the Hulme Hippodrome from April 15th. A reviewer from the local paper said, *"Frank Randle rescues 'Home Service Scandals' from the mediocre... His whimsicality is a delight and as an 82 year old 'ancient warrior' we see him at his best".* When the show opened at Blackpool's Palace Theatre on April 29th 1940, Randle had the opportunity to confront Jack Taylor face to face regarding the Opera House situation. During this meeting Taylor insisted that Randle would not be playing the venue. Instead he offered him an alternative show which Randle categorically refused. Although enraged, he did however, agree to accept a weekly payment of £150 for the duration of the Opera House summer season. While the amount was far less than he would have received for performing he would in essence be collecting this for doing nothing. While accepting this offer Randle was far from being satisfied with the situation and he instructed his solicitors to take legal action against 'The Blackpool Tower Company'

At the end of the tour of *'Home Service Scandals'*, Frank and Queenie took a holiday returning in time for the filming of Randle's first feature film *'Somewhere in England'* which commenced at the Walton-on-Thames studio on Monday May 27th 1940. For the short time it took to shoot the film, Randle would have had a diversion from his dispute with Jack Taylor and the 'Blackpool Tower Company'. However, we wonder just what was going through his mind when he attended the film's premiere, ironically held in Blackpool in August at the height of the season.

Randle starred with Harry Korris in his first film 'Somewhere in England'

Although picking up payment for his non-appearances on the Opera House stage his annoyance had been rising on a daily basis. Living in the resort was not helping matters – if he had spent the time elsewhere it may have been easier for him to take. Being at home with time on his hands and the whole affair troubling his mind he turned to the bottle. Like many people in show business or indeed any walk of life, Randle enjoyed a drink. In reality he was a very heavy drinker and there was always at least one crate of Guinness in his dressing room. He drank real beer in his act and too much of it off stage, yet he seemed to be able to handle the situation without it taking too much effect on his daily routines. From time to time having had one too many he would miss odd performances and quite often have to be pulled out of nearby pubs for the start of a show's second half. However, it was a different matter altogether if on top of his beer intake he also hit the whisky. In years to come there would be many

Frank Randle caught on camera by Arthur Goulding during a Blackpool walkabout in summer 1940

drink related incidents, some evidently true but also a good many fabrications. Throughout the summer Randle continued to show his displeasure at 'The Blackpool Tower Company' by turning up at the Opera House somewhat worse for drink. According to Arthur Askey, Randle used to stand by the stage door with a bottle of Guinness in hand in order to irritate them. It is claimed that this whole incident was the one that established the comedian's dislike of impresarios, agents and theatre managers. It probably pleased Randle to see 'The Blackpool Tower Company' encountering copyright problems in the use of the *'Bandwagon'* name. After being forced to drop the original title the show stumbled through several title changes before eventually settling down as *'The Super Show of 1940'*. More problems beset the production when due to ill-health Arthur Askey had to end his season several performances early. None of the troubles surrounding the mounting of this show had endeared Taylor to 'The Blackpool Tower Company' and he soon felt their wrath. In what turned out to be a very hostile split they told him that he would never have another summer season show at their theatre. Undaunted Taylor was soon producing shows in opposition to the New Opera House at the resort's South Pier Theatre and the Hippodrome Theatre.

For the oncoming 1940/41 winter tour Legate and Randle assembled what was essentially the same line-up as used on the successful *'Home Service Scandals'*. With a schedule taking it through to the spring/summer of 1941 the tour ran under two differing titles. At some venues, like the Palace Sheffield, the show was billed as *'North West Follies'* while at others it was known as *'Randle's Scandals'* and described in one review at Salford as *"The very epitome of comedy"*. Who can take credit for the *'Randle's Scandals'* title, star or producer, is unknown however, under this name the show was destined to become a theatrical phenomenon touring annually for over a decade.

The 'Scandals' shows provided work for many artistes who would practically become Randle's stock company of stooges and artistes - over the years these have included Ernie Dale, Billy Pardoe, banjoist Arthur Cannon, organist Rita Shearer, Sally Barnes, The Ben Abdrahman Wozzan Troupe of acrobats, Hal & Winnie Mack and the Dancing Demons, Stan Stafford the singing navvy, Arthur Wilton, Jon Boden, Leo Fitzpatrick, Hal Swain and his Swing Sisters, soprano Irene Mansel and her husband (Randle's musical director) Billy Dixon Wood, Peter Brothers, Philip Kelly, Florence Whiteley's Zio Angels, Sonny Roy - the funny boy, pint sized Jimmy Clitheroe - later to find stardom as the eternal schoolboy in the 'Clitheroe Kid', Pat Williams, The Dagenham

Gus Aubrey – 'The Lady'

Girl Pipers, The Kerry Pipers and not forgetting 'The Lady' drag artiste Gus Aubrey.

On the 1940/41 winter tour Randle introduced his 'Grandpa's Birthday' sketch which was featured for the first time at the Theatre Royal, Rochdale when the show opened on Monday 24th February 1941. Arthur Goulding who appeared with Randle at the time recalled, *"My mother Lily was the first person to play Grandma to Randle's Grandpa in his sketch".* Randle's aged characterisation was based on his own Grandfather Arthur Hughes and his adopted 'Grandpa Heath'. Presented at this time as 'Grandfer's Birthday' the sketch centres on the old man returning home from the pub to be greeted by friends and family who have gathered to celebrate his birthday.

The opening scene is set in a parlour where a group of people are dancing and singing to the strains of *'Knees up Mother Brown'* after which 'family friend' Arthur Cannon entertains them with a banjo solo. *"Well seeing it's Grandpa's Birthday - where is he?"* cries out Ernie Dale. *"He'll be in the pub celebrating - but he should have been here by now,"* replies Grandmother. *"He's here now! He's coming up the garden path"* Ernie Dale proclaims. A door opens and Grandpa - Frank Randle - enters carrying a glowing red road lamp and a bottle of beer. The whole company welcome him with cries of *"come on Grandpa".*

Grandpa (Randle): *"By gum I've 'ad some ale to'neet.* *"Eeh look what some damn fool left near a hole in't road".*
Poor old Grandpa with a little too much ale is staggering as he hands the lamp to his Grandson (Ernie Dale) and says: *"Go and lie down, you'll feel better".*
Grandson: *"What the...?"*
Grandpa takes a drink from the bottle.
Grandpa: *"See I can do the Swallow. Is it 12 o'clock yet?"*
Grandson: *"12 o'clock? Why, Grandpa?"*

Grandpa: *"Well I want to wish you all a happy and prosperous New Year".*

Grandson: *"No, no, Grandpa, it's your birthday".*

Grandpa: *"Many happy returns".*

The local vicar steps forward and in placing his hand on Grandpa's shoulder somewhat startles the old gent, who reacts with a surprised vocalisation of *"Who the Hell's that".*

Grandson: *"Shush, you mustn't say that.   Thank the Vicar, Mr Clutterbuck".*

Eyeing up Grandma, Grandpa says: *"I'll clutter thy buck.   "I've got a surprise for thee, thy likes to hear of a man winning money at dominoes"?*

Grandma: *"By gum, I do an all".*

Grandpa: *"Well, Bob Gutteridge has won my pension off me".* Grandpa is tapped on the shoulder by his Grandson who invites him to take a seat.   Grandpa sits down then quickly rising again says, *"I've sat on a bobbin of cotton".*

Grandson: *"No, no, there's nowt there Grandpa".* Grandpa grabs the front of his trousers and as he looks down, a voice from the crowd asks, *'What's the matter Grandpa, what's the matter?'*

Grandpa: *"I've been tampered with".*

Grandson: *"Come on folks lets do what we said"*

The whole company then joined together in singing 'Happy Birthday to You'.

Grandpa: *"And a prosperous New Year".*

Grandpa then takes a drink from his bottle just as a knock is heard at the door.   The door opens to reveal Gus Aubrey as Widow Twillop a one time youthful but now elderly dancing girl.   Grandpa on seeing her almost chokes on his beer (Randle literally spitting it out onto the stage).

Grandpa: *"Eh, look who's come, it's Mrs Miniver".*

Widow Twillop: *"Aye and I've come to see thee.   "Eh when I look at thee thar as beautiful as ever tha were".*

Grandma: *"Now then none of that".*

Widow Twillop: *"Nay, what's up with thee Sarah? "Don't get thee rag out, he were courting me afore thee".*

Grandpa: *"Hey shut up, tha'll get me throttled"*

Widow Twillop: *"Well tha were courting me, weren't tha?"*

Grandpa: *"Well tha doesn't need to keep on harping on it"*

Widow Twillop: *"He were a young clip in them days".*

Grandpa: *"I'll give thee a crack on the head with this bottle in a minute. "I could tell a few tales about thee tha knows".*

Widow Twillop: *"Not here though.*

Randle as Grandpa

Grandpa: *"Does thee remember when I pinched that elastic off thee for my catapult".*
Widow Twillop: *"Eh I can. "It's all as though it were only yesterday. "We'd be about that high* - (indicating height with his hands) - *we used to play together in the nude".*
Grandpa: *"Where"?*
Grandson: *"She says you used to play together in the nude"*

Grandpa: *"Eeh, you wouldn't know the old place now, they've built a picture palace on there".*

Widow Twillop: *"He were only a little 'un. But he had his moments".*

Grandpa apologetically turns to Grandma and says: *"It were only a bit o' fun"*

Widow Twillop: *"We were very young. "Well we knew no better".*

Grandpa: *"No - but I'd a damn good idea".*

Grandma: *"Now then none of that".*

The Grandson approaches the Old Dame indicating she should get herself a drink and as she walks to the drinks table she removers her coat. Watching her every move Grandpa says: *"By gum we 'ad some ale toneet".*

Grandson: *"Aye tha's getting too much ale thee".*

Grandpa: *"I can't get enough".*

Grandson: *"No, I mean tha's getting to old to keep taking too much".*

Grandpa: *"Too Old? "Who?"*

Grandson: *Thee"*

Grandpa: *"I'll fight thee any time thee likes".*

As Grandpa raises his fist the assembled company cry out in unison *"No, no".* Grandpa stands defiant before his Grandson.

Grandson: *"Now then wi thi' tupping"*

Grandpa: *"Well tha shouldn't keep saying I'm too old"*

A voice from among the assembled company shouts: *"Now then Grandpa, sit down and behave yourself".*

Grandpa dutifully or perhaps needfully complies and finds himself a comfortable seat, yet almost instantaneously rises up to say, *"I'll 'av a do at thee, never mind him".* The Grandson manages to hold him back as Grandpa exclaims, *"Don't, let go".*

Grandson: *"Come on Grandpa we want no fighting here".*

Grandpa: *"No, we'll have no fighting. "I can't fight".*

Grandson: *No, tha can't fight Grandpa'.*

Grandpa: *"But I can make it blasted awkward for them that can".*

Widow Twillop: *"Sit down and shut up thee old gob".*

Grandma jumps up seizing the bottle and attempts to hit the Old Dame.

Widow Twillop: *"Oh, that's nice to a Lady".*

Grandpa: *"What a face to go ratting with".*

Widow Twillop: *"Well I can't help it".*

Grandpa: *"No, but you could stop it".*

The door suddenly opens and an old man enters.

Grandson: *"Look who's here".*

Grandpa: *"Eeh, it's my father. "What are you doing out of bed at this time of night"?*

Great Grandpa: *"I've been 'aving a bit of bother with thi mother".*

Grandpa: *"Why, what's up wi 'er?"*

Great Grandpa: *"She wants me to stop playing football with mi father.* *"Anyhow seeing as how its thi birthday, I think I'll have a sup wi' thi and then...*
Grandpa: *"And then, what"*
Great Grandpa: *"And then I'll 'av another".*
Grandpa: *"Tha'll be lucky if tha gets first 'un".*
Great Grandpa: *"What! You refuse me?* He goes to hit Grandpa - people from company carry him out through door.
Grandpa: *"I'll knock his stomach off his chest".*
Grandma: *"I'm ashamed of you".*
Grandpa: *"Well I've 'ad some ale toneet".*
Grandma: *"Aye and you'll suffer for it in the morning".*
Grandpa: *"We want no fighting here".*
Grandson: *"No. Look at that lovely cake that Grandma's made for you".*
Grandpa: *"Fetch it over I'll eat it 'ere".*
Grandma: *"Nay, they all want some of that".*
Grandson: *"I've a good idea Grandpa, how about cutting the cake with that sword you had at Balaclava"?*
Grandpa: *"Aye. I will, I'll cut t'cake with the sword I had at Balaclava.* *"I had a sword at Balaclava I was there".*
Voice from the company: *"Of course you were Grandpa".*
Grandpa: *"They were a fine body of men. I can see it as though it were yesterday ... it was on a hill between two valleys".* As he is speaking, Grandpa is handed the sword, *"We had as many as three on the end of that...",* he says as he begins to wave it around quite erratically. *"Balaclava... "Aye... I was the first man in..."*
Grandson: *"Aye"*
Grandpa: *"I was the first out again".*
From the orchestra pit comes the sound of a bugle - sounding the charge.
Grandpa: *"Did you here that my lads? "The charge - the charge of the Light Brigade. Boots and Saddles"*
As he is brandishing the sword, thrusting and parrying, screams are heard from the company - Grandpa pauses.
Grandpa: *"I'll cut all yer ruddy 'eads off"*
Grandson: *"Get the sword off him - give him his ale".*
The Old Dame hands him a drink and does business of poking eye out.
Grandson: *"Come on folks, let's have some Lancers."* The whole company take up their positions and start to dance 'The Lancers'. Grandpa and Widow Twillop dance together before he chases her off the stage. Widow Twillop soon re-enters rushing across stage closely followed by Grandpa who is holding a long pair of comedy bloomers on the end of his sword.

46

The above sketch is from a version presented in 1942 in which the then 68-years-old Pat Williams played Great Grandpa. Dublin born Pat had been in show business most of his life making his first stage appearance in 1892. For many years he performed as a solo comedian before later becoming associated with several double acts including 'Williams and Brown' and 'Williams and Warden'. Pat also appeared in many stage farces, straight plays and musicals. After retiring from the business he moved into a home for retired theatricals but found life away from the stage boring. He approached his old friend Frank Randle in the hope he may find something for him in his 'Scandals' shows. Randle didn't hesitate in offering Pat a position for he felt indebted to the aged comic. Apparently, many years earlier during a period when Randle was still struggling to climb the showbiz ladder Pat had shared a chicken with Frank and Queenie at a time when they were practically penniless and virtually starving. This act had never been forgotten by Randle and the pair remained friends all their lives.

Before the 1940/41 winter tour ended Randle received the news that his solicitors had won the case against 'The Blackpool Tower Company' which resulted in Randle securing a spot in 'Hullabaloo' the 1941 Opera House summer show. This production, which was publicised as 'Blackpool's Laughter Blitz', had no top billing and Randle was just one of several stars which also included Webster Booth & Anne Ziegler, Nervo & Knox of Crazy Gang fame and xylophonist Teddy Brown. The show had its Grand Gala Opening on Friday June 20th. Randle's performance was confined to the second half, in which assisted by Arthur Wilton, Gus Aubrey, Bill Pardoe, Ernie Dale and Arthur Cannon he presented his new sketch 'Grand Pa's Birthday'. Of Randle's 'Grandpa' performance one reviewer said, *"Randle [is given] opportunity to get every ounce of fun from his clever character study"*. Although Randle experienced a good season from the point of view of audience reception he still disliked the limitations that had been placed on his performances. Another likewise thinking show reviewer, after first stating that Randle's delicious performance was one of the biggest hits of the show, knowingly added, *"We should like to have seen more of Frank"*. The show ran for an extended season ending on October 9th. Randle was never to forgive or forget the treatment he had received from 'The Blackpool Tower Company' over the whole affair. However, he did see one opportunity to have a final swipe at those responsible and gain a modicum of revenge. This occurred at the conclusion of the run of 'Hullabaloo' at an end of season party. It had been announced that male members of the production were expected to accompany the female members to the lavish affair. However, as the party got underway Frank was notably absent. It was actually in full swing by the time the great man made his uncertain entrance, together with his - *"young lady"* - as he announced her. She was a reeking, staggering drunken old tramp. In the stunned silence that followed she ploughed into the free food and drink with uninhibited gusto. Frank had had some form of retribution.

The success of the 1940 film '*Somewhere in England* had prompted more of the same and Frank was back in the studios in October 1941 with just a few Variety dates to take him up to Christmas. During his career Randle acquired a good reputation for his many fine pantomime performances. Most notable amongst these would be his 'Buttons' from '*Cinderella*' followed closely by 'Widow Twanky' from '*Aladdin*'. The pantomime this particular year was a touring version of '*Red Riding Hood*' for Jack Taylor and John D. Robertson. Playing the part of 'Simple Simon' the complete opposite to Randle's usual 'ancient geriatrics' seemed to have put a youthful sparkle into everything he did on stage. The show opened at the Lido, Bolton on Christmas Eve 1941 to a crowded and responsive audience. Frank was supported by an able cast, which included Irene Mansell as the Fairy Queen, Bebe Terry as Red Riding Hood, Freda Barrie as Maid Marion and Bob Cromwell as Dame Trot. The local newspaper noted, "*...without 'Simple Simon' 'Red Riding Hood' would be nowhere. "At least that is what Frank Randle and his associates make of the simple-minded soul whose comedy became so infectious that many an aside was lost in the laughter"*. The traditional Christmas fare was more than well received in Bolton and in just over the two weeks that it played at the Lido it generated over £6,000. The show continued on its tour playing to similar audiences and creating like profits much to the satisfaction of Randle himself. For not only was Frank being paid £350 a week, he was also getting a percentage of all the takings - a deal which had been struck between him and Jack Taylor. When the pantomime played at the Manchester Hippodrome early in 1942 Jack Taylor said of Randle's pay packet "*I don't think it's a penny too much"*. To which a reviewer in one Manchester paper most heartily agreed adding, "*Here surely is the King Pin of 'low comedy"*. Both Jack Taylor and John D. Robertson were delighted with the success of the production, so much so that the same formula was recreated the following Christmas. Frank Randle again starred as 'Simple Simon' with the added benefit of Gus Aubrey taking over the role of Dame Trot. Freda Barrie and Bebe Terry reprised their roles while Billy Pardoe was the Squire. The Wilton Bothers appeared as the Robbers, Sylvia Hylton as the Fairy Queen and Ernie Dale as King Wolf. The show also featured a number of specialty acts, notably Al Wright's comedy circus, juggling by Marjora and the talented banjo playing of Arthur Cannon, though to incorporate these meant straying from the story. After opening at the Leeds Empire for a two week Christmas run on December 21st 1942 the show toured until February 1st 1943.

1943 was the year which saw Randle taking on the mantle of solo producer for his 'Randle's Scandals' shows. Unfortunately Randle's fellow artistes from this period are now virtually all deceased though happily as we write, 84-years-old Arthur Goulding who performed as Arthur Wilton, is alive and well and full of memories. Arthur came from a show business background as his mother Lily had initially been a soubrette touring under the name Monica Wilton until taking temporary retirement and raising three children. However, from a very young age the children were all taught to play musical instruments and actively encouraged to perform. So much so that by 1927, when Arthur was just six-years-old, the family were presenting an act entitled 'The Wilton Brothers and Ma'. The talented brothers, Arthur, Ron and Gordon, could play an assortment of musical instruments including piano-accordion, banjo, violin, guitar and drums. By 1933 Arthur was appearing more often with his brothers and introduced a strong element of comedy to their routines. The family joined Randle in 1939 with Arthur's father Tom acting as the show's stage manager and Frank's dresser. Listening to Arthur recall the time spent with Randle during the first four years of World War II and the story which unfolded was one of violence, bullying and drink. Though of course there were also some happy times.

Arthur Wilton poses with Frank's Chevrolet

"*I used to drive his car to take us to the various towns*", said Arthur. "*There'd be me and Frank in the front with Queenie and my mother in the back. "We actually stayed with them in their caravan while on tour".* Petrol rationing had been introduced in Britain almost as soon as war had been declared which only allowed for around 200 miles of travel for the private motorist per month. One can only guess at how Randle obtained enough fuel to travel the length and breadth of the country with a caravan in tow. "*I don't know how he managed to get all the petrol"* added Arthur, *"it could only have been the black market – he never actually told me".* If indeed it was black market fuel then Randle was taking a huge risk. Fame was no protection from prosecution as proven by well-known songwriter Ivor Novello when he was given an eight-week prison sentence for dishonestly obtaining petrol for his Rolls-Royce. Another story recounted to us concerns a group of war-time motorcyclists who pulled into the car park of a public house to affect a repair. While one chap remained outside to mend his puncture the others went inside the pub. While working on his bike the lone motorcyclist noticed a rather large car with what looked like an adapted fuel tank. On completing the patch up he entered the bar to find his friends laughing and joking with Frank Randle – who had bought everyone beer and pies. After some time in his company they decided it was time that they were on their way. Randle followed them into the car park and told them all to remove their petrol caps. He then produced a piece of rubber tubing and proceeded to siphon fuel from his own car's petrol tank. The cyclists were taken aback by this act of generosity and although wondering where Randle obtained such a quantity of fuel they were not going to look a gift horse in the mouth. Talking this over later several of the cyclists were of the opinion that the petrol they had been given was actually aviation fuel and that they were fortunate to have had enough of their own petrol left in their tanks to dilute it.

Listening to Arthur Goulding reminisce it became clear that while he respected Randle as a performer, he thought him as a person to be *"very devious, deceitful and very cunning with a streak of evil which he was vary careful to hide".* He went on to say of how Frank Waters, a former miner from Scotland who appeared in several early 'Scandals' shows, had received an offer to work at the London Palladium. *"He could certainly sing",* enthused Wilton, *"Randle in a broad Lancashire accent said to Frank Waters, 'oh congratulations owd lad'. "Talk about being two-faced, poor Frank told me that from that moment on Randle made his life hell".* It was only a select few of Randle's close cronies that had the privilege of calling the comedian by his first name, these included Ernie Dale, Bill Pardoe, Arthur Cannon and of course Gus Aubrey. However, most members of the company had to address him formally as Mr Randle. Obviously, he was the one in charge and he certainly let them know this, a strange situation for someone who supposedly disliked those in authority. Arthur Goulding said, *"He was a despot, a dictator and it was his nature to be like that".* An indication of this was given in a story related to us by Winnie Mack. Winnie and her father Hal Mack had joined the shows in 1942 and remained for eleven tours. Winnie remembers that Randle once instructed all the male members of the company to meet him at 9.00am next day at the theatre. Hal wasn't looking forward to this for usually after a long performance he liked to stay in bed late the following day studying the racing pages as he was a great man for the horses. However, as Winnie recalled, *"He had to join them or Randle would not have been too pleased".* Reluctantly, Hal arrived at the theatre and before long every male member was congregated together awaiting Randle's appearance. When he finally arrived he was carrying a bag from which he pulled out a number of teaspoons. He proceeded to pass these out to his bemused looking company. What followed next must have totally baffled the by now irate gathering and it proved that no one dare not do as Randle said. On each spoon he placed senna pods and ordered that everyone was to eat them. One can only imagine the look on their faces. Strangely none of them spoke out when Randle informed them that they were now all about to go on a cross country run, a measure of the hold he had on them. *"I only hope none of them was caught short before they got back",* said Winnie laughing. But what was it all about, why should Randle have done this? Only he would have known and it was something he never explained. He was in a position where he could do such things and obviously did so – and all without anyone's objections.

One of the most popular sketches to be featured over the 'Scandals' years was 'In the Jungle/At the Medical Board'. Here was a sketch which obviously struck a chord during the war years and even post-war when National Service was still in force. In the 1941 version Billy Pardoe played the Medical Officer, Ernie Dale the orderly with Privates Randle, Aubrey and Wilton causing the havoc. In the following extract as the three privates are marched on stage to face the MO, Randle trips and falls down...

MO (Billy Pardoe): *"What's that man doing down there?"*
Randle: *"Getting up"*
MO: *"Getting up indeed... what's the idea of barging in here like that?"*
Randle: *"Well... we haven't been feeling so well and the Sergeant sent us down to see the MO".* Randle taps the officer on the head as he says, *"I'm talking to you".*
MO: *"Don't do that I'm the MO".* - *"Now then, what is your baptismal cognomen?"*
Randle: *"If it comes to big words... Friars Balsam".*
Orderly (Ernie Dale): *"Oh the illiterate"*
Randle: *"What's that you say?"*
Orderly: *"I said you were illiterate".*
Randle: *"My father and mother were married".*
MO: *"What is your baptismal cognomen?"*

Randle: *"I don't know"*
Orderly: *"He means... what is your name"*
Randle: *"Will you please shut your gob"*
Orderly: *"Oh that's nice for the modern army"*.
Randle: *"I'm talking to the engineer not the oil rag"*.
MO: *"What is your name?"*
Randle: *"Henry"*
MO: *"Henry What?"*
Randle: *"You've guessed it"*
MO: *"Guessed what?"*
Randle: *"My name"*
MO: *"Well, What is it?"*
Randle: *"It is"*
MO: *"What?"*
Randle: *"Aye, that's it"*
MO: *"I demand to know your name"*.
Randle: *"You bladder of lard... lend me your pen... get off mi foot...Move up there"*. Gets into MO's chair.
MO: *"Get out of it"*.
Randle: *"I'll draw you a duck"*

In the Jungle/At the Medical Board

MO: *"I don't want a duck"*
Randle: *"Two oo's and a Watt"*
Orderly: *"I've got it... Sir... Watt... W. A. T. T."*
Randle: *"You clever little thing... Boyeee"*
MO: *"Number one in the ranks there... where do you live?   Here you, Curly... what did you do before you joined the army?"*
Aubrey: (Stammering) *"I was working on the r.r.r.r.railway"*
Randle: *"He was working on the railway"*
Aubrey: *"I was o.o.o.o.opening c.c.c.arriage d.d.doors"*
MO: *"What for?"*
Aubrey: *"T.t.t.to see if they were s.s.shut"*.
Randle: *"He's nearly as daft as thee"*.
Orderly: *"Where were you born?"*
Randle: *"In bed"*
Orderly: *"Were you staying with your parents at the time?"*
Randle: *"No I was staying with my aunt Fanny"*
MO: *"Who is your father?"*

Randle: "My uncle Bill"
MO: "Were you born in wedlock"
Randle: "No, Matlock"
MO: "Get these man ready for medical examination"
Orderly: "I want to know your pedigree"
Randle: "What do you think we are Whippets?"
Orderly: "He want's to know your forefathers"
Randle: "There's only three of us"
MO: "Everybody has forefathers. He's got forefathers. I've got forefathers".
Randle: "I though he was a well built fellow"
Arthur Wilton as the third private commences to do a few stitches of knitting and is spotted by the MO.
MO: "Knitting", says the MO as he throws up hands in despair.
Randle: Picks up his hat.
MO: "Put that down... Attention... Left turn... Quick march". The sketch ends as all are marched off stage

When performing this sketch at Manchester, Arthur Wilton recalled that he messed things up somewhat. What followed then not only showed Arthur's youthful cockiness but also Randle's short temper and violent streak. After walking off stage Randle remonstrated with Arthur over his mistakes. Arthur in return stated how he hadn't intended to mess up and appropriately apologised adding, "Alright I'll be careful next time Mr Randle". However, in doing so, he heavily emphasised the word Mr. That lit the touch paper with Randle and livid he turned to Arthur Wilton and threw a punch, which knocked the skinny youth to the ground. He then continued to make his way to his dressing room as if nothing had happened. Over the four years that Arthur Wilton worked with Randle he became as close as anyone to the man. Not close in respects of a confidante but in proximity through their work, daily routines and the fact they shared Randle's caravan. First hand he learned of Randle's violent temper. Not only had he himself been assaulted by the man he also recalled that Randle hit Queenie. Vividly he described the caravan, 20 foot long with a double bed at one end taking up the whole width where of course Frank and Queenie slept. At the other end two single beds running down each side of the van with an aisle between, here slept Arthur and his mother Lily. Most of the time whilst touring Randle would park the caravan on the car park of a public house. Arthur Cannon (Jnr.) whose father was a close friend of Randle's and part of his entourage for many years also remembered, "The caravan was a massive four-wheeler which totally filled a Chelsea public house car park when he was playing at the Chelsea Palace". He also recalled that on occasions his father had said that Randle could be quite volatile, which adds substance to what Arthur Wilton recollects... *"Randle had been at the pub drinking one night after a show, on his return to the van his forehead was red".* Apparently this was a sure sign that Randle had been drinking whisky, *"We knew this and knew there would be trouble",* said Arthur. Almost immediately on entering the caravan Randle and Queenie were involved in an argument during which Randle hit her several times. The argument seems to have been caused by the fact Randle had not noticed Queenie standing in the wings during his performance. Arthur Wilton said, *"She daren't leave the side of the stage while he was performing and he insisted that she be in view in case somebody pinched her... stole her from him... it's a fact... she had to watch his act through every time".* Many people were in agreement that Randle was a man's man, Arthur Wilton remarked, *"He wasn't a womaniser. "He liked male company especially when visiting a pub which to him was a manly thing - fine with mates but definitely not with females".* Occasionally, on a Saturday night after the last performance of the week Randle and those privileged to call him Frank would go out for a beer. From time to time Arthur Wilton was asked to join them. Making their way back from one such night out Gus Aubrey had them all in fits of laughter. Gus, whom Wilton referred to as a 'Nancy Boy' also added, *"He was a nice lad and wasn't afraid of Frank, he wasn't frightened at all".* *"He was tall and thin with plenty of humour in him".* This particular night Aubrey's humour came flooding out in abundance. As the friends were walking down a back street singing and acting the fool, a bedroom window was suddenly flung open quickly followed by a woman's protruding head which bellowed, 'will you all shut up you noisy pigs'. Instantly Gus turned around looked up towards the window and in the most over the top effeminate voice shrieked, 'Oh shut up yourself you silly old cow'. Continuing in the same feminine manner he had everyone in stitches as they stood aside to witness two 'women' having a rare old public slanging match.

Randle's wartime shows were obviously tailored to suit the times as one reviewer for a performance in Oldham noted, *"It's a khaki show; chorus girls in nurses uniforms decorate the background, while Frank as a not so simple recruit finds fat targets for his humour amongst Colonels, Sergeants, Orderlies and his own fellow privates. Mr Randle blazes a trail of laughter through Barrack Square and orderly room - Yes fundamentally it is the same Frank Randle of pre-war. Not just a purveyor of jokes but a skilled character actor".*

These shows also featured much patriotic flag waving and morale-boosting elements, especially during their finales. Nightly the audience would bring the house down after their rousing rendition of 'Rule Britannia' and 'The National Anthem'.

The finale began with the entire company joining together on stage to sing, 'Soldiers of the Queen', 'I do like to be Beside the Sea'. 'Pack up your Troubles' and 'Land of Hope and Glory'. Randle certainly knew what the audience required during these times and their involvement was testimony to their appreciation. Once the applause had finally subsided Arthur Cannon stepped forward to recite the monologue 'I Vow to Thee my Country'. During which, he waved his arm to gesture on to the stage two artistes respectively representing Winston Churchill and Joseph Stalin - the latter played by Randle himself. Neither actually spoke but merely crossed the stage acknowledging the vast applause, which greeted them. *"There is still another great statesman standing side by side*

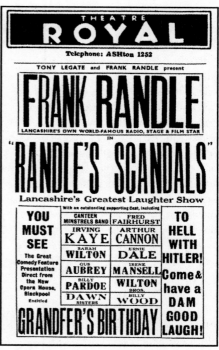

Theatre Royal, Ashton-under-Lyne,
April 13th 1942

with Britain today", cried out Arthur Cannon, *"President Roosevelt".* Ernie Dale as Roosevelt enters to the same thunderous welcome. Arthur Cannon then proceeded to bring the audience to a fever pitch as he praised the statesmen, the navy, air force, army and lastly the workers of the British Empire. *"We'll stick at it and we'll lick 'em in the end"* he proclaimed. One can well imagine the audience's response to this. The band then burst into the last few bars of 'Rule Britannia' as a backcloth was lowered on which was painted a large portrait of the Royal Family. *"Ladies and Gentlemen - The King",* said Arthur Cannon - as all the assembled acts turned their backs to the audience and faced the Royal portrait. The audience en-masse rose from their seats as artistes and public collectively sang 'God Save the King'. Taking their bows the company's ears must have been ringing as Randle in an acknowledgment to the crowd, brought yet another tidal wave of appreciation.

Since moving to 32 Forest Gate, Frank and Queenie's lifestyle had continued much as before with more time spent on the road in their caravan than at their Blackpool home. This of course had left Rhoda as usual living alone for most of the time though now in a very large house. This then may have been a contributing factor in why Randle upped sticks yet again. It cannot be said when exactly this move took place but by 1943 they were already settled at 50 Grenfell Avenue; a smaller house and similar in size and character to that of Ellesmere Road. Randle's life on the road also made his turn out with the Blackpool Home Guard somewhat erratic. He was a member of 'C' Company based in Marton, Blackpool and it was probably his uncertainty of turnout with the company that saw him assigned duties in the cookhouse on the occasions he did manage to join them. Much like George Formby, who, when he turned out, acted as a dispatch rider. On one occasion when the full Blackpool Platoon were on a weekend of tactical exercises at Fletcher's Holiday Camp, Little Singleton, Blackpool during July 1942, Randle was again on cookhouse duties. After a gruelling march to the camp the tired volunteers were

Randle with Home Guard colleagues pictured at Fletcher's Holiday Camp

greeted by a lively and chirpy Randle ready to dole out the ubiquitous 'cup of cha and a wad'. Although sleeping with his colleagues and helping to feed them Randle never actually indulged in any active part of the manoeuvres.   While his comrades were crawling about in simulated battle conditions, Frank was busy peeling mounds of potatoes.   As the weekend came to its end and the weary contingent were about to leave, rumour abounded that Randle was ill.   If this was the case then he seemed to make a quick recovery for as the group were marching back to the centre of Blackpool, Randle passed them in his large convertible car and with the top down was smiling and waving as he sped by.   Unfortunately touring Britain in his shows meant even less time was being spent with the Home Guard and eventually he reluctantly relinquished his position.   However, he certainly had plenty of thoughts on how Britain could defeat the enemy.   He continually inundated his friend at the local newspaper office with elaborately self-drawn drawn plans of his innovative ideas aimed at helping to win the war accompanied by the earnest plea for them to be forwarded to the war office.   Randle's journalist friend publicly pointed out that... *"Some had the germ of merit, and all showed a new facet of Frank's many-sided character".*   Locally the RAF was training at Lytham with many of the men being quartered in the large seafront hotels.   Randle on several occasions took it upon himself to organise entertainment for them and for the American Army Air Corps who came later in the war.   One can only wonder at what they thought of his Lancashire humour. Randle and his company were to eventually give hundreds of shows entertaining the British troops and he accepted as many invitations as possible, no matter when or where it was.   He personally bore the brunt for the travelling expenses for the full company when he took them off to visit various naval and military hospitals even when travelling as far as Falkirk in Scotland.

For the summer of 1943 Jack Taylor had once again booked Frank Randle to appear in his season offering at the South Pier Theatre *'The Show that Jack Built'.* The early 1940s also saw the arrival in Blackpool of Harry Barnes as the new Chief Constable of the Borough Police Force. Over the next few years he would prove to be a constant thorn in Randle's side.   During his career in the resort Barnes made few friends either within the force or with the public.   From his arrival he had his own ideas on how he was going to run things and soon made a huge impact on the resort.   It mattered little to him if people disagreed with his methods or points of view.   Quite laudably he soon started to weed out the town's criminal element and hardly a day passed without him making a court appearance in some case or other.   Less admirably, he had little regard for public relations and the humble police constables would be reprimanded for simply chatting to the public. Barnes was a staunch churchgoer with a marked Victorian outlook and certainly a prudish aversion for alcohol and its purveyors.   He was overscrupulous in enforcing long outdated byelaws and the Sunday entertainment law.   The one person who Barnes really formed a close friendship with was Alderman Quayle, Chairman of the local Watch Committee.   Like Barnes, Alderman Quayle was far from being a popular figure.   The two would meet for lunch almost daily and on many occasions even holidayed together.   No doubt many of the lunches would have included discussion on the summer shows and of course, Randle.

With such a strict morality, Barnes it seems had taken an instant dislike to Randle. To see someone standing in the glare of the spotlights, beer bottle in hand, burping, gurgling and, as Randle was prone to do, throwing false teeth into the audience, was so unacceptable - yet there was little he could do about it. The only way Barnes could take Randle to task was if the star strayed away from the show's script.

We should point out that at this time any play that was to be performed on stage had to submit its script for approval and licensing to the office of the Lord Chamberlain. After reading the script, if it was regarded as having any content unsuitable, then the license would not be issued until amendments were carried out.   In variety or revues any act appearing did not need a license, but a sketch being performed may possibly have needed one. We say, possibly, as there seems to have been much confusion within the Lord Chamberlain's office as to when a sketch actually became a play.   Whereas one person would take a sketch as being just that, another could easily say it was a play. Interpretation of the rules was somewhat ambiguous and there appears to have been no rigid guidelines. If this was confusing for those in the Lord Chamberlain's office it was to mystify the poor performers like Frank Randle. Many a producer and theatre manager in reality did not know where they stood and many would submit a script for a sketch or even a whole road show revue for approval just to be on the safe side - while others thought there was no need and refrained.

During the run of Randle's Blackpool summer shows Barnes would have police officers in the audience almost nightly in the hope that Randle would include some unlicensed material.   We have received several letters from people who state that over the years it seemed to be a personal crusade for Barnes, and Randle, more than any other was his nemesis. It is hardly surprising that Randle's dislike of authority figures increased.   The first encounter between the two seems to have happened shortly after the opening of *The Show that Jack Built'* on Friday June 11th 1943.   *"Another Jack Taylor Triumph"* proclaimed the headline in the local press reporting on the first night's performance.

The reviewer said, *"In the brand of humour that he has made particularly his own Randle pulls out all the stops. Whether fighting the rigours of military life, grouching with grandpa or getting a drink he rolls with roving eye along the lanes of laughter. They include a rich sense of caricature, a devastatingly facial expression and a broad - sometimes very broad - sense of comedy. 'The Show that Jack Built' was ably blue printed by Taylor and smoothly constructed by a talented company of builders which included Billy Scott Coomber, Jeanette Haley, Ronaldé and of course Randle's stooges".* The report concluded that the show was given the happiest of send offs by the packed audience, which included the Mayor of Blackpool Alderman P Round. All looked well for a successful season, before the intervention of Chief Constable Barnes changed things completely. Barnes sent a communication to the theatre management drawing their attention to certain incidents in the show that he thought were of an unsavoury nature; and pointed out to them the terms of their license. He stated that he had received complaints from the magisterial bench and from the public. Barnes asked that the material should be deleted and enquired as to what action the directors proposed to take.

Jack Taylor

Jack Taylor spoke to Randle and discussed the correspondence from Barnes. As a result of that conversation Taylor later left a letter at the theatre for Randle that stated that his contract was terminated with immediate effect. Consequently Frank Randle did not appear in the show from that night Thursday 17th June. The show continued with Billy Scott Coomber filling in until Taylor could bring in Norman Evans a few weeks later.

Randle was bewildered by the whole situation and he said, *"There are people who may object to some kinds of humour, this cannot be avoided and, of course I stand to be shot at should I be in disfavour with anyone. "Naturally we are supposed to keep within the limit and I have never set myself out to be a dirty comedian. Most of my fan mail is from young children".* He went on to say that he had proof that the material in question had been used many times before in Blackpool - without complaint from anyone. On this occasion again he had received not one complaint concerning the material or for anything else within the show. He stated however, that he was willing to cut the so-called offending material and was not opposed to leave out anything else they might consider to be objectionable. But due to Taylor's abrupt response he was not given any opportunity to do so. *"There are lots and lots worse material than mine,* Said Randle, *"I do not wish to offend my public I only want to make them laugh and feel a little happier in times like these. "I am willing to keep faith with the chief constable, the public, the pier directors and Mr Taylor",* he added. But the die had been cast and Randle left the show.

Arthur Wilton remembered, *"When the show abruptly finished and before Randle could plan anything else, we got away".* Arthur was under the impression that because Randle didn't want them to leave, he acted meanly towards them. The war was still on and a lot of theatrical agents, like Mannie Jay and Hyman Zahl had come up from London to Blackpool to avoid the bombs. Arthur believed that Randle influenced these agents into not booking the Wilton's and as the agents themselves may one day want to book Randle they took notice. This according to Arthur is the main reason they had to spend the next five years appearing in resident shows in Scotland. Arthur Goulding's opinion of Randle after their time together was that, *"He was always on the think, always trying to pull a fast one, he was pretty awful and plainly a mess". "I even heard Gus Aubrey, who was close to Randle, once say to someone, 'How would you like to work for an idiot', meaning Randle of course".*

Around this time producer John D. Robertson's fifteen year old son Jack was employed as a general dogsbody at the Birley Street office which was shared with Jack Taylor. The young man, later to become famous in his own right as comedy actor Jack Douglas, had quite a differing opinion of Randle than did Arthur Goulding. Jack recalled, *"I was a sort of runner for my father and Jack Taylor and also Frank Randle. For some reason Frank became like a father to me, he was absolutely marvellous. I don't know if you know, but whenever there was a full moon Frank went very weird. It's perfectly true! He became a different person".* Apparently when Frank was taken like this, it was only the young Jack who could handle him. As a result both his father and Taylor called upon him every time Randle felt the moon's influences. Not that Jack had any magic formula for controlling the comedian. *"He simply didn't act up with me, for some strange reason he behaved*

60

perfectly normal", said Jack. *"But with Jack Taylor, my father or anyone else when there was a full moon he became suspicious, argumentative, mistrusting, all of those things"*. It has long been asserted both in print and by people who knew him that Frank Randle was undeniably influenced by the moon. All round entertainer Roy Castle who for a while worked with the comedian once said, *"He was a very strange character. They all said he was moon mad because every now and again he'd just go potty and disappear"*. Even today, in writing this book countless people have informed us that they too believe that the moon definitely had an effect on his life. These include Arthur Cannon (jnr.) whose father worked alongside Randle in many of his shows, Wynne Mertz employee at the studios of Mancunian Films and the comedian Bob Monkhouse who said, *"Randle was a genius but very definitely wired to the moon"*. Contrary to these thoughts however, Arthur Goulding was of the opinion that Randle was simply mad, *"I was there with him for four years and I think the moon was an excuse, somebody's fairytale, to my mind he was a straightjacket job"*. Another person who believed Randle was just crazy was Sadie Corré a comedienne, singer and tap dancer, who worked briefly with Randle in the early 1950s. When talking with us Sadie was quite forthright and outspoken regarding Randle. *"You know he was quite mad don't you?"*, was one of her opening remarks. She told of a time that she along with several others were in a dressing room with Randle. He asked her to get him a pair of socks from out of his trunk. As Sadie was only about four feet tall she was hidden from his view behind the large trunk especially with the lid up. Not being able to see her Randle erupted and in a wild rage produced a revolver, an action which quickly emptied the room – apart from the shaking Sadie. He proceeded to lock the door and began to shout at the top of his voice, 'where are you. I'll get you, you little bastard'. A tearful Sadie huddled behind the trunk started screaming fearful of her life. *"I started screaming and thank God the night door keeper heard me and came to let me out. "They had to sedate Randle or give him something to quieten him down he was in a terrible state. It was all very frightening you know"*. We remarked about how some people connected his actions to the moon. *"Oh well the moon must have been full then"*, she replied. There were without doubt so many times that Randle did the oddest of things with the recurrent sackings of Gus Aubrey being one. A great many people have spoken of such incidents yet not one knew the reasons behind the periodic dismissals. On one occasion the raised voices of both Randle and Aubrey could be heard emanating from the dressing room. After a tirade of blue language Gus was seen leaving the room with Randle shouting after him that he needn't come back. Aubrey's response was that he had no intention of ever coming back. Yet a couple of

61

performances later and the pair were together again acting as if nothing had ever taken place.

With no proposals for a 1944 summer season the year was to be spent on the road touring. Randle's itinerary was full with dates from January through the summer months leading up to panto time. There was the occasional break, not so much a holiday with Britain still at war, but a welcoming respite nonetheless. Overall however, 1944 was spent working the theatres in towns and cities which included Liverpool, Manchester, Leeds and Morecambe. Summer months embraced the likes of Peterborough, Grimsby, Dundee and Aberdeen, while autumn brought visits to places like Bolton, Lincoln and Wolverhampton. Pantomime for the year was to be *'Mother Goose'* which opened on Christmas Day for a season at the Leeds Empire. In their review 'The Yorkshire Post and Leeds Mercury' said, *"The inimitable style of Frank's homely comedy as Idle Jack is reinforced by the almost equally distinctive humour of Gus Aubrey, who, as Mother Goose, is a great Dame".* Adding their support were regulars Ernie Dale, Irene Mansel, Pat Williams, Bob Hulme and Stan Stafford. Also featured was Jon Boden as the Demon King. Relative newcomer Jon was destined to become associated with the 'Scandals' tours on and off for several years. An ex Mansfield coalminer, Jon had gained experience with ENSA before entering showbusiness as a professional singer. When the pantomime came to its end in January 1945 Randle seemed again to be on course for months of travelling the country. As in the previous year, there was to be no Blackpool summer show on offer and it now seemed evident that Chief Constable Barnes had succeeded in ending Randle's summers in the resort. That is, until Jack Taylor decided Randle was just what his ailing show at the South Pier Theatre needed. Taylor had already made arrangements for Randle to play in his 1945 pantomime due to open at Bolton that Christmas. However, he knew in his mind that he needed Randle's services now! His summer show *'Taylor Made'* starring Renné Houston and Donald Stewart had not been doing the expected business and casting aside any thoughts of possible troubles involving Barnes and Randle, Taylor took a chance and brought Frank in to replace Stewart and Houston. Randle made his first appearance in the revamped show, which also featured Albert Burdon and Jimmy Clitheroe, on July 23rd. Back in Blackpool, Randle resumed his friendship with Jack Douglas. *"I used to do things for him"* Jack told us, *"I remember one day after the show had finished he said to me, 'look I've got to go to London on Sunday and I've hurt my wrist, would you drive me down'. We got to London and I dropped him off and he said, 'right take the car go where you want and I'll see you in 24 hours time'. So, there I was at about 18 years of age entrusted with his* beautiful Mercedes. *I was in paradise. We were great, great friends and I admired him tremendously".* After the show ended its season on September 29th, Randle and most of the cast took to the road in a touring version. *'Taylor Made'* had brought together Randle and Clitheroe for the first time appearing in a sketch entitled 'At Easter Time'. Gus Aubrey was by his side in 'The Hiker' while Freda Barrie, another who appeared often in Randle's shows, played the barmaid in 'At the Bar' a sketch which also featured Albert Burdon.

5-45 ——— S O U T H   P I E R ——— 8-0.

Matinee : Wednesday at 2-30.   Special Sunday Performance at 7-0
JACK TAYLOR Presents—

"TAYLOR MADE"

A Magnificent Spectacular and Comedy Revue.

F R A N K | A L B E R T
R A N D L E | B U R D O N
K A R I N A   ●   DONALD PEERS

Freda Barrie : Gladys Church : Vadio & Hertz
The Wazzan Troupe

JIMMY CLITHEROE   ●   THREE JACKS

Frank was brought in to help boost the 1945 Blackpool South Pier Summer Show

After travelling the length and breadth of the country with *'Taylor Made'* it was once again panto time. Therefore, from December 22nd, Randle could relax a little, at least for the four-week run of the pantomime and relish the luxury of being in one place for a fixed period. The place in question was Bolton's Theatre Royal with Jack Taylor and John D. Robertson's *'Cinderella'.* This gave Randle the opportunity to play one of his favourite panto characters, that being the role of 'Buttons'. Gus Aubrey was 'Ethel' one of the Ugly Sisters while husband and wife team Billy Rhodes and Chika Lane played 'Baron Hardup' and 'Cinderella' respectively. Of all the pantomimes Frank Randle had appeared in throughout his career, *'Cinderella'* was one of his personal favourites. So much so that he often included in his 'Scandals' road shows a sketch taken more or less directly from *'Cinderella'* entitled 'A Page from Pantomime'. Of the many oft repeated tales told of Randle, one concerns his role of 'Buttons'. The Lord Chamberlain's Office had scrutinised the script for one particular presentation and had been busy with their blue pencil crossing out lines which they deemed unsuitable. As was often the case Randle could see nothing wrong with the material they wanted deleted. During the kitchen scene having delivered the lines, *"There she is poor little Cinders... all by herself and nobody with her..."* Randle stopped the action and walked to the front of the stage to address the audience

63

thus; "*Ladies and Gentlemen, I would just like to say that at this moment I am supposed to say to Cinderella, 'I've come to cut your water off', but the buggers wont let me'* - an oration which brought the house down. A similar scenario was to occur again during the summer when back in Blackpool, Randle was starring in Taylor's seasonal offering *'Tinker Taylor'* at the South Pier Theatre. The show which also starred Norman Evans opened on June 10th and the review in the local press said, *"Frank Randle with his amiable toothless grin and outsize boots opened the show and started the laughs.* "*Aided and abetted by Gus Aubrey, Billy Pardoe and his "dad" Pat Williams he was at his wittiest and best".* Unfortunately, Randle at his best wasn't good enough for some and it wasn't long before trouble was looming. Frank, Gus, Billy and Jack Taylor would soon find themselves appearing at another of Blackpool's venues, the local Magistrates Court for contravening the Theatres Act. The case for the prosecution was that the script as originally licensed by the Lord Chamberlain's Office had been added too and varied by the performers. It was stated that two police officers acting on instructions from Chief Constable Barnes - following purported complaints - witnessed the show on Friday June 16th where they made notes. They stated that three sketches in particular, 'The Prodigal Son', 'At the Bar' and 'Grandpa's Party', did not coincide with the original script and implied the additions were offensive. When questioned, Gus Aubrey said he'd never even seen a script but knew it from its inclusion in a Randle film. He did not agree that any of the actions were indecent. Billy Pardoe also denied there was anything suggestive or anything that could be taken exception too. Randle himself asserted that the three sketches had been played in many places in the same way. No one had ever complained. He said he could perform them at a church concert. There was nothing in his acts that he knew of that anyone could take exception too. "*It seems that a filthy construction has been put on everything I did"*, he said.

Norman Evans

Norman Evans said in court that he had seen Randle's sketches and there was nothing in them that he would not take his wife to see. Taylor had told Randle to keep the show as clean as he could and not to include anything that would cause

64

offence. Randle's reply was that he would go on stage with a halo. Taylor also said in court that sketches couldn't always be presented as written... the personalities of the person playing the parts must be taken into consideration. He went on to say *"We were all under the impression that we were being persecuted by the police, and I took two sketches out"*. On Monday August 12th Randle was fined £30, with Gus Aubrey and Billy Pardoe each being fined £5.00 and Jack Taylor £1.00. All had jointly to pay costs. As if the court action had not been enough to worry about through August, Randle also had a problem with his health. Having suffered throat problems for several weeks, a doctor had diagnosed a quinsy. This is an abscess in the connective tissue around the tonsil usually resulting from a bacterial infection and often accompanied by fever, pain and swelling. Frank was in such severe pain that he was unable to perform and from Monday August 26th the theatre announced that he was temporarily indisposed and would not be appearing. The original diagnoses however, proved to be incorrect. Randle was in fact suffering from a far more serious complaint and had to undergo two operations, after which he told the press, *"The specialist tells me that I acquired millions of rare germs and believe me I have been conscious of a raging battle inside me"*. Even though he had specialist care and nursing and was taking antibiotics, Randle's recovery came too late for a return to *'Tinker Taylor'* – which ended its run on September 26th. At this time Frank's house was being overrun with visitors almost on a daily basis as fans and colleagues called to wish him well, *"I didn't know I had so many friends"* he said. Frequent visitors were Gus Aubrey and his sister Rene, as well as her husband Billy Sibley. Rene had played Grandma to Randle's 'Grandpa' in *'Tinker Taylor'*. This was a part she had performed previously including the 1945 *'Randle's Scandals'* during which she also acted as secretary to Randle while husband Billy, also on the bill was his manager.

Many of the visitors to the prostrated Frank would be paying their last visit to his Grenfell Avenue home for the couple would soon be moving house. Their relocation was to a property less than two miles away on Whitegate Drive. 'Westwood', as it was named, was an imposing bay windowed detached house standing in its own grounds. An indication of its size can be gained when it is realised that in later years the house was converted into a convalescent home housing up to thirty people at a time. The rear garden was also impressive with its lawns, trees, shrubs, paths and central water feature. Indeed its layout was similar to a small well kept park complete with several large greenhouses. Obtaining such a property and its continued upkeep reflected Randle's earning power at this time.

The imposing 'Westwood' and the impressive gardens

Chapter Three:

Barnes! A Pain in the Heart.

The 1947 version of *'Randle's Scandals'* opened with a short Moss Empire's tour which took in theatres in Leeds, Sheffield, Newcastle, Glasgow, Birmingham, Wolverhampton, Liverpool and Manchester. After one particular performance in Manchester, Randle, who was staying at the Grosvenor Hotel, invited Arthur Mertz back for supper. Arthur was a friend and colleague from the company which made and distributed Randle's films. He had already ordered traditional Lancashire Hot Pot and although rationing was still in force at this time he had been assured it would contain plenty of meat – this had been firmly understood when extra payment had passed hands. As the hotel dining room was rather cold Frank suggested they should have the food sent up to his suite. Shortly after their arrival Randle answered a knock at the door and he beckoned in the waiter pushing a trolley containing a huge tureen. With the waiter's departure and two large drinks poured, Frank lifted the lid of the tureen and proceeded to dip the ladle in and out of the steaming collation. A puzzled Arthur Mertz asked, 'What are you doing' to which the comedian responded, 'There's no bloody meat in this', while at the same time lifting the tureen from the trolley and flinging it at the wall. Gravy ran down the expensive wallpaper, pieces of potato and onions slowly slid towards the thick pile carpet, every ingredient that made up this typical northern dish, except the meat, was everywhere. Mertz remembered that around six weeks later he and his wife were dining at the home of friend Harold Richies, to whom he repeated the tale. Harold, who was also Frank Randle's solicitor, listened intently and then said, 'it's funny you should tell me that story, I received the bill for that just this week'.

A newcomer to the 1947 'Scandals' tour was Sally Barnes a young entertainer who had joined Randle's company as his female foil. Instantly Randle could feel an attraction towards her and after just a few shows this feeling grew to the extent that he fell head over heels in love with her. However, as she was more than twenty years his junior she at first snubbed his overtures. Later in her career Sally Barnes became a successful stage performer and had her own TV shows. As a child she had experienced a hard upbringing. From a family of five - with one child dying - living in various houses in Brighton, they moved quite regularly because they couldn't afford the rent. This despite her mother desperately scraping to make ends meet. Being something of an acrobat – entertainer, she joined ENSA, possibly to give her some security. The job with Randle was one of the first back in civvy street and one she hoped would help advance her career. Although initially rejecting Randle's amorous advances she did eventually succumb to his charms. Later however, she ended the relationship as she had fallen for a younger man, entertainer Bobby Beaumont whom she eventually married in September 1950. In February 1953 she gave birth to a daughter Laura. Had Sally Barnes really fallen for Randle's charms or had she simply seen an opportunity to further her career in show business? Putting these thoughts to Sally's daughter Laura, she said, *"Whether or not she threw herself wholeheartedly into the relationship I don't know. He was certainly a man with money and would have been able to treat her well taking her out for meals and lavishing gifts and presents on her. Also, he was quite an enigmatic and popular guy so you can see why he would have been quite seductive to her".* As for furthering her career? *"Exactly, it could easily be true, she was ambitious, very ambitious. If there was a sort of possibility of going on to do bigger things I'm sure she would have taken the bull by the horns".* By the summer of 1947 Randle and Barnes were seeing each other whenever possible; a task made easier as they were both appearing in Jack Taylor's Blackpool summer show *'Regal Revue'* at the South Pier. The show opened on Whit Monday, May 26th and the local

Sally Barnes

press said of Randle's opening night performance, *"The mirthquake had the audience rocking with laughter all the time he was on the stage".* Two standout sketches in 'Regal Revue' were 'At the Rose and Crown', in which Randle played a crafty Chelsea pensioner who liked his ale and proceeded to get it for free, while in 'A Page from Pantomime', Randle introduced a twist to the part of Buttons. This time, playing him dressed in a Sherlock Holmes overcoat. The scene from Cinderella has Sally Barnes playing Cinders with Gus Aubrey and Arthur Cannon as the Ugly Sisters. The press along with the

Elementary my dear Gus

opening night audience were unaware that not everyone in the theatre was laughing. For amongst the crowd, the Pier directors were far from being amused at Randle's onstage antics as he appeared to be straying from the script. Worried and annoyed, the directors called for an emergency board meeting the very next day. They knew that if Randle persisted with his off-script ad-libs, a court action would again be looming and the police could even close the show meaning a big loss of profit. On their part they didn't want to sack Randle, for this too would have meant profit losses. They had booked Randle in the first place because he was a huge attraction but they were left with the problem of ensuring he would behave. Their only option was to instruct Jack Taylor to keep on top of Randle, making sure he did not step out of line again during the length of the season. This Taylor did and although these measures ensured the comedian kept within the script, Randle was furious at the situation and the restrictions. Another often repeated anecdote relating to this situation is that Randle during rehearsals for the show could be seen carrying a crudely wrapped brown paper parcel under his arm. Onlookers waited wondering what the joke would be. Randle however, did nothing with the parcel and it carried no punch line or gag. With run through completed and the parcel still under his arm some brave soul asked what it was for and where was the joke. Randle supposedly replied that it was no gag while simultaneously unwrapping the parcel to reveal an axe, adding that it was for Jack Taylor, 'just in case he starts laying the law down, I'll lay this down on him'. As a result of the restraints placed upon him Randle said he would never again do a Blackpool summer season. Consequently, four summers were to pass before he eventually returned to the resort.

On stage Randle may indeed have been unhappy regarding the limits imposed upon him, but off stage he was under no restraints when it came to the blossoming relationship with Sally Barnes. As the season progressed more and more people became aware of his 'secret affair'. Randle and Barnes would spend time at his yacht 'The Namoura'; they would go to local restaurants and pubs, all this on home ground. At the end of the day however, he would return home to Queenie. With the affair with Barnes blossoming and a wife at home, it seemed as though he wanted the best of both worlds. Indeed this is probably what he thought he had, two women, both his, his possessions, his to love and he wanted to hold on to them both. During the summer Randle had arranged with film producer John E. Blakeley for Barnes to be given a part in his next picture 'Holidays with Pay' which was to begin filming immediately after the close of the South Pier show. This not only gave Sally a further career boost it also presented more opportunities for them both to be together. This was a situation made the most of by Randle, as there was no travelling back home to Queenie and Blackpool after a day of filming at the Manchester studio. Instead he opted to live in his caravan... with Barnes as his guest - only returning to Queenie at the weekends. Jeff Nuttall author of the Randle biography 'King Twist' said that Queenie only agreed to talk to him provided he made no references in print to 'that woman' and certainly not by name. This would imply that Queenie either knew what was going on at the time or certainly learned of it later. Consequently Nuttall only alluded to the Barnes affair in his completed work. Since Sally Barnes had arrived on the scene she and Randle had constantly been in each other's company. They had initially been together touring with Scandals, then during the eighteen weeks summer season they spent innumerable evenings together, followed by a further ten weeks at Randle's caravan in Manchester. To Randle, the affair with Barnes was more than a casual fling; he had said that it was love. Certainly the amount of time 'living together' would have increased such feelings for her. It would seem that Sally eventually returned this love and to those who knew of the affair she appeared to be happy with Randle.

The relationship after 1947 faltered slightly due to their differing work schedules, which now gave them less opportunities of spending the same amount of time together. They did see each other whenever possible and from April 1948 were again in Manchester filming Randle's new picture 'Somewhere in Politics'. However, as shooting ended it brought an end to their close working relationship. Randle having no resident holiday season this year, toured the provinces, with summer dates in towns like Nottingham and Wolverhampton replacing the coastal resorts. Randle's appearance at the Nottingham Empire had not gone unnoticed by Mr Terry Felton who was stationed at the nearby Whatton RAF camp. Mr Felton recalled how he had boasted to his mates about knowing Frank Randle as the comedian had been a good friend of his father's. "Of course they didn't believe me", he said. Nonetheless they all went along to watch a performance after which they accompanied him to the stage door. After Terry had explained to the door keeper that he knew Frank Randle, he asked if he could see him. When Frank heard his name, Terry and his RAF mates were all invited into his dressing room. Mr Felton recalled, "There were beer crates stacked up and he had a projector in there. "He said to me, 'what you doing in the RAF, why aren't you in the family business". While the pair were reminiscing about times in Blackpool, from where Mr Felton's father and Randle knew each other, they were interrupted by a knock at the dressing room door. Hal Swain the saxophonist who

Hal Swain and his Swing Sisters

along with his 'Swing Sister' was appearing on the bill entered. Hal proceeded to tell Randle that one of the 'sisters' was experiencing a bad time financially. Randle's response was quick and simple, 'Oh dear', he said, 'Better give 'em some more money'. *"The way I remember Randle, this didn't come as a surprise to me"*, said Terry. *"He was a very kind and generous person. "I wouldn't have a word spoken against him"*, he added. The tour eventually ended in Newcastle on Saturday November 4th after which Randle travelled to Sheffield to star in the Pantomime *'Mother Goose'* at the city's Lyceum Theatre.

Randle's pantomime was in direct opposition to Emile Littler's *'Aladdin'* at the larger Empire Theatre. This production starring Nat Mills & Bobbie – with Mills having being described as the best dame since Dan Leno - was expected to be the city's Christmas hit. Randle however, had other ideas and his winning ways with every audience soon ensured that *'Mother Goose'* was the show to see. The Sheffield Star said, *"This is versatile Frank Randle at his best"*. In the role of Jack, Randle really had little to do with the plot but what did that matter? The reviewer for the Sheffield Telegraph said, *"Frank...is the Frank of the halls, of radio and of films fitting in to the gilded stage of pantomime the turns that have rocketed him to favour"*. The Sheffield people loved Randle and his every appearance was greeted with howls of laughter and applause. Gus Aubrey, apparently appeared as a 'new look dame'. Most traditional pantomime dames were of the more substantial and robust variety unlike the lanky, slender Aubrey. The show also featured actor Bill Kerr as Squire Skinflint who just a few years later would make a name for himself alongside Tony Hancock in the comedian's radio shows. Bill's parents were both entertainers and his mother actually gave birth to him while they toured South Africa in 1922, though Bill was brought up in Australia where he still lives today. During the Second World War he entertained troops whilst serving with the Air Force Reserve. Coming to England in 1947 with just a few pounds to his name he eventually got a part in BBC Radio's 'Navy Mixture' which in turn lead to his appearances on 'Variety Bandbox' with his catchphrases *"I've only got 4 minutes"* and *"I don't want to worry yer".* He became a household name with his appearances as Hancock's lodger in 'Hancock's Half Hour' and went on to appear in countless films including *'The Dam Busters'*, *'Doctor in Distress'*, *'Gallipoli'* and the 2003 version of *'Peter Pan'.* Tracking down the 82 year old actor we discovered he lived happily in Perth, having returned to Australia in 1979. He is still very active in television and films and after forty-seven years still had fond memories of working with Randle. Bill recalled, *"Randle always struck me as a very good looking man; he always wore good clothes and seemed particularly fond of a well cut Prince of Wales check suit, which he wore quite often. He gave me the impression that he wanted to look like a respectable gentleman - you know, somebody like a bank manager or something like that. He was certainly considerate to those who worked with him. I remember that he was the only one of the cast who came to visit me when towards the end of the run of 'Mother Goose' I caught pneumonia. Of course I won't be telling you anything new when I say he*

Mother Goose, Lyceum Theatre, Sheffield, 1948

always had a crate of Guinness in his dressing room but it is quite true". Of the show itself Bill recalled it as his first pantomime, *"In fact this was one of my first engagements and I didn't do very much in panto after that",* he said. *"There were two memorable scenes in the panto. The first was 'Buzzing the Bee' which he just stopped in the middle of the show while the audience were still in fits of laughter, walking to the front of the stage he said 'I must tell you that this is the best this sketch has ever been played by young Bill Kerr and myself' - I was basically his feed but it was a very nice gesture and still got a laugh".* *"The other sketch was the School Room scene with Randle playing the headmaster. This particular night as the curtain went up he had simply vanished. We were all on stage and as we looked down into the front stalls we could see him sitting in a front seat watching the show. Somebody asked him 'what are you doing Frank' and he said 'I've never seen the show from the front'. A very wonderfully funny man; a king. He was king".*

1949 started with what was to be a major event in Randle's life; an emotional meeting with his now twenty-one-year-old son. Prior to his coming of age, Arthur and Danny his elder half-brother had for a time been brought up alone by their mother Eva. When she eventually married, taking her husband's name of Burgon, Arthur and Danny retained the name of Delaney, although accepting Chris Burgon as their stepfather. While living at New York Street, Chorlton-on-Medlock an area of Manchester which then housed many theatrical people, Rennie Jukes struck up a friendship with Arthur. *"I grew up with Arthur Delaney as we lived opposite them"*, she recalled. *"There was Chris and Peter Burgon and Danny and Arthur who were known as Delaney. "But it was common knowledge to everyone that Frank Randle was Arthur's father".* Rennie wasn't really sure if Arthur as a child knew the truth but she did recall that over the years Randle made many visits to the house. This was confirmed by Jeff Nuttall who was told by Arthur Delaney that during his childhood 'Uncle Arthur' would often call in on them. The young Arthur had even on occasions seen 'Uncle Arthur' perform. His first recollections being as a six year old and seeing the 'Any More for Sailing' sketch at a Manchester theatre. However, Arthur told Jeff that he only learned the real truth about his father when he came of age.

The meeting when 'Uncle Arthur' faced Arthur Delaney as his father would surely not have been held in the confines of a dingy theatre dressing room. In all probabilities it would have been at 'Westwood', Randle's Blackpool home on Whitegate Drive. Delaney was soon to become a frequent visitor here and at their new home 'Craig Royston' on Blackpool's Lytham Road. It didn't take long before a strong friendship between father and son developed. There was certainly no animosity between anyone as Eva Burgon often accompanied her son on visits to the Randle home and got on well with Queenie. Over the oncoming years if Randle was not working, he and Queenie often invited them round to stay. Of course Delaney was meeting his father at a time when Randle's emotional life was somewhat in turmoil with his relationship with Sally Barnes.

Although the professional relationship between Randle and Sally Barnes had ended, their love affair was still lingering with Frank determined to see her at every given opportunity. The wedding of Sally's sister Joan in April 1949 at least gave them the chance to spend another night together. Laura Beaumont recalled, *"My mum had never hidden her relationship with Randle from the family. In fact they all willingly accepted him and a closeness between them formed. Randle even paid for my Auntie Joan and Uncle Paul to get married and both had nothing but praise for him. They thought Randle was a really lovely chap, a really nice bloke, very generous really sweet and lovely".* *"Aunty Joan said that when they had the wedding reception, Randle and mum stayed in the same room together – which implies something was going on".*

Whilst touring the provincial towns and major cities with his 'Scandals of 1949' Randle was now given an opportunity of appearing at probably the world's most famous variety stage - that of the London Palladium. The offer came from impresario and director of Moss Empire's Theatres, Val Parnell, who wanted Randle to top the bill at the famous venue from August 29th through to September 11th. However, in late July Randle regrettably announced that he had to decline the chance of appearing at the mecca of variety due to his filming commitments. 'School for Randle', in production at Film Studios Manchester, had begun filming late and due to delays it was unknown when shooting would be completed. It is probably an understatement to say that it was a disappointment for Randle when he reluctantly turned down the Palladium date. One can only wonder how Randle's West End Palladium appearance may have been received when topping a variety bill at the most prestigious of variety theatres, especially with hindsight of Randle's actual and disastrous West End appearance in 1952.

It was while filming that Frank heard from Sally Barnes the news that she wanted to end their relationship. Having been working in stage shows away from Randle she had been mixing in different circles and meeting other people both professionally and socially. While appearing in one show she had become romantically involved with entertainer Bobby Beaumont. Sally Barnes obviously knew that ending the relationship with Randle was not going to be an easy task, bearing in mind the possessiveness of the man. Here was a man with a wife and mistress both of whom he regarded as his possessions. Randle flew into a rage; he most definitely did not want her to leave him and found the situation difficult to accept. Not only did Randle love Barnes he now began to show he was really obsessed by her. Laura Beaumont recalled, *"When I was young my mother used to tell me how he used to chase her around. She had to hide from him as he had a temper and she was scared. He was obviously giving her a bad time and just wouldn't let go".* Randle even went as far as telephoning the landladies of the theatrical boarding houses where she was staying to see if she

Sally Barnes as her own 'Mrs Mopp' type creation

was with anyone. Even after Sally had married Bobby Beaumont, he could not leave the matter alone taking such drastic action as trying to run both of them down when he spotted them crossing the road. Laura said, *"I'm sure he and my dad ended up having a blazing row or altercation or something. I think he was obviously majorly obsessed with my mum".* It was an obsession that never left Randle or perhaps fairer would be to say his love for Sally never waned - albeit now from afar. Impressionist Ronné Coyles was appearing in Randle's show in October 1956 at the Norwich Hippodrome. After the second house had finished on the first night Frank approached Ronné to ask if he would accompany him to the nearby Theatre Royal. Ronné agreed and in no time they were both standing across the road from the Royal's stage door. Ronné recalled, *"I said to Frank, why are we here? He said, 'I just want to see somebody'. So there we were standing in the darkness peering across the road. When the artistes from the show began to leave Frank asked, 'Is that Sally Barnes Ron?' I said 'it is, are we going over'? He said, 'no, no stay here - who is she with? I said she's with another lady and a couple of others. He said 'who are they'. I said they're probably on the bill with her. He just said, 'aye, aye', well come on and off we went home. Every night that week he had me outside that theatre with him waiting for them to come out just so he could see her. He never approached her but I believe he did have a thing about her. I knew he was married of course but I never met his wife and he never ever spoke of her in front of me - not ever".*

76

The unwanted break-up with Sally Barnes coupled with the disappointment of having to turn down the Palladium was probably why Randle was somewhat highly strung and volatile on the set of 'School for Randle'. It appears that Fred Harries, the film's Musical Director, bore the brunt of his temper with Randle demanding and obtaining, the dismissal of the musician on what some described as 'trumped up charges'. Ironically the shooting on 'School for Randle' ended on the very day the Palladium show opened - though now headlined by the Ink Spots. If drink was the great reliever then so too was work and Frank tried to push things to the back of his mind and ventured back on the road with his usual road show, though this time with a difference. Apart from the final week at the Finsbury Park Empire on December 5th 1949 the short tour consisted of fortnightly dates which commenced at the Sheffield Empire on September 26th, with two-weekly performances following at Nottingham, Leeds, Sunderland and Newcastle.

Betty Boden wife of singer Jon Boden who had travelled with her husband on the tours recalled, "I didn't know about Sally Barnes, but on this [1949] tour Randle did have a girlfriend". From what Betty told us the 'girlfriend' was Nina Rathbone, "He introduced her as the stage director, but she didn't do anything, she just walked around with her dog, Swanky, and a whistle around her neck. I think she only got the job because she was his girlfriend", she explained. Having been rejected by Sally Barnes and with Queenie at home in Blackpool had Randle found someone on the rebound? Did Randle feel the need to bring someone in to satisfy his sexual needs - for as Bob Monkhouse is later to explain he felt they had a sexless marriage. As it was, the show already had a stage director in James Munro, who was also acting as the star's manager. Before joining Randle, Munro had worked for producer Jack Taylor with a break of three years during the war when he served with the Allied Military Government in Italy. Munro was a well-known theatre critic, reviewing shows for a weekly syndicated newspaper column and was also the Blackpool correspondent for the theatrical paper, 'The Performer'. With the introduction of Nina Rathbone, Munro concentrated his efforts for Randle on those of business and personal manager. This was a position he continued with until around 1952 coincidentally leaving about the same time as Nina Rathbone. It is possible that when Nina first joined the team she perhaps didn't have much experience. If so, then as time progressed she certainly became competent enough in the duties of stage director. While chatting with Betty Boden she also informed us that under the direction of Frank Randle it had been her husband Jon who had put together 'The Mandalay Singers'. The singers included Irene Mansel, Don Carlos, Leo Fitzpatrick, Ray Waller and Jon himself brought a

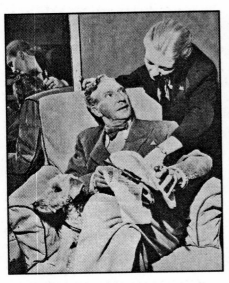

Frank with Nina Rathbone and Swanky

touch of class to the 'Scandals' productions with varied renditions of operatic arias. Their most popular piece was their interpretation of 'The Hallelujah Chorus' which usually brought the house down. When several years later Jon decided to leave the business, Randle kept faith with the group. 'The Mandalay Singers', albeit with differing personnel, would remain involved with the 'Scandals' shows until 1954.

Although Arthur Delaney only gained closeness to his father for an all too short nine years he retained for the rest of his life fond memories of the time spent with him. While others recall bottles of beer in Randle's dressing rooms Delaney remembered those in his bedroom. Of his father asking if he'd like a pre-breakfast drink while at the same time reaching for one from under the bed and opening it with the bottle opener strung around his neck. The bedroom like the whole house was beautifully decorated and full of fine furniture, though his bed had a simple straw mattress, which Randle believed gave him a better night's sleep. Delaney worked in Manchester as a textile designer where he had learned the trade having been employed at the same firm since the age of thirteen. As a result of this, the weekends were really the only time he could spend with his father. Of course, even this was subject to Randle appearing in the area; which when he was, also meant there could be the occasional evening visits to see him. There were other times when Arthur Delaney actually drove Randle to his shows, especially during his driving ban in 1952/53. Night drives together, plenty of talk, long conversations over a drink or two, or maybe more, in cramped dressing rooms, acted as belated bonding sessions between father and son. Randle once sent Delaney out front at one theatre to sit among the audience with the brief to see how long he could stand on stage without doing anything - yet still get the laughs. A father losing his temper and smashing up a dressing room - getting to know you - getting to know all about you - sung Delaney, well maybe not but the words rang true. There is no doubting that Delaney became extremely proud of his father of what he had achieved and of who he was. This was of course with no disrespect to

Arthur Delaney pictured in later life

his stepfather, who in Delaney's own words *"was a smashing bloke".* Had Randle lived longer we are sure that he himself would have been equally proud of his son, if not more so. Arthur McEvoy Delaney went on to become a well-known, popular and respected artist, influenced by both L. S. Lowry and the streets of Manchester where he grew up. Sadly Delaney died in 1987 but his works live on and have increased in value and praise and continually sell worldwide at auction - his father would indeed have been proud.

Christmas of 1949 gave Delaney and Randle the chance to be together for the festivities, this being made all the easier with the comedian's pantomime role at the Salford Palace theatre. Rehearsals for Jack Taylor's *'Aladdin'* began on Monday December 19th and the show opened that same week on Christmas Eve. Like most pantomimes, the bill included a troupe of juvenile dancers. In this instance they were a group called the Manchester Follies, although they were listed in the programme as 'The 12 Beautiful Babes'. Lizzie Burthom's job was to chaperone these children and generally look after them backstage as well as being their wardrobe mistress. Her daughter Brenda spent a considerable amount of time with her mother backstage during rehearsals and actual performances. She spoke with us of her memories of this time and of the things her mother had told her. It was plain to see by her enthusiasm and her choice of words that Brenda was one of the many people who believed that Randle was mostly harmless and not half as bad as he had been painted. Lizzie would never have a wrong word said against him. Of all the time spent working on the show with Randle he was always the perfect gentleman. He would never use any bad language in front of the children and would always stop anyone else from doing so. If any of the stage hands or the older girls from the chorus line or even the other principals were swearing within earshot of the children Randle would approach them and insist that they stop immediately. He always asked them politely, a request they adhered to. Another side of Randle's nature well remembered by Brenda and her mother and echoed throughout his life by those whom it was bestowed upon, was that of

TOP: *Aladdin, Salford 1949, Frank in costume with 'The 12 Beautiful Babes'.*
BOTTOM *(Front Left) Leo Fitzpatrick, Frank Randle, Freda Barrie, Kay Sothern, Gus Aubrey, with Jimmy Clitheroe holding Frank's hand. At the rear (left) Don Carlos, Alex Munro, Jon Boden, Ray Waller and Tommy Wills.*

his generosity and kindness. With sweet rationing only ending earlier that year, the children in the troupe had all grown up knowing only two ounces of sweets now and again. Suddenly, here they were placed into an environment totally alien to most of them, in the company of a star entertainer who would present them with a huge box of sweets after the Saturday shows. Brenda remembered, *"Of course it was like the crown jewels to the children. At the end of the very last show he gave them all big boxes of chocolates – the children's eyes were on stalks".* Also appearing in the pantomime were many of Taylor's and Randle's stable of artistes including Alex Munro and Tommy Wills as the Chinese Policemen. Kay Sothern appeared as Aladdin, Jimmy Clitheroe as Wishee Washee and Freda Barrie as Princess Balroubadour. The Mandalay Singers also appeared, with Jon Boden, Ray Waller and Leo Fitzpatrick as Abanazer, The Emperor of China and The Grand Vizier respectively. Others included were Karina as the Slave of the Ring, Barbra Forde as Nurse Emma and Tom Hertz and the Slave of the Lamp. A part was especially written for Gus Aubrey who played Miss Twankey, sister to Frank's Widow Twankey. The contrast between the two could perhaps be compared to 'Cinders' and one of the Ugly Sisters from 'Cinderella'. Gus dressed over the top as the so-called 'beautiful one', as Randle, though not exactly in rags as the 'plain Jane', wore a simple gingham dress. However, as the story unfolded, Randle's Twankey also took the opportunity to become 'lady like' in a stunning gown. Two years later Lizzie Burthom and the troupe of children again appeared for Jack Taylor in pantomime. Once more it was 'Aladdin' at Salford's Hippodrome theatre with Dave Morris as the star. Brenda Burthom recalled, *"My mother couldn't get over it. It was so different to the Randle show. Morris was obnoxious and used to push the children out of the way and he had such a foul mouth. Morris was the complete opposite to Frank Randle who had been so good and kind all the time.* Brenda added, *"Even when he had been drinking he was no different".* Neither Lizzie nor Brenda ever saw Randle drunk. It was never a secret that he always had ample supplies of beer in his dressing room and Brenda to this day, can remember vividly the rattling of Guinness bottles as the dressing room door slammed against the wooden crates holding them. She also recollected that her younger brother who shared the same January 30th birthday as Frank Randle, gift wrapped a bottle of Guinness and offered it to the comedian as a birthday present. *"After taking the wrapping paper off",* said Brenda, *"Randle gave such a huge smile, thanked my brother generously saying how he would look forward to enjoying it later".* I'm sure he was genuinely touched; you'd have thought he'd been given a fortune".* The 'Randle' Aladdin ran for eight weeks and proved so popular that the matinee performances were increased from twice a week to daily. The pantomime made its final bow on Friday 17th February 1950.

Two days later, Randle, Aubrey and Clitheroe along with Kay Sothern, Jon Boden and Ray Waller from the *'Aladdin'* cast, made the short hop across to the Hulme Hippodrome. Here together with the rest of the 'Scandals' team of 1950 they opened a tour, which would run for almost six months. Included on this tour was the now customary 'A Page from Pantomime' however, this time around a change of pantomime was implemented. 'Cinderella' was rested in favour of 'Aladdin', which the main players had just closed with at Salford. The scene obviously needed no rehearsal as the quartet of players now had the routine off to perfection. Randle's main contribution to the 1950 roadshow alternated between 'Grandpa's Birthday' and 'The Old Hiker'. As usual Frank was involved in other elements of the show, one of which, the 'acting' routine where he and Gus showed what 'lousy actors they were', had been used on many previous occasions. As in former years the tour must have

Frank on stage at the Hulme Hippodrome as captured by son Arthur Delaney

been exhausting for those involved for as usual it was quite an extensive schedule taking in all points of the compass. Along with the usual northern dates there were four in London, including the Hackney Empire, where it was reported, *"This tough London audience lapped up his ancient hiker and everything else Frank offered and howled for more. On the last night they wouldn't go home, and mobbed the orchestra pit stretching over the footlights to shake Randle's hand".* After Leaving the Capital it was off to the coast to take in Brighton and Portsmouth. Wales was also included in the itinerary with visits to both Swansea and Cardiff before heading back up to Northampton and the Midlands, finishing in Coventry a week before the opening of the summer season. Randle had previously announced that this would be at Morecambe, co-starring with Josef Locke. Newcomer to the 'Scandals' tour this year was comedian Sonny Roy. Roy was often billed as 'Sonny Roy - The Funny Boy' or 'Wonder Boy' and was a

A few of the regular performers from the Randle's Scandals Shows'

Top Left: *Stalwart Ernie Dale and banjoist Arthur Cannon.*

Top Right: *A.J. Powell Xylophonist whose sister Doris also appeared many times with Randle.* Middle Right: *Rita Shearer who travelled with one of the largest Hammond organs in the country.*

Bottom Left: *Irene Mansel "National Golden Voice" and Eisteddfod winner. She also made appearances as one of Randle's 'Mandalay Singers'. All appeared at Brighton 1950* (Poster Middle Left)

different style of comedian to Randle in that he was more the straightforward stand-up gagster. He was also an accomplished singer and banjoist. His real name was Herbert Maxwell and he soon became a regular in Randle's stable of acts making many appearances with the 'Scandals' shows. Many people have informed us that Sonny Roy and Frank Randle would on numerous occasions carry out a routine that audiences' thought was ad-libbed. So good was it that it did indeed come across as an impromptu or unrehearsed piece of work. However, in truth it was an oft-performed brief piece of material that always raised a laugh and teased the audience with glimpses of the man himself. Sonny Roy having been on stage a good ten minutes or so had already given the audience a rendition of 'Fifty Percent of it's Mine', a few hearty laughs with his tales and one-liners and another song, 'Princess Lulu'. Now it was almost time to wind up the act with a bit more patter: *"Do you like the suit"?* He asks the audience. *"It's a present from the wife. I went home the other night unexpected and there it was on the foot of the bed".* It delivers enough amusement to

the audience for him to carry on in the same vain. *"Do you like the socks?"* he asks, lifting one leg to show off a sock. *"They cost a shilling a pair"* he adds, as he lifts the other leg to show a sockless foot. *"I only had a tanner".* A deafening roar of laughter filled the auditorium far too much for such a weak joke. The reason being that behind Roy's back in full view of the audience Randle's head has appeared through the curtains. In feigned surprise, Roy looks over his shoulder to see what had caused such a hearty response. The pair face off to each other. Staring in silence the head swivels from side to side, and then looks the bemused comic up and

*Sonny Roy the Funny Boy -
Real name Herbert Maxwell.*

down before uttering the words, *"How do.* Two little words which are nonetheless greeted with a huge chorus of laughter. As the laughter begins to ebb, the disembodied head raises slowly upward and then down again as if operated by some magic force. The laughter rises again, as does the head as the action is repeated. *"Come on now, what you doing, you owd fool?"* Asks Sonny Roy. *"Haven't you got a bottle to open?"* With that the head vanishes as quickly as it arrived. Turning to the still laughing audience Sonny Roy asks, *"Now what was I saying, I've forgotten".* I'm getting very forgetful lately. *I was shaving last night, I cut myself and I forgot to bleed".* His time on stage is almost up. He knew once the audience had seen Randle he couldn't overstay his welcome. Just time for one more gag and a closing song. *"I met a nice girl last night, she was wearing a dress cut very low. It was called the New Look, yes, one look and I knew".* Picking up his banjo he adds, *"Well its nearly time - He wont be long - so I'd like to finish with this little song",* before belting out his rendition of 'Five Little Minutes From Now' an indication of how long it would be before they would see Randle in full flow.

An unusual diversion for Frank came towards the end of the tour when on Saturday June 10th 1950 he made his television debut. Travelling down to London he was to star for the BBC in their show 'Music Hall' which was broadcast live that night. The sale of television sets in the north of England had not really gained momentum at this time, so very few people in Randle's home territory would have witnessed his first appearance on the small screen. Indeed across the whole of the country there were only 350,000 combined radio and TV licences held at this time. Someone at the BBC however, must have realised that Randle's aged characters were popular south of Birmingham. His slot on this show was a good promotion for his forthcoming summer season at Morecambe.

Randle had just a few weeks earlier released his planned Morecambe co-star Josef Locke from his contract, enabling the singer to head his own Blackpool summer show. It was agreed however, that Locke would appear in Morecambe for Randle in special Sunday only concerts. Locke and Randle had become firm friends after Locke had bought a house at St Anne's, in close proximity to Blackpool and Randle's home. They soon became great drinking pals and when not performing the two could often be seen together in Blackpool's public houses. Even when on tour, if they were appearing in towns in close proximity to each other, they would soon meet up for a few pints... or

Josef Locke

more. Their drinking bouts became legendary and whenever there was a chance to get together they would make the most of it. It would often be that the pair would end up brawling or arguing about something or other, for their similar temperaments didn't make for just sitting and having a quiet drink. The Artisan's Rest was a public house close to the Empire Theatre in Oldham, which Randle while appearing in the town would regularly visit. On one such occasion Josef Locke joined him and after a few drinks the two ended up throwing chairs and punches at each other, seemingly, all because both had eyes for the same pretty young woman who was sitting at the bar. With seven Sunday appearances by Jo Locke planned for Morecambe there must surely have been more than a few occasions when the pair held one of their legendary drinking sessions.

The opening night of 'Randle's Summer Scandals' at the three thousand capacity Winter Gardens, Morecambe almost went ahead without Frank Randle, for the week previous during rehearsals at Coventry he sustained an injury to his right hand. Although in some discomfort he chose to ignore it. However on the morning of June 26th just hours before the show's opening it had become so painful it was decided an x-ray was required. The result showed that Randle had sustained a bone fracture necessitating the application of a plaster cast. With having to wear the cast for three-weeks it was the Doctor's opinion that Randle should take the opportunity to rest and refrain from his stage appearances. Ever the ultimate showman, Randle of course chose to disregard this advice.

Devised and produced by Randle this summer show was to be his most ambitious project to date starring ninety artistes and costing over £5,000 to stage. An abundance of colour was evident in the scenery and costumes. Two rolls of canvas and 150 gallons of paint were used on the scenery and over 100 yards of genuine Highland tartan cloth was among the material used in the making of the costumes. A notable effect in one scene was the use of 10,000 glass beads specially moulded to represent a tropical rainfall. Knowing what the public expected from him he did not disappoint them and presented a couple of his well-known elderly characters that soon had the audiences in raptures. Randle also performed a very popular but today often overlooked sketch as an old ventriloquist. The curtains open to a scene of a grimy old attic or storeroom. Several trunks and theatrical baskets fill the floor and there are piles of old papers and photos stacked on a table. Randle enters weary and sad-looking. He picks up one of the photographs and blows dust from it. There is a faint hint of a smile on his face as it is evident that the old trouper is surrounded by a lifetime of memories. Wiping cobwebs from the top of one trunk the lonely figure proceeds to open it. Now his face has brightened and with a broader smile he gently lifts out his old vent's dummy. It is a rather battered looking dummy and one that appears to have had its own

86

Ventriloquist and Dummy –
AKA Frank Randle and Jimmy Clitheroe

lifetime. Somewhat standard in appearance as far as dummies go, it has the grotesque look of over exaggeration, rosy red cheeks, wide eyes, loose limbs and the telltale lines of the obvious false jaw. Sitting the doll on his knee he goes into his old routine and soon has the audience in fits of laughter. Randle's character acting ability shines through and at the end of the act after reminiscing with his doll the old ventriloquist sighs, slumps forwards and dies. The laughter that had filled the air disappears as a sense of sadness now pervades the auditorium. Then suddenly there is a slight moan from the lifeless doll and as its head drops down the curtains close. For a brief moment the audience is silent before erupting into deafening applause. Even greater applause - from those not knowing - followed as Randle and the dummy played by Jimmy Clitheroe come back on stage to take their bows.

To help the comedy side of proceedings Randle was aided and abetted throughout the show by Gus Aubrey, Sonny Roy, Ernie Dale, Arthur Cannon and Jimmy Clitheroe. Music and dance was featured heavily and the enlarged Winter Garden's Orchestra was conducted by Randle's own musical director Billy Dixon Wood. One outstanding scene was that of an Aztec sacrifice notable for its effects as well as the performances, which featured the Wazzan Tunisian Troupe and the exotic Karina. Making up the bill were many specialty acts and artistes that had appeared in previous Randle shows, though this without doubt was one of his most successful productions.

Randle's Musical director Billy Dixon-Wood was married to 'Scandals' stalwart Irene Mansel.

A colourful representation of Scotland sets the scene for the finale to the show. A young couple walk towards a crofter's cottage singing as they go. They join an elderly pair sitting outside the cottage as in turn other members of the cast enter singing or dancing Scottish favourites. The audience's warm response is increased when Frank Randle appears in full Highland regalia to lead the singing. With the whole cast now assembled on

Bonnie Scotland Randle style

stage they collectively bow in appreciation to the audience. The applause however, is soon drowned by the sounds of bagpipes as the cast step back to allow on stage the Kerry Pipers. The entertainers as well as the audience clap along in time as the band leave the stage, followed closely by the full company, and proceed to make their way through the auditorium and around the audience. Back on stage Randle takes several minutes trying to subdue the applause. Slowly a hush descends and stepping forward he addresses his audience. It is now almost twenty minutes to midnight and Frank, himself now tired, apologises for the late finish to the show. The opening night performance had lasted for over four hours. *"Why apologise Frank?"* cried a voice from the auditorium as every member of the paying public join in with an impromptu rendition of *'For he's a Jolly Good Fellow'* - a perfect ending for his first night. The show was an outstanding triumph and the reviewer for the local paper was in no doubt why, *"One touch of Randle makes the people laugh - and the more they get of him, the more they like it, because he is so human, so natural, so true-to-life. ...With his inimitable expressions, loveable idiosyncrasies and natural sense of mimicry he had everyone laughing - from the lads and lassies who paid two shillings to sit in the 'gods' to the Mayor and Mayoress and civic dignitaries in the stalls"*.

Many of the artistes appearing in the show that summer had deemed to stay in caravans on the nearby Ferries Holmes site. Randle along with Queenie and Kitty Risk, her companion, had an impressive Coventry Knight caravan. Adjacent to them were Jimmy Clitheroe and his mother, with Rita Shearer and her family next door. As the season progressed they might well have wished they had opted for theatrical digs for it rained almost non-stop turning the field into a virtual quagmire. Rita Shearer's daughter Helen, now Helen Taylor, attended boarding school and used to write regularly to her mother at the various theatres. During school holidays she joined her parents on tour, quite often with Randle's Scandals. Helen retains many fond memories of these times and informed us of how Randle was a very close family friend and that she and her sister would call him Uncle Frank. *"He was very attached to my mother and father, George my dad who was not a performer probably saw a side to Randle others didn't see – he got on really well with him".* Helen remembered how much Randle loved children and the many occasions he would be surrounded by them. This feeling was mutual as seemingly everywhere Randle went the children just loved him and enjoyed being with him. His love and kindness towards children was evident at Morecambe when he decided to throw a party for those connected with the show. With around 90 people involved with the production, many with children, this resulted in a good response to Randle's invitation. *"There were lots of us"*, recalled Helen. To say the children enjoyed themselves would be an understatement but none enjoyed it more than Randle himself. At Morecambe, and throughout her time on the road with her parents, Helen also saw another side to Uncle Frank. *"At Morecambe one day he suddenly started to smash up a radio he had, literally smashing it to pieces on the fence.* It was probably something to do with Queenie, thought Helen, *"They were always arguing. My sister and I combed Uncle Frank's hair which soothed him"*, she recalled. Vivian White remembered another way of

Rita Shearer

soothing the star after he had shown a fit of temper at the Theatre Royal, Rochdale. *"My father Jack North worked at the theatre and he told me the only way they could soothe Randle was by giving him ice cream".* Helen Taylor added, *"I saw him smash things up many times over the years. I don't know if it was anything to do with Queenie or not but they were always at loggerheads".*

During the Morecambe holiday season Randle made full use of the Winter Gardens facilities when he introduced for Friday nights 'Frank

WINTER GARDENS
MORECAMBE
Proprietors: THE WINTER GARDENS (MORECAMBE & HEYSHAM) LTD

| Joint Managing Directors: | Manager ... EDWARD COPUS |
| J. W. CARLETON & H. SMIRK | Secretary ... ... C. A. INGRAM |

TELEPHONE NUMBERS:
Morecambe 8 — Booking Office.   Morecambe 1114 — General Office.
Morecambe 1842 — Stage Door.   Morecambe 677 — Restaurant.

COMMENCING 26th. JUNE, 1950
6-0 — Twice Nightly — 8-30
For a Season

FRANK RANDLE PRODUCTIONS present
the
Personal Appearance of the Famous Stage, Screen, Radio and Television
Star Comedian

FRANK RANDLE

in his Spectacular Summer Season Show

"Randle's Summer Scandals"

1 **OVERTURE** ... ... The Winter Gardens Orchestra

2 **THE SHOW-BOAT — "RIVER BELLE"** arrives, with the Entire Company - featuring **Hal Swain** and his **Swing Sisters, Hal Mack** and his **Dancing Demons, Jon Boden, Jimmy Clitheroe, Gus Aubrey, Karina, Sonny Roy, Kay Sothern, Winnie Silver, Rita Shearer, Doris Powell, A. J. Powell, Johnny Peters, Irene Mansel, Raymond Waller, Bobby Collins** — **Frank Randle** as "Texas Dan"

3 **FRANK RANDLE** and **GUS AUBREY** will now show you what shocking actors they are — and there's worse to come

4 **THE FOUR GRAHAM BROTHERS**

5 **THE TOY SHOP**
The Toy Maker ... ... **Arthur Cannon**
A Friend... ... . **Pat Williams**
—and featuring **Jimmy Clitheroe, Jon Boden, Kay Sothern, Winnie Silver, Kitty Pemberton, Rita Shearer** and six **Zio Angels**

6 **SONNY ROY** ... ... The Funny Boy

7 **A CROFTER'S COTTAGE IN THE HIGHLANDS,** featuring the Entire Company — and introducing **The Kerry Pipers Band**

8 **INTERMISSION**

9 **AN OLD FRENCH COURT-YARD,** featuring **Jon Boden, Irene Mansel, Lino Farrugia, Don Carlos, Raymond Waller, Ernie Dale, Bob Hulme** with **Rita Shearer** at the Organ
Villagers, Dancers, etc.

10 **FRANK RANDLE** in his famous characterisation "THE OLD HIKER"

11 **AN AZTEC SACRIFICE IN THE JUNGLE**

The High Priest	**Ernie Dale**
A Beachcomber	**Arthur Cannon**
The Witch Doctor	**Jon Boden**

Specialities by The Exotic **Karina** with **Vadio & Hertz** — and **The Wazzan Tunisianis Troupe**

12 **STAN STAFFORD** ... ... The 'Silver-voiced' navvy

13 **THE PHANTOM GUARD** ... presented by Florence Whiteley — with the **16 Zio Angels**

14 **FINALE** ... featuring **A. J. Powell**, Xylophone Ace, with **Johnny Peters** on the Drums, **Rita Shearer** and her Hammond Organ, the **Zio Angels**, the Entire Company — and — **Frank Randle**

The Entire Show Devised and Personally Produced by
FRANK RANDLE and THE COMPANY

The Augmented Winter Gardens Orchestra under the direction of
BILLY DIXON WOOD

Scenery devised by Frank Randle — built and executed by Keystudios Ltd, London. Ladies and Gentlemen's period costumes by Pageantry Ltd, London. Wigs by Nathanwigs Ltd, London. The Show-boat, Toy Shop and Highland Scene costumes designed and executed by Miss Winnie Silver. Choreography by Miss Kay Sothern. Special Lighting effects by Arthur Kershaw, Blackpool. Revolver and ammunition supplied by W. Richards Ltd, Liverpool. Musical arrangements by Billy Dixon Wood and Rita Shearer

---

Manager ... ...)		(...	...	JAMES MUNRO
Stage Director	For	...		NINA RATHBONE
Stage Manager	Mr. Frank	...	...	ERIC REYNELL
Wardrobe Mistress ...)	Randle	(...	...	Madame Madid
Publicity Manager ... ...)		...	...	TOM PHILLIPS

Programme subject to alteration

Fully Licensed RESTAURANT Open All Day

Randle's Party and 50-50 Ball'. From Friday August 11th to Friday September 8th 'Randle's Productions' staged these popular events where for three shillings and six pence patrons could join in the revelry dancing from 8.00pm to 1.00am. There was also a cheaper admission price for any of his 'Scandals' audience who wished to join in the later fun after the conclusion of his show. Randle the impresario was a busy man that summer for he was also responsible for staging special Sunday concerts throughout July and August. On the Sundays of July 9th, 16th, 23rd and August 6th, 13th, 20th and 27th, he booked Irish Tenor Josef Locke into the Theatre. Sundays July 30th and August 20th he brought in comedienne and singer Tessie O'Shea. Obviously Jo and Frank were pals and even Tessie O'Shea was well known to both of them as all three had appeared together in two films made by the Mancunian Film Corporation. O'Shea and Randle had also been together for Lawrence Wright's ill fated 1938 Blackpool summer show.

During the summer months of 1950, Jack Taylor had signed both Randle and Josef Locke to a £1,000 per week deal for the pair to appear in his production of Cinderella. True to form, this occasion was celebrated in Randle and Locke's usual fashion and after much drinking things got slightly out of hand resulting in the breaking of a large ornate mirror. Although presented with a bill for damages both stars seemed unperturbed as presumably they were still on a high with their lucrative deal.

Randle's extremely successful Morecambe season ended with the performance of September 9th after which he and Queenie took off on a well deserved holiday. When Frank and Queenie returned to Blackpool it was to a new home, 'Craig Royston'. The purchase of this property on Lytham Road had been completed during their stay in Morecambe. When talking of 'Craig Royston' Randle described it as being their ideal home. The property a detached house in Accrington brick contained two attic rooms, four bedrooms, four large ground floor rooms, large hall and the usual utility rooms, bathroom and kitchen and would soon become a source of pride and joy for the pair. Having previously stopped touring the country with her husband, Queenie was left to organise things in the new home adding her own personal touches to the property, furnishing it with luxurious carpets, good quality furniture and expensive fixtures and fittings. For many years the lifestyle of the pair had been far removed from their working class origins and Queenie, though not forgetting her background, obviously enjoyed her stylish existence and radiated ladylike charm. In describing her, countless people simply summed her up as a 'Lady'. Frank could equally be the well dressed gentleman, but at home could

Randle's beloved Craig Royston

often revert to his comfortable roots. Many was the time that visitors would see him in his vest sitting in the kitchen drinking tea from a pint mug while the milk bottle and sugar bag cluttered the table, which obviously did not please Queenie who liked things in the house to be just right. Especially when they entertained friends which she like to do.

On one occasion though, when Randle invited someone around, it turned out to be something of an embarrassment. After being out with Jo Locke and George Shearer, Randle suggested that they should all go back to his house for a bite to eat. On their arrival Randle asked Queenie to make some food available for his guests. Somewhat uncomfortably she informed her husband that there was no food as there was nothing in. Outraged with incredulity Randle yelled at her demanding that she find and prepare something. Queenie left the room still insistent there was nothing while Randle could only mutter in disbelief that there had to be something in the house. He already felt some embarrassment and doubtful of the situation as he made small talk with his friends. However, his embarrassment deepened somewhat when Queenie re-entered the room, for the food she had brought for the hungry threesome was nothing more than a small piece of cheese.

Randle and Queenie often gave the outward signs of a happily married couple but all was not as it seemed. We know that Frank had a violent temper and had on occasions hit Queenie. Arthur Delaney in later life spoke of a bad marriage. There were constant arguments as Helen Taylor recalled, *"They were always falling out and quarrelling"*. The arguments no doubt fuelled by Frank's jealous and possessive nature. Queenie was Randle's and she belonged to him. Although they had been married for nineteen years he still had thoughts she could be taken from him. In the past he had demanded that Queenie should accompany him on tour keeping her continuously by his side. Perhaps his illegitimacy and the insecurities he had grown up with were the reasons for these actions. Since Queenie had stopped touring she had in effect become a prisoner in her own home – a fact she herself admitted many years after Randle's death. Frank installed Kitty Risk, a one time wardrobe mistress from his 'Scandals' tours, as a full time companion for her. Mrs Risk was instructed to accompany Queenie everywhere she went thus ensuring that no one could attempt to lure her away. It has been said that on occasions when Randle was out and about on business or visiting friends he would suddenly make an excuse to leave having remembered that a tradesman was due to call. His insecurities meant he couldn't actually cope with the fact that Queenie had to interact with men thinking she might stray. There appears nothing to suggest that this is something Queenie would ever have contemplated except in Randle's mind. However, the same cannot be said for Randle who had recently been involved in a relationship with Sally Barnes. The late entertainer Bob Monkhouse said, *"I was once told by a very well-known person, who I'm not going to name, that Randle and his wife had a sexless marriage. The love was there, no, I think the word he used was affection, but no sex. So I suppose like any red blooded male if the sex dries up at home you look elsewhere"*. If this is true then it could also account for the fact that the couple never had any children.

Outward signs of a happily married couple

Time out for relaxation

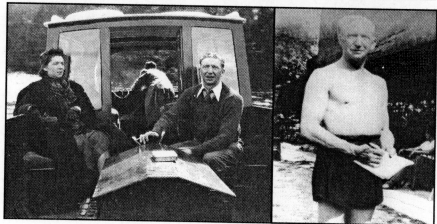

Top: *After show relaxation with friends. From right, Frank, Kitty Pemberton and Doris Powell. With Gus Aubrey extreme left.*

Bottom left: *Frank and Queenie enjoy the delights of Lake Windermere – Frank always had a love of boats and 'sailing' and was the proud owner of his own yacht the 'Namoura'.*

Bottom right: *Frank in summer mood captured by son Arthur Delaney*

Frank had a soft spot for animals – his chair

Indeed, the only patter of little feet in their household came from their dogs Patsy and Fifi. The story of how Patsy came to be part of the Randle household shows again the kind hearted side to the man. Frank at one point had spent sometime staying with friends in Scotland. One day while looking through the window he noticed a man roughly treating a dog while practically dragging it along by a length of string. Dashing outside Randle remonstrated with the chap over his handling of the defenceless animal. While the pair stood talking the poor canine was whimpering and shaking with fear probably sensing this was its last walk. During the ensuing explanation it transpired the dog had been suspected of worrying sheep on the nearby farms. Not wanting to see the dog destroyed Randle gave one of his best performances which had the desired effect – as the irate farmer granted a stay of execution on condition that Randle promised to take the dog away from the area. Given the name Patsy, the Welsh sheep dog soon settled into its new home and became a constant companion to the comedian. Patsy would soon be joined by a black French poodle, Fifi. As a surprise Randle had purchased the dog thinking it would keep his wife company while he was away from home.

During the oncoming months prior to rehearsals for the Hulme pantomime which began on December 11th, Randle embarked on a short tour which included Bolton, Salford and a sell-out week at the Accrington Hippodrome.

'Cinderella' at the Hulme Hippodrome had Randle playing Buttons with Locke as Baron Hardup. However, from the very first performance through to the end of its run the part of Baron was actually undertaken by Ernie Dale. Ernie had been drafted in at such short notice that although he played the role in every performance, his name never appeared in the programme. It was a strange situation, for Josef Locke was still part of the show but only with a singing spot for around thirty minutes at every performance. There are differing accounts as to why this situation evolved. One, simply put, is that the two stars supposedly argued and fought so much that they vowed never to appear on the same stage together. Being under contract a compromise had to be found, hence Locke's appearance in a solo singing role. It is true; as we have stated that the two stars could argue and fight especially when under the influence of drink. Yes, there was even a bust up between them at Hulme but at this point that event was still three years away. This version has no real merit and since being first told has been expanded and altered in similar fashion to so many other tales which involve Randle. The truth of the matter was that Randle had no part whatsoever in the circumstances surrounding Locke's position in the pantomime. Josef had in fact been having second thoughts about actually playing the

Ernie Dale complete with toupe

part of the Baron. He said at the time, *"Originally we were going to play Aladdin and in that I could have been the Emperor in a role that would have been more suitable for me".* More importantly though, was the concern he had over his voice. He felt troubled that if he undertook the demanding role of Baron Hardup, it may have irreparably harmed his power of song. After taking medical advice Josef Locke made the decision not to play the Baron. However, not to displease or disappoint his fans or indeed the production he settled for a singing spot only. Randle even went into print in defence of his drinking buddy saying, *"I personally applaud Mr Locke's good sense in taking the sound advice of his specialist. Although he is quite capable of playing the part (see him play the sergeant and you are convinced) his throat would have lasted about two weeks in pantomime, especially with speaking over the noise of thousands of kiddies. He would have found great difficulty in speaking, let alone singing. Therefore he would have been forced to withdraw from the pantomime for perhaps the remainder of the season, giving the knockers another chance of blaming it on temperament".* Locke's appearances in the show now saw him front of curtains smartly dressed in lounge suit belting out many of his popular songs. After several performances it was thought that this was not in keeping with the show's presentation. So, in order to create an appearance more acceptable to the fairytale setting it was decided that he would enter on stage dressed in white fur. He would also be seated in a snow cart pulled by children in the guise of ponies. The pantomime, which opened on December 23rd 1950, ran until March

Both Frank and Jo were earning £1,000 per week for this lavish production

17th 1951 other principal players included Jean Williams as Cinderella, June Barrie as Prince Charming, Marie Joy as Dandini and the Ugly sisters played by Peter Webster and Gus Aubrey. The whole show was a magnificent, spectacular production, which drew high praise and plaudits from both the public and the local press. One reviewer wrote, *"At times like an anaemic ostrich, at others like a battered edition of Sherlock Holmes, Frank Randle, high master of low comedy, shattered all inhibitions at Hulme Hippodrome in Cinderella. No comedian could be more of a low brow than Randle, but his comedy is honest, robust, if rude. His slapstick contains none of the back-of-the-hand material that sometimes gets by in Revue. His fooling is never worse than just 'common!'"* It may have only been pantomime but to Frank Randle it could have been the greatest play ever written - for he gave an acclaimed performance - not just in one show but in every presentation. Tears of laughter could be generated by Randle's outrageous and often crude performances, yet he was also capable of provoking tears of sentimentality with a gentler, softer, caring type of humour. The kitchen scene from Cinderella is one such occasion and was recalled by many people. Here Randle is not the old lecher but a tender and affectionate Buttons in love with Cinderella; he still plays for laughs but on a different level. As Cinders stands in the kitchen she is seen gently sobbing. Buttons warmly takes her in his arms and places her head on his shoulder, *"Don't cry Cinders"*, he says. *"I don't care if you won't marry me... I'll come back for you one day... and when I do.* Buttons stops mid-sentence as tries to give her an affectionate kiss and misses. *"I do that every blinking night,"* he says to the audience before resuming his conversation. *"...When I do I'll take you away to a lovely spot I know deep in the heart of the country... a place where the sun always shines... a place where beautiful streams abound... and lovely trees go flowing by ... boyee... can you hear the wind in the trees? A place where the grass is always green... have you ever been to Salford?".* There is a very apt passage in Jeff Nuttall's book 'King Twist' which is worth repeating. Derek Andrews of Chorlton-cum-Hardy told Jeff, *"I have seen many fine performances in over thirty years of theatregoing and my favourite performances are as follows, Wolfit's Lear, Olivier's Othello and Frank Randle's Buttons, it was indeed a brilliant piece of theatre."* Another press review added that it had been a pleasure to watch him with the kiddies whom he coaxed into singing on stage with him. One such child was 5-years-old Victor Coulton who to this day holds fond memories of his moments in the spotlight with the great comedian. *"I remember very vividly a point in the show when Frank asked for some young children to join him on the stage. Being stage struck, even at that young age, I made my way onto the stage and joined a line of other young children. I do believe that one was so excited that he wet his pants on the side of the stage! Anyway, Frank made his way along the line of children until he came to speak to me. I remember his broad Lancashire accent saying to me, "Na lad, by gum that's a long tongue tha's getten theer? It was a bright red tie that I was wearing! He then asked if I knew any songs and I said that I knew Rudolph the Red Nosed Reindeer. He had a word with the orchestra leader and they played the tune while I sang the song. It brought the house down and when I got back to my seat I was surprised to see my mother crying her eyes out - I didn't think my rendition was that bad!"*

After *'Cinderella'* had completed its run in March 1951 Randle took to the road with the year's production of 'Scandals'. The one and three quarter hour shows saw Randle performing 'Grandpa's Birthday', 'The Old Ventriloquist' and 'In the Jungle'. The latter sometimes performed as 'At the Medical Board' had been a mainstay of Randle's for many years, though obviously going through many dialogue changes. The script as submitted to the Lord Chamberlain's Office for 1950/51 had as usual been subjected to the blue pencil. Here is a short extract with the ordered cuts underlined.

Medical Officer: *"Quiet... Quiet... Qui... Qua...Quack... Quack..."* (In shouting quiet the MO goes into effect of making it sound like he is quacking)
Randle: *"he's a quack doctor"*
MO: *"Now pay attention"*
Randle: *"I'm paying nowt"*
MO: *"What do you want?"*
Randle: *"What have you got?"*
MO: *"I'll show you what I've got"* -
Randle: *"I don't want to see it"*
MO: *"Quiet, Quiet, Quiet".*
Randle: *"He's got the fowl pest"*
MO: *"What's the matter with you?"*
Randle: *"I have been tampered with"* (Does Business with baggy part of trousers). *"I've twisted myself... eeh I'm back to front"*
MO: *"Number one forward... You are one aren't you?"*
Randle: *"Oh yes... he's one as well"* (Sergeant walks round) *"Do you wish to go somewhere?"*
MO: *"Stand to attention"*
Randle: *"It's my uniform that's at ease"*
MO: *"Look at the stains on your tunic... what are they?"*
Randle: *"Canteen medals".*
MO: *"Through drinking beer I suppose?"*
Randle: *"No through spilling it"*
MO: *"Now then, what is your baptismal cognomen?"*
Randle: *"If it comes to big words... Friars Balsam"*
Orderly: *"Oh the illiterate"*
Randle: *"What's that you say"*
Orderly: *"I said you were illiterate".*
Randle: *"My father and mother were married".*
MO: *"What is your baptismal cognomen".*
Randle: *"I don't know"*
Orderly: *"He means... what is your name"*
Randle: *"Will you please shut your gob"*
Orderly: *"Oh that's nice for the modern army".*
Randle: *"I'm talking to the engineer not the oil rag".*
MO: *"What is your name?"*
Randle: *"Henry"*
MO: *"Henry What?"*
Randle: *"You've guess it"*
MO: *"Guessed what?"*

Randle: *"My name"*
MO: *"Well, What is it"*
Randle: *"It is"*
MO: *"What"*
Randle: *"Aye, that's it"*
MO: *"I demand to know your name".*
Randle: *"You bladder of lard... lend me your pen... get off mi foot...Move up there"* (Gets into MO's chair)
MO: *"Get out of it".*
Randle: *"I'll draw you a duck"*
MO: *"I don't want a duck"*
Randle: *"Two oo's and a Watt"*
Orderly: *"I've got it.. Sir... Watt... W. A. T. T."*
Randle: *"You clever little thing... Boyeee"*
MO: *"What's that?"*
Randle: *"It's that cheese I had for my tea... Hindberger... Steinberger*
Orderly: *"You mean Lindberger"*
Randle: *"That's the berger"*

From Monday August 20th the show was practically resident in London playing Shepherds Bush, Kingston, Metropolitan (Edgware Road), Chelsea, West Ham and Brixton. During the course of this 1951 tour Randle had been voicing his opinion regarding the normal twice-nightly performances staged in Britain's theatres. He thought that in having two shows not enough time was being given for 'acts' to perform to their best ability. In order to fit every act onto a bill, many, if not all, had to work within restricted time slots thus cutting their performance short. Randle had suggested that it would be far better if only one show on each night was performed enabling everyone on the bill to complete their full act. By increasing the admission charges for the show, he believed that takings would not be harmed and may even be improved. To demonstrate this point he revamped his show and for the week beginning November 19th it opened at the Oldham Empire. This lavishly staged offering allowed each act more time on stage and the sketches and dance routines were extended. A new scene 'The Toy Shop' was included which saw Arthur Cannon playing the old toymaker. Here he tried to restore sanity when all the life-sized toys, played by other members of the cast, ran riot after some bungling fool had accidentally switched them on. The end result of all this was that the performance time had greatly increased to three and one quarter hours. The experiment seemed to work though as the packed house enjoyed the show and the week overall was a successful one. When the actual takings were published, a sum of £1,702 had been made. Randle was delighted, saying, *"The new venture creates history".*

101

Randle would pursue the idea of once nightly shows until the end of the year. Whereas today one show per evening is the acceptable norm, theatre managers and promoters of the time were not convinced.

Prior to the Oldham show it appears that Randle and Gus Aubrey had suffered yet another disagreement – which resulted in Gus leaving the tour. Aubrey's name however still appeared in some publicity for Randle's shows as was evident with advertisement appearing in the December 1st issue of The Redditch Indicator. Aubrey was billed as part of the supporting act for the show due to open on Monday December 3rd at the Palace Theatre, Redditch. However, in that same week's publication of The Stage issued on Thursday 6th there was an announcement from Aubrey in which he stated that he was definitely no longer associated with Frank Randle. Betty Boden recalled, *"It seemed as though every week or other that Gus Aubrey was being fired by Randle, it was almost a set routine"*. Apparently Randle was never too worried as in Stan Stafford he had a suitable replacement for the esteemed drag artist. As soon as Gus was sacked, walked out, or at the first sign of disagreement, Stan would have donned a dress and doubling up for Gus would be in the wings waiting for his entrance. *"If it happened on a Friday or Saturday Frank knew that Gus would be back by Monday. But sometimes Frank would not let him into the theatre because he knew he had Stan. Next day however, everything would be fine again between them both"*.

Stan Stafford in make-up as the Singing Navvy

The visit to the small Redditch theatre with its seating capacity of around 500 was a first for Randle and came at a time of uncertainty for the future of the venue. It was planned that after Randle's week, the Palace would close, though whether this was to be on a permanent or short term basis was unclear. However, by the time the curtain had come down on the Saturday at the end of an extremely successful production of 'Randle's Scandals of 1951' the theatre's proprietor Jack Leuty had made a decision. Mr Leuty announced from the stage that the Palace would close, but only for a refurbishment and would reopen in three weeks time when once again Frank Randle would be appearing. When accepting the original 'Scandals' booking for the Palace, Randle had not been fully aware of the complications which would present themselves due to the restrictive dimensions of the

Though advertised on the bill Gus Aubrey had at this time again split from Randle

theatre stage. As was reported by the local press, *"Mr Randle was forced to abandon many of the production scenes which are featured in his regular show and to substitute items in keeping with the stage space available. The show as presented is consequently but a shadow of its real self, but nevertheless substantial enough to merit all the publicity which preceded its visit to the town".* Amongst several changes that were made out went 'At the Lido' and 'The Toy Shop' as well as 'Grandpa's Birthday' with its scenery, props and supporting cast, being replaced instead with Randle's solo offering in his 'Old Hiker' routine. Some scenes that were presented, even if drastically altered, were the 'Show Boat' opening and the 'A Crofters Cottage in the Highlands' finale with the full cast and a slightly depleted Dagenham Girl Pipers. The diminutive Jimmy Clitheroe who had left the tour mid way through, had been replaced by an artiste of equal stature, Sadie Corré. Jimmy had given Sadie words of advice on what to expect of Randle and as she had no kilt of her own for use in the Scottish Highland finale scene he offered Sadie the loan of his. Sadie informed us of how she and another girl whom she believed to be Kay Sothern performed together in a sketch, *"She was very good, very good indeed, she was marvellous and easy to work with".* However, it wasn't long before the working relationship between them was halted, *"Frank took her out of the sketch and brought in his new bit of crumpet. I'm not sure of her name now",* said Sadie. *"But she was terrible to work with, it was real hard going. She had no idea, but he fancied her and he put her in the show",* added Sadie. Nina Rathbone whom it is alleged Randle was having a relationship with since the break up with Sally Barnes, was still with the company at this point. So if there was anything between her and Randle she would not have been too happy with this new arrival. It is interesting to note that within a few months of the newcomer settling in, Nina Rathbone left the company. Whilst not working long for Randle Sadie Corré admitted that he made a lasting impression on her in more ways than one. *"I did the ventriloquist sketch with me playing the dummy. It was very hard that fake dummy thing. It wasn't a mask it was all make-up. Randle used to come in and make me up himself and he'd bang my face about while he was doing it"*. Hardly surprising is that Sadie remembered that Randle drank heavily and also recalled just how unpredictable he could be, *"You never knew what he was going to do"* she said. Randle could on a whim change the running order of the shows. It was not uncommon for him to do this even during a performance. On one occasion a front of cloth act was told from the wings to stretch their performance. Meanwhile behind the curtains, where the stage had been set for the next sketch, Randle at the last minute had decided to alter things. As a result stage hands were frantically trying to rearrange the set while performers rushed to get into different costumes. All this having to be achieved before the poor artistes on stage had completed their extended act. *"He used to make us do a running order"*, said Sadie. *"During the Monday morning rehearsals we'd have to sit in the stalls while he sat on the edge of the stage talking to us. He'd ask us all to write down what we thought would be the best running order for the show that week. Eight times out of ten he'd pick mine which I was ever so pleased about"*. What didn't please Sadie however, was how Randle insisted she make her entrance in the show. This he was adamant about, something on which he would not change his mind and because of his stance the reason why Sadie left the show. Her entrance saw her being thrown to and fro between two male acrobats while they descended a staircase, unfortunately on one occasion she was dropped and injured her wrist. It was eventually discovered that she had suffered a fracture but at the time as Sadie recalled, *"It was just bound up as it was assumed it was just sprained and it would soon get better, but it didn't"*. In some discomfort Sadie asked Frank Randle to alter things to make a better entrance for her explaining how continually being thrown was causing her pain. Randle's reply was a flat refusal, stating that she could continue in the same way or 'she knew what she could do'. Not wanting to upset Randle any further Sadie soldiered on until eventually her mother insisted she seek medical attention and made an appointment for her. Sadie said, *"When I told Randle this he said, 'you what!'. I said I'm sorry and he said, 'of course you're sorry, you're sacked'. So I left. Sadie continued, "I went to meet Jimmy Clitheroe to give him his kilt back and he said, 'I didn't think you'd last long with him"*. Sadie made it perfectly clear to us that she was pleased to leave Randle adding, *"Quite candidly he was mad"*.

Randle had devised a slightly different show for the planned return visit to Redditch. *'Frank Randle's Road Show – Christmas Party'* was an out-and-out variety show. However, due to the theatre's restrictions the show was without the usual large production scenes though still big on music, dancing, fun and laughter.

Chapter Four:

The Court Jester.

While in Redditch for the start of the New Year Randle had every reason to think 1952 would be a very good year. He was booked to appear once again in a Blackpool summer season and London's West End was beckoning.

However, at the end of the first week in Redditch, over the weekend of January 5th and 6th, Randle made a decision to cancel the scheduled second week's engagement, a move which forced the newly reopened Palace Theatre to close for the week. Making a phone call to Jack Taylor, arrangements were instead made for Randle and his company to move to Manchester and join forces with Taylor's pantomime, 'Aladdin', playing at the Hulme Hippodrome. Randle's reasoning for this being that during the day, his team could use the Hippodrome's larger stage to rehearse for his scheduled London show. It was a strange decision to make, for rehearsal time had already been designated for the week prior to the proposed London opening date. It seems odd that Randle thought extra time was needed for rehearsal of sketches he and his team had already performed countless times. At this time Randle was also perhaps being a little presumptuous. He blatantly informed London he was on his way, through a series of photographs which appeared in the national press showing the 'Old Hiker' at various London landmarks including 10 Downing Street, meeting a llama and a goat at London Zoo, feeding the pigeons in Trafalgar Square, strolling in Hyde Park, visiting the waxworks at Madame Tussauds, having a shoe shine in Piccadilly Circus and posing at the Herculean Memorial commemorating Duke of Wellington's victory at Waterloo - All this taking place despite the fact that meetings regarding his London show were yet ongoing. There were still certain points which he and Jack Hylton needed to iron out and things had not yet been finalised other than the opening date of February 4th.

Randle's arrival at the Hulme Hippodrome brought him and Gus Aubrey back together after their latest fallout. Aubrey was playing the part of Widow Twankey and the show featured Karina who had appeared with the comedian on numerous occasions. Albert Whelan the pantomime's Abanazer was also a long time friend of Randle's. Monday January 7th was total mayhem backstage as forty-four people from Randle's company mixed with an almost identical number from the original cast – all trying hard to adjust. The show which had a usual running time of approximately two hours now became considerably longer, turning into a late night affair – which was nothing new for a show featuring Randle. Aladdin gave the opportunity for Randle to play 'sister' to Gus and repeat routines they had worked often in the past. Anyone in the audience for the two remaining weeks of the panto – it was due to close on January 19th – and seeing them perform would not have believed that the two had recently fallen-out as they worked so well together.

Get off mi foot

While in Manchester several meetings were arranged between Jack Hylton and Frank Randle in order that the pair could finalise arrangements for the Adelphi show. Hylton had a format worked out whereby the first half of the show would feature variety acts, a Randle sketch and a stage version of the popular TV programme 'What's My Line?'. Randle thought that many of his 'Scandals' company should be given their own spots and that the 'What's My Line?' segment should not be included at all. The first of these meetings took place on Tuesday January 8th at the Midland Hotel at which Mr Hylton was quoted as saying, *"Nothing has been settled yet. I want to get him [Randle] to town with the people who work with him in his sketches. I think they'll do very well"*. However, He didn't want to use Randle's company other than in the sketches. Randle on the other hand, wanted his assault on the capital to be *his* show, in essence 'Randle's West End Scandals'.

Both he and Hylton were adamant and the talks were on and off over a number of days with much travelling back and forth to the Midland Hotel. When Hylton had to briefly return to London, negotiations continued with agent Harry Foster as intermediary. Ultimately

Jack Hylton won the day

however, it was Hylton who won the day. Although happy to be playing London's West End, Randle was disappointed in having to give way to Hylton's format for the show. However he bore no ill feelings about the matter. In fact Frank accompanied by Queenie and son Arthur Delaney joined Jack Hylton, Harry Foster and several others for a formal meal on the Saturday evening in the hotel Restaurant. Saturday night's at the Midland Hotel like most prestigious hotels of the time were rather special occasions. The residents and their guests were attired in their finery. Evening dress was de rigueur for the gentlemen with elegant dresses for the ladies. Never a member of the dinner-jacket club Randle was nevertheless smartly dressed in a simple lounge suit yet still thought of by many to be improperly clothed. Nonetheless, the dapper Randle escorted Queenie to the table that had been reserved for their party. During the lavish meal which followed, champagne corks popped while afterwards came the brandy and inevitable cigars. When Harry Foster offered Randle an expensive looking cigar from an equally expensive looking leather case, the comedian's reaction was instant. *'No thank you'*, he said *'but would you like one of mine?'*, while simultaneously producing a battered old tobacco tin in which he kept the 'dog ends' of his Woodbines cigarettes. None of the formally evening suited gentlemen present took up his offer though he himself carefully chose a Woodbine which still had a decent length to it. As their waiter once again tended the table Randle asked, 'would *you* like one owd lad?' To which the waiter replied, 'Yes, Mr Randle, if you don't mind I'll save it for later'. With this, Randle, with all the dexterity of a magician deftly substituted the tobacco tin for a solid gold cigarette case, which he quickly flicked open and proffered to the waiter.

As indicated by the show's eventual title 'Televariety', it was to be a hybrid of stage variety and television show. Hylton had been determined to exploit the ever increasing TV audiences of the time by bringing 'What's My Line?' to the stage. The simple format to the panel game saw the team trying to discover the occupation of participants by the mimes they performed. It was nothing more than a parlour game played out before a large audience who in general found it amusing

FRANK RANDLE

The Lad from Wigan

in

GRANDPA'S BIRTHDAY
TWERP OF THE JUNGLE

with

IRENE MANSELL	BILLY WOOD
DORIS POWELL	STAN STAFFORD
ARTHUR CANNON	JAMES EDGAR
JOHNNY PETERS	ERNIE DALE
KAY SOTHERN	BOB HULME
RAY WALLER	DON CARLOS
NINA RATHBONE	A. J. POWELL
JEAN CHADWICK	PAT WILLIAMS
WINNIE SILVER	PETER HINDLEY

★

GILBERT
HARDING

★ **ELIZABETH**

ALLAN

★

BRYAN MICHIE

invite you to take part in

★

WHAT'S
★ MY LINE?

(By arrangement with Maurice Winnick)

JACK KELLY	JOAN TURNER
Novelty from the Continent	The New Singing Star

FRANK COOK	ALI BEN HASSAN'S
With Guitar and Harmonica	WHIRLWIND MOROCCANS
Frank Randle's MANDALAY SINGERS	Breath-taking Acrobats

ADELPHI THEATRE ORCHESTRA UNDER THE DIRECTION OF CHARLES SHADWELL

Frank's disastrous West End engagement

especially with the dry wit of Gilbert Harding. Most critics however, seemed to agree that this was not Variety and questioned its place in Theatre. Unanimously they thought that on this occasion Mr Hylton had put together a mismatched show. 'Televariety' opened with Ali Ben Hassan's Whirlwind Moroccans - an acrobatic and balancing act. Next on stage was Jack Kelly, billed as 'novelty from the continent' performing an amazing and amusing juggling routine. This in turn was followed with Randle's first entrance in the sketch 'Twerp of the Jungle' which also brought on stage for their first appearances Arthur Cannon, Ernie Dale, Stan Stafford, Johnny Peters, Ray Waller and James Edgar, all regulars from the 'Scandals' shows. Then it was the turn of Joan Turner a vocalist with a good line in impressions including Vera Lynn, Rose Murphy and Gracie Fields. Joan Turner would later make a name for herself starring in TV shows and topping theatre bills. The first half was brought to its end by Gilbert Harding introducing 'the panel' Elizabeth Allan, Bryan Michie, Gladys Young and Peter Casson for the 'What's My Line?' segment. The Mandalay Singers opened the second half of the show. Randle himself then took to the stage with just enough time to perform his 'Sewing on a button' routine and introduce the next act, Frank Cook a harmonica and guitar virtuoso. 'Grandpa's Birthday' proceeded to bring 'Televariety' to its finale. Featured alongside Randle in his famous sketch were stalwarts of his company. Doris Powell (Grandma), Irene Mansel (The Old Flame), Ernie Dale (Grandpa's pal), Arthur Cannon (Grandpa's son-in-law), Stan Stafford (Grandpa's pub pal), Jean Chadwick (Grandpa's niece), Jackie Herrick (another niece), Kay Sothern (family friend), Bob Hulme (Engine Driver), A. J. Powell (Vicar) and Pat Williams (Grandpa's Father).

Most of Fleet Street's show critics seemed to have had inbuilt preconceptions of Frank Randle and it certainly showed in the tone of their reviews. The Daily Telegraph wrote, *"Mr Randle relies almost entirely on vulgarity for his laughs. For tastelessness and crudity his performance would take some beating".* The Daily Mail stated, *"Mr Randle and his audience obviously had some difficulty in getting to know each other last night and his material did woefully little to bring about understanding".* While the Daily Express noted, *"Frank Randle the Lancashire comedian - a spry toothless old popeye - did several turns and apologised for their length and bad taste. Rightly I'm afraid".* The notices which Randle received in the press were according to 'The Stage' *"particularly rude and crude".* They went on to say, *"What the majority of the critics failed to recognise, let alone give credit for was one of the most expressive talents in present day variety".* Commenting on the 'Grandpa's Birthday' sketch, 'The Stage' while favourable of Randle's performance felt he was actually let down by a supporting company that were *"sadly lacking in technique and personality"* – and these were members of his own 'Scandals' team. The paper was also surprised by Randle's apology to the audience for some of his supposed crudities. They were of the opinion that there was *"no need for this"* adding, *"You like his work or you don't like it; there can be no halfway; and as it belongs to the real rosy tradition of music hall most variety enthusiasts love it".* Perhaps Arthur Askey had it right when he said that if anyone was wrong for the West End then it was Frank Randle. Taking his teeth out on stage and placing them on a velvet cushion was not perhaps what a West End audience expected. No doubt class distinction was also playing its part here as there was certainly a difference between the Adelphi audience and those who usually attended the likes of say the Brixton Empire. What may have been good enough for one was clearly not acceptable to the other even allowing for a good performance from Randle.

The opening night reviews would certainly not have helped the show but there was yet to be another hammer blow. On Wednesday February 6th the country was stunned to hear of the death of King George VI and as a mark of respect all theatres and cinemas remained closed that evening. When the Adelphi reopened on Thursday it was to a nation in sombre mood with many people feeling it discourteous to be enjoying themselves. During the show's second week the King's body was lying in state and London had thousands of visitors, hardly any of whom were seeking out entertainment. This left the theatres of the West End playing to less than full houses without exception. The already established shows would in time begin to win back the crowds, but for 'Televariety' the damage had been done. The sad demise of King George VI and the show's poor reviews was too much. The weak attendance figures, being £2,400 below the figure at which it was agreed Randle would leave the show, never looked like increasing. Consequently the show was pulled with the final performance being held on Saturday February 16th, the day after the King had been laid to rest. Once the decision to close the show had been made, Randle as ever undeterred, assembled his entire company and had soon put together a new road show, 'Randle's New 1952 Scandals'. Randle may not have conquered the West End but he certainly won over the rest of the capital. For of fourteen dates worked before his Blackpool Summer Season, eight were in London with another in Brighton and one in Portsmouth. The week following the closure at the Adelphi his new 'Scandals' show was playing to a packed Metropolitan Theatre on the Edgware Road where there were the unlikely scenes of police being needed to keep him from being mobbed at the stage door. Fair to good weeks quickly followed at theatres at Chelsea, Finsbury Park, Brixton, East Ham, Kingston and Chiswick. At Manchester where his show opened at The Hippodrome on March 10th, he ended up breaking the box-office records for a Saturday night performance. After the Adelphi flop Randle commented, *"I don't mind what happened in the West End. If I couldn't take it I'd have no business in show business, it's all experience. You haven't to take it too seriously.* He continued, *"Even in Lancashire in my own midden, I've done badly. Nine months later I've returned to the same theatre with the same act, word for word, gesture for gesture, and I've been a riot".*

While doing the rounds of London's variety theatres Randle found time to visit Kitty McShane who herself was appearing locally. Now split from her partner and husband Arthur Lucan, alias Old Mother Riley, McShane had begun performing with an alternative 'Old Mother Riley'. Slim Ingram, friend of Arthur Lucan and also his tour manager in the 1950s, recounted an intriguing story which he remembered well. Randle had gone to see Kitty at one of her London dates. Once backstage the pair soon ended up drinking heavily, not just after the show but also while it was ongoing with Kitty going back and forth between stage and dressing room. Shortly before completing her performance and now quite visibly under the influence, she announced to the audience that she would in future be presenting a brand new act with a new partner. Amidst murmurings from the audience she went on to say, 'I would like to introduce him to you now, please ladies and gentlemen welcome my new partner... Frank Randle'. Instantly the audience joined as one in loud applause as an intoxicated Randle staggered on stage to take his bow. From both artistes at that moment in time it may well have been their intention to team up together.

A nightmare partnership that never was

However, in the cold light of day - no doubt the very next day, after the effects of the alcohol had worn off, reality obviously dawned. Nothing ever came of this and it was never mentioned again. Of similar temperament and both with a liking for the bottle, one could only imagine what a nightmare of a partnership that one would have been.

The summer of 1952 heralded Frank Randle's return to Blackpool for the season at The Central Pier Theatre in *'Randle's Summer Scandals'.* This was his first season in the resort since his fallout in 1947.

The show which was devised and produced by Frank himself opened on June 14th before an eagerly awaiting audience whose holidays in Blackpool had not been the same over the past couple of years without Randle. This first house was also attended by several civic dignitaries headed most notably by the Mayor and Mayoress. Those watching the second house performance were given an unexpected treat. The full

111

company, including the McFarlane Pipers, were on stage completing the rousing Scottish Highland finale. Randle in full Scottish regalia was about to step forward to give his usual address to the audience when suddenly an unanticipated cheer filled the theatre. For on stage walked comedians Terry-Thomas and Harry Korris accompanied by producer Jack Taylor. Randle's face gave the impression that he was just as surprised as the audience were – but this is doubtful. For as it transpired the trio were there on behalf of the Variety Artistes Benevolent Fund to promote their forthcoming charity Garden Party.

Offering Randle good support on the show were 'The Kandy Sisters and Eddie', 'The Peter Brothers', 'Sonny Roy', 'Bobbie Collins' 'Sally Summers and Dizzi' and newcomer 'Phil Kelly'. Phil, who today still lives in Blackpool, was very much a singer in the mould of Josef Locke. Indeed, as he informed us it was Jo who had discovered him back in their native Ireland and suggested he should try his luck in England. Phil actually understudied for Jo during the 1950/51 pantomime at Hulme, Manchester, something which is not widely known. *"Jo had been having trouble with his voice at this time and I was there just in case it gave out"*, said Phil. *"That was my first time with Randle"*, he added. *"Jo and Frank were right rogues together and I got pissed with them many a time"*. *They were all right together, really good pals although they did have the occasional fall-outs"*. 'Randle's Summer Scandals' was Phil's first ever summer season *"... and I was another Jo Locke to him"*, recalled the six foot three inch Irishman. A lasting memory of that season for the singer was when Randle upstaged him and as Phil began to explain, he could hardly refrain from laughing.

Phil Kelly

The singer had been well into his act and had the packed holiday crowd in the palms of his hands, when midway through a ballad the audience suddenly burst out laughing. A puzzled Phil not knowing what had caused such a reaction continued with his song. A few more notes, then even louder laughter, a worried Phil took a quick glance to the wings, nothing. By this time the whole theatre was in uproar but Phil could only think of finishing the song before confronting the audience. However, before he could warble the last few lines he soon found out the reason for the audience's reaction. A startled Phil physically jumped when from behind him came an outstretched hand which rested on his shoulder. Quickly turning around he saw what the audience had seen those seemingly long minutes earlier. There was

Randle in all his glory as 'The Old Hiker'. In his relatively short time in showbusiness Phil had never experienced anything like this and he was stuck as what to say or do.... besides laugh. However, Randle for the next few minutes took control and as Phil remembered it said, *"We'll do a bit of Bing Crosby and Barry Fitgerald"*. As he continued the tale, Phil still in good voice, imitated Randle, *"We'll sing 'Too-Ra-Loo-Ra-Loo-Ra'*, he said *"He'd be doing all the business and I'd sing it in as low a key as possible, like Crosby and he, with no teeth in, would be singing all out of tune. You had to see it to appreciate it but it was the talk of Blackpool all week"*, Phil proudly boasted. *"I should say that before the season came to its end we became great friends Randle and I. I got on marvellously with him and on occasions when my dad came out with us, people would ask if Randle was his brother"*.

'Randle's Summer Scandals' didn't disappoint the audiences and Frank gave them full value by presenting several sketches including 'In the Jungle/At the Medical Board', the reintroduction of an old skit 'Set a Thief to catch a Thief' though now presented as a 'new drama' and 'The Village Scene' which as always wound up the first half of the show. In this closing segment the whole company were on stage either as band members' or villagers. A female from the group introduces the arrival of Randle with the words *"look, here comes our dear old Vicar"*. Dressed as the vicar Randle walks on stage and greets the assembly with a cheery *"Good morning everybody are we ready"?*. With all ready they begin to play as the vicar conducts. However, the music has no sooner started before it abruptly stops as the comedy dame comes rushing across the stage, *"Sorry I'm late, I've been on my rounds collecting for a bell tent"*. While taking her hand to kiss it the vicar adds, *"I do hope it fits you"*. After the kiss he quickly pushes her hand away with the words, *"have you been milking a nanny goat?"*. The dame, as the harpist, takes her place with the band. As she sits with the instrument between her legs her long skirt rises to knee height. The vicar noticing the indiscretion taps on the harp with his baton and points to the skirt. The dame shrugs and pulls down the skirt a few inches. This however, still does not please the vicar and again he taps on the harp. Once more the dame pulls down the skirt a couple more inches. The vicar obviously not satisfied leans over and pulls at the skirt himself bringing it down to ankle length and while doing so he says, *"I see you've got them on again"*. *"Yes vicar"* replies the dame, *"and they're my last pair of nylons"*. With the dame seated correctly the vicar asks, *"Right are we all ready now?"*. The band begins to play with the vicar conducting. However, before they can really get into their stride an old man walks on stage, sits with the band and apologises for being late. *"That's quite alright"*, says the vicar. *"I*

thank you", says the old man, *"and mother thanks you too".* Yet no sooner as the old man seated himself than he gets up again and walks off stage. Wondering what he was doing the vicar watches as the old man walks away and the band stop playing, *"He's gone back to his almanacs",* the vicar proclaims, *"I'm sure we all understand".* As the old man returns the vicar says to the band *"shall we play our other tune, the one we practised for so long – The William T'Hell Overture".* *"No, no vicar",* cries the band. *"Well then T'Hell with William"* says the vicar. The band then proceed to give their own musical interpretation of the William Tell Overture, at the conclusion of which the vicar says, *"Now I think the band should retire for refreshment and perhaps while we are gone our own Mandalay Singers will practice for the All Britain Festival".* As the singers take their positions, the vicar and his band leave the stage. After two or three songs, the singers finish with 'The Village Blacksmith' during which the vicar re-enters. *"I don't think we*

The Mandalay Choir – with Jon Boden second from right

114

have any fear about winning the festival do you?".   To which, the singers all reply, *"No vicar"*. The vicar continues to address the band asking, *"Shall we just sing one more number – our favourite song, The Hallelujah Chorus?"*.   With the singers in agreement a voice is heard from the orchestra pit as the Musical director asks of the vicar, *"Would you like to conduct this song?"*. The vicar happily accepts the invitation and taking the baton conducts the orchestra and singers in 'The Hallelujah Chorus'.   When the song was completed the assembled troupe all step forward to take their bows and accept the warm applause as the curtains close heralding the interval.   However, as Frank Randle had been conducting the orchestra he was now obviously still in view to certain members of the audience, to whom he turns and says, *"Well that's the first half finished I'm off to the bar"* and promptly sets of up the aisle at a run.   Randle in his sketches was aided and abetted by his usual contingent of stooges including Gus Aubrey, Ernie Dale and Arthur Cannon.

Frank's happiness at the early successes of the summer shows was soon to rapidly diminish when once again he fell foul of the law. After visits to theatre by the police on two occasions (June 17th and 18th) summonses were issued against Randle for presenting unlicensed material. Although by June 20th a hastily applied for licence had been obtained further trouble lay ahead. On July 10th and 11th police in the audience witnessed Randle and company deviate from the licensed script which resulted in further charges being made.   Randle was summoned to appear at the town's Magistrates Court on September 3rd to answer charges of contravening the Theatre Act.

Never needing an excuse to take a drink Randle on the night of Wednesday August 27th perhaps had good reason to turn to the bottle. For his impending court appearance was now only one week away and he was still in the throes of trying to rewrite parts of the show. He arrived at the theatre around 6.00pm, appeared on stage in the two scheduled performances before returning to his dressing room where he worked on the show's scripts until 5.00am.   During this period he consumed a large quantity of alcohol, he was later to admit only to having nine bottles of Guinness and one large gin and tonic. In the early hours of Thursday 28th feeling somewhat tired and rather annoyed with the world, he left the theatre for home.   Although Blackpool's streets were practically deserted, within minutes of driving away from the theatre he was involved in a road traffic accident that would make headline news and bring about yet another court appearance.

115

On September 3rd 1952 Frank Randle, Gus Aubrey and Sonny Roy, along with John Capstack, Director of the Central Pier, appeared at Blackpool Magistrates Court accused of contravening the Theatre Act - departing from the script and performing a sketch before it had been licensed. In court the prosecution cited several occurrences when deviations were made. These included Randle's vicar in the English village scene saying, *"What the hell's going off here?"* he then preceded to conduct his Mandalay choir, adding *"We will sing this as it has never been sung before. What a lot of new faces in my flock tonight. What a collection!"* It is unclear whether it was the use of the word hell that was found offensive or whether it was simply that none of the dialogue was included in the script. However there were other instances including Gus Aubrey in apparent homosexual overtones dressed in tight Boy Scout outfit and Randle again with, *"There was a young man named Vickers who took his girl to the flickers. He saw some wool and started to pull - I nearly made a bloomer there".* However, the major part of the hearing was taken up by arguments concerning the offence of performing an unlicensed sketch. Randle's contention was that he did not believe the sketches needed a license being part of a revue. The prosecutor's opinions were the opposite and perhaps as to be expected judgment went against him. Surviving documents today show that a license for 'Randle's Summer Scandals' and 'Randle's Scandals of 1952' was applied for, obviously belatedly. Interestingly there is no indication or suggestion from the Lord Chamberlain's office that the offending rhyme previously mentioned should be cut and it seems to have been passed thus: *"There was a young fellow named Vickers who took his girl to the flickers he found some wool and started to pull and found he'd unravelled her ... knitting. Ah you though I was going to say Knickers didn't you - Oh I've said it - I made a bloomer there".* Other offensive items mentioned in the court case were however, purged including, *"Is that King Farouk"* spoken as a Chinaman walks across the stage.

One month later Randle was again back in a courtroom on the charge relating to the road accident of Thursday August 28th. Electing for trial by jury and pleading not guilty the case opened at Blackpool's Quarter Sessions on Thursday 2nd October.

The story of the events unfolded thus. At around 5.10am one of Blackpool's grinder trams, or maintenance vehicles used through the night to clean the town's tram rails, was stationary on Lytham Road. Frank Randle in his Lagonda, entered the road from the Promenade. On approaching the tram the car swerved to the wrong side of the road, swerved back to the right side just missing a lamp post, then

Frank outside the Pier Theatre in a happier moment posing with his Lagonda.

swerved back to the wrong side and made contact with the tram scraping along the full length of the vehicle before carrying on for a further 60 feet or more before finally coming to a halt. As if arriving on cue Randle was quickly confronted by a policeman. The tram driver soon joined them giving his view to the constable of what he had witnessed, whilst at the same time strongly asserting that Randle was the worse the wear for drink. Randle looked at the constable and stated that the tram was actually moving and had hit his car. Upset at the tram driver's accusation that he had been drinking he endeavoured to show the constable how steady he actually was and commenced a series of ballet movements in the road. These gyrations were performed to prove his sobriety and he even asked the police officer if he could manage to do them. He also recited several tongue twisters and again asked the constable if he could repeat them.

The prosecution cited these events, the swerving of the car, the actual hitting of the tram, the dancing in the street and the claim that the tram actually hit him, as all pointing to someone who had too much alcohol. In defence Randle asserted that the swerving had been due to the car 'snatching to the right' having run over some obstruction in the road, a brick or piece of wood. The ballet movements were not

117

drunken silliness but a test to show how steady he was on his feet and likewise the tongue twisters were also an aid to prove his sobriety. The statement about the tram was said in theatrical jest not to be taken seriously.

Arriving at the police station the prosecution alleged the duty Sergeant thought Randle had difficulty with his speech, his eyes had a fixed expression and he smelled of drink. The police doctor, Dr O'Riordan examined Randle for thirty-five minutes and during the tests Randle allegedly made a joke of the whole procedure going through bouts of expanding his chest and commenting on what a fine figure of a man he was. He spoke rapidly and constantly in a mock Irish accent calling the doctor a 'Broth of a boy'. The doctor's conclusion was that Randle was not fit to be in charge of a motor vehicle - in cross-examination he was to reveal that he thought Randle only just over the border of drink. The defence maintained that much of Randle's behaviour was not down to drink but to his nerves and mental state. He was naturally theatrical in his expressions and the manner in which he spoke. His own doctor, Dr Harris, who had examined him shortly after the police doctor, was of the opinion that Randle did not appear to him to be any different than normal. At the end of the subsequent court case the jury could not come to a unanimous decision and consequently a retrial was set for the first week of January 1953.

There have over the years, been several suggestions that Randle may at some point have had psychiatric care or mental treatment. This idea has no doubt stemmed from his three-day stay at Birch Hill Hospital, Rochdale in 1952. His admission to hospital was not for treatment of any kind but simply for assessment by the senior physician Mr Robert M. Maher - who had been called as a defence witness during the 'drink driving' court case. Having had Randle under observation from September 22nd 1952 Mr Maher was confident that his road side antics, his arabesque movements, tongue-twisters, Irish brogue and the showing off of his athletic prowess were not those of someone who had had too much alcohol - though they could easily be mistaken for such - but were brought about by the man's mental make-up. He said, *"McEvoy was a type of man who would want to demonstrate to the police that he was not under the influence of drink. If a man was suffering from alcoholism he would not be able to say tongue-twisters accurately. I know actors who ask for the ordinary things in life in tones and terms they use on the stage. McEvoy is a type of character who could get himself into trouble without alcohol by the way he behaves in ordinary life".*

118

During the three months leading to the retrial, Randle's life continued as normal with touring, stage shows and drinking. He was as ever his own worst enemy and no matter how many times he appeared in court it never seemed to be a deterrent. Prior to the oncoming Blackpool trial he would be making an appearance before the magistrates bench in the City of Manchester, charged with being drunk and disorderly. The arresting officer at the time, Police Constable Bill Oldham recalled to us the time he arrested his favourite comedian. Arriving at Mill Street Police Station, Bradford, Manchester at 5.45am to commence his day's duties, PC Oldham was immediately informed of a disturbance and directed to investigate. The police emergency car was in those days locked away and not often used, so when informed to use the car Bill obviously jumped at the chance to get behind the wheel. The early morning Manchester streets were still fairly quiet which meant Bill could put his foot down and sped off in the direction of Hyde Road. Reports had been received of a man who, apparently in a drunken state, had been driven around this part of the city in a taxi since around 2am stopping frequently to bang on the door of an off licence. Quickly arriving at the scene PC Oldham knocked at the off licence door only to receive verbal abuse from an upper bedroom window. On realising they were addressing the law and not the antagonist the voice bellowed that the culprit was at that moment in the adjacent newsagents shop. Instructing his colleague, a young probationer, to be on his guard the two entered the shop. Immediately the lone figure standing at the counter turned around to face them. *"It's Frank Randle"*, PC Oldham informed his young colleague. *"At that time I thought he was a fantastic comedian, so I thought I'd just warn him and send him on his way. I knew about the case in Blackpool and Randle's accusations against the police and I didn't want anything like that"*. With this in mind PC Oldham held out his hand to Randle saying, *"Great to see you Frank"* as he gently walked him out to his still awaiting taxi. By this time a long queue of people had formed at the nearby bus stop and the sight of such a crowd meant only one thing to Randle... an audience. Suddenly there was a change in Randle, 'who the fuck's sent for you bastards' he said taking a threatening attitude. Due to his change in behaviour and his course language, PC Oldham had no alternative than to arrest Randle, pushing him into their car. At the back of his mind was Randle's response to his arrest in Blackpool. *"I told the probationer to sit on him as I didn't want any bother – but just in case Randle started anything, I didn't want the young bobby losing it so I whispered 'on no account hit him'"*. Back at the station as constable Oldham was giving his statement and charging Randle, the comedian once again started his unruly and threatening behaviour. *"He was swearing wildly at everyone and he said that if he had a knife he would*

119

stick it in my stomach". This remark prompted the Inspector to almost leap over the desk and it was only the quick response from PC Oldham that prevented him from doing so. The cell man, who had dealt with all kind of villains, was also trying to confront Randle with the aim of teaching him some manners. Keeping everyone apart PC Oldham explained to his superior of the problems the Blackpool force had encountered with the star, eventually diffusing a potential explosive situation. When things calmed down somewhat it was decided to fast track a court appearance for Randle rather than keep him in the cells. Later that day in court Randle, charged as usual under his real name of Arthur McEvoy, was asked if he had anything to say. 'Yes' said Randle. *"I thought shit here we go"*, remarked Bill Oldham. Randle told the bench 'I would like to say that the officer treated me like a gentleman' as Bill gave a huge sigh of relief. Regrettably, PC Oldham's recollections did not extend to the outcome of the case.

Back in Blackpool for the retrial, much of the same ground was trodden with Randle's theatrics again to the fore. He gave his evidence as if playing to the gallery - demonstrating his roadside arabesque movements from the witness box. At the conclusion the jury in returning a guilty verdict also added a strong recommendation for mercy, asking for leniency in view of his physical and mental condition. He was fined £25 and his licence was suspended for twelve months. This was to be the final slap in the face for Randle, bringing the events of 1952 to a close. A year, which had started out full of great expectations was in fact a disaster and as time would tell, it was in effect the start of Randle's decline.

The week following his ill-fated court appearance, Randle was embarking on yet another nationwide tour with his lavishly produced show - Randle's Scandals of 1953. In which, there were many spectacular scenes and none more so than the finale which had on stage the Dagenham Girl Pipers. The tour brought together once again his usual supporting troupe including Gus Aubrey, Ernie Dale, Arthur Cannon and Sonny Roy. The fact that Randle was booked solid for the first few months of 1953 did little to suppress his growing depression. He really was finding it difficult to come to terms with the way variety was going – although he would ensure his audiences enjoyed this tour – and it was now becoming clearer in his mind that this was something he was no longer totally happy with. Over all he was gradually becoming disillusioned not just with variety in general but how at times his own shows, and he personally, had been besieged with problems. A thought he had harboured for a while was now forcing its way to the surface. In actual fact, he was thinking the time may now be right to change the direction of his career. Would people accept him as an actor? He knew at this time it was something he had to try. The whole situation was one that deeply saddened Randle and the more he gave it thought the more it added to his depression and propensity to drink. Unlike many heavy drinkers Randle always had a general idea of the personal costs of his weekly intake. However, on one occasion, after the show at the Hulme Hippodrome had concluded its week's run, he had reason to question a bar bill. This incident is well documented and is a story often told, however in its telling there are a number of discrepancies, remarkably from people who even witnessed the occurrence. While many don't put a date to this bout of Randle madness, most attribute it to 1956. However, Marjorie Kendall, who joined the show in November 1953, recalled the incident was already a topic of conversation with the troupe. Her remembrance of this would therefore suggest it took place on that very tour. The show finished its run at Hulme on Saturday 2nd May 1953. Everyone present at the after show gathering in the star dressing room that night was in a

The Hulme Hippodrome – where Frank had a smashing time

happy mood. The air was full of laughter and genial conversation as Randle played the perfect host. In his presence were theatre manager Mr Powell, stage manager Frank Taylor along with his wife Hilda who was in charge of the theatre bar. Frank Randle's son Arthur Delaney was also present along with his mother Eva, as too of course was

Frank's wife Queenie. Some sources also say theatre owner Jimmy Brennan was in the room. Unexpectedly, the warm amicable environment altered as a penetrating coldness surrounded everyone. Randle was yelling at the top of his voice 'I've not drunk that much'. Family and friends apprehensively glanced towards him then immediately away again agitated as Randle, waving the bill at Powell from whom it had been received, cried, 'that's not my bill, I've not drunk that much - I'm not mad'. Varying accounts have the bill as £96, £110 and even £130 all exceptionally large amounts for the early 1950s. Although there was no denying Randle could go through crates of beer a week and a bottle of spirits a day, he nonetheless protested, insisting others must have been putting drinks on his account without his knowledge - which perhaps could have been the case. With a sprint in his stride Randle walked from one side of the room to the other and then swiftly walked back again to face a nervous Powell. In trying to diffuse the situation Powell simply suggested he should pay the bill and sort out any discrepancies later. Queenie - perhaps used to her own man - sat nonchalantly gazing into the dressing room mirror as if nothing was happening. The aggrieved Randle moved closer to her side took out his chequebook and proceeded quite reluctantly to write out the cheque. Handing it over to Powell, or Hilda Taylor, as eyewitness views differ on this as they do on what happened next. One certainty is that damage was done - it is just in how it was done that people have their differences. Randle hurled his whisky glass at the dressing room mirror then stepped out of the dressing room to the fire point and with a crazed look on his face, returned clutching a fire axe, (or in an alternative version picked up the huge weight from the fire door,) he then proceeded to smash up the whole room, the sink, mirrors and wardrobe are demolished, possibly a settee also, carpets and curtains are in shreds. Silently and in a state of disbelief, those present stand amazed. Job completed, Randle as if waiting for applause, admires his work. He puts on his overcoat then arm in arm with Queenie bids his farewells to Powell (or Brennan), adding what a good week it had been and he would see them all in September or as others recalled, October. At a later date Queenie made it known that in due course Randle paid for all the damage he had caused that night but that Brennan later returned his cheque.

From Hulme the show moved over the Pennines to Halifax, opening on Monday May 4th at the Palace Theatre for a two week stay. Clive Roberts at this time was working on the stage lighting and one night was operating in the gallery keeping Randle in the main spotlight. According to Mr Roberts, both houses ran late which caused problems for the small orchestra. Not many of the musicians had cars and as time edged closer to their last buses home many began to leave the orchestra pit. This did not cause Randle too much concern as Rita Shearer on her Hammond organ continued to provide accompaniment. Mr Roberts recalled, *"I also had a last bus to catch and so the Chief electrician sent one of the back stage staff up to the gallery to tell me to go home".* As soon as Mr Roberts had turned his light out Randle said to the audience, 'as you can see the band has already left and now the lights have gone off, therefore we shall have to close the show'. Mr Roberts, added, *"I felt badly that it was due to me that the show had ended".* It wasn't until later the next day that he discovered the chap who brought him the message to go home was actually supposed to have taken over on the spotlight.

During one performance at Halifax of 'The Village Scene' where Randle as the vicar conducts his band, he seemed to upset a member of the theatre orchestra. According to the pianist Randle in the way he was conducting, had brought in the violins too soon. The pianist was already irked with the overrunning of several performances which he blamed solely on Randle. Now, to his mind, he and the band had to follow the inept conducting of the comedian. Showing his anger he snatched the baton from Randle's hand, passed it back to the legitimate conductor and stormed off. He returned for the second half as Randle was now confined to his on stage antics. At the next performance of the Hallelujah Chorus the pianist sat and played as normal but at its conclusion showed his displeasure by refusing to stand with the others to bow. Not being satisfied by his answer, when asked why he had refused to stand in acknowledging the applause of the audience, Randle asked that the musician should be removed from the orchestra. This action however, resulted in the whole band refusing to play – in effect they went on strike missing several performances. To resolve matters the Musicians Union had to be called upon. Consequently all members of the band were informed that Randle could carry on conducting the band and that the musicians should all stand to take their bows.

By May, having worked virtually non-stop, Randle publicly announced that he was thinking of quitting the variety stage to concentrate on acting. The theatrical paper 'The Stage' reported him as saying, *"I am fed up with cheap prices, poor houses and following nude shows, which are prostituting art and are by no means the type of entertainment to which a man can take his family".* On May 25th he undertook the first steps into what he intended to be a new career - that of an actor. Playing the part of Joss Skinthorne in James R. Gregson's *'The Devil a Saint'* which opened at the Theatre Royal, Hyde. The rest of the cast were members of Randle's own 'Scandals' company. As was the custom with many shows *'The Devil a Saint'* had an opening night attended by many local dignitaries, including the town's Mayor and Mayoress, along with Mr W. H. Coleman director and general manager of James Brennan's Theatres. James R. Gregson and his wife were also in attendance, as was Randle's wife 'Queenie'. Along with the audience, they witnessed what was an apparent under-rehearsed performance. With Randle's touring commitments, this was probably understandable and it was all too obvious that he required much help from the prompter. One local critic on summing up Randle's performance said, *"One must be honest and record that it was not of the stuff that sends the audience into a ferment. It was adequate and moulded to suit the artist's own technique. There were flashes of genius and there were periods when the acting dragged intolerably slowly. However, these are early days and Frank is a seasoned enough campaigner to sense the weak spots and inject more strength into them".* Of the Hyde performance, Randle told well-known show business columnist Weston Taylor, *"I was really full of enthusiasm for the play but I was the one who knew least about it. I didn't learn my script properly because I devoted more time to getting the rest of the cast right. But towards the end of the week I'd begun to get a grip on it".* Hoping eventually to take the play to Blackpool for a season Randle first offered it to the provincial theatres. Entering the film studios in June to shoot what was ultimately to be his last film *'It's a Grand Life';* Randle eagerly awaited the response from the theatres.

Randle played Joss Skinthorne in James R. Gregson's 'The Devil a Saint' - 1953

124

Chapter Five:

Franky Goes to Jollywood.

The films made by Frank Randle were a phenomenon all of their own and as such deserve looking at in isolation.

When Randle entered the studio in 1953 to film *It's a Grand Life* he was, even if unknowingly, bringing this part of his career to a close. When talking about his films and the money made from them Frank once simply said, *"I've made a packet".* This in all reality would have been no exaggeration for although never blockbusters, almost every film he made packed out the cinemas, especially those in northern England, the Midlands and Wales. As a seasoned music hall performer it is generally agreed that Randle was never at his best in the medium of film – though a Randle at second best was still pretty good and his surviving films are a lasting legacy to a great comedian.

In total Randle made ten films, eight of which were for John E. Blakeley's Mancunian Film Corporation. John E. Blakeley had been responsible for initiating the film career of George Formby – he had seen several of his stage shows and thought he would be ideal for film. He was to be proved right and though Formby only made two pictures for Blakeley, *'Boots! Boots!'* and *'Off the Dole'* they both proved to be extremely popular. So much so that Formby was whisked away by Basil Dean to be a huge hit at the Ealing studios. Though disappointed at losing Formby, Blakeley now knew just what the public wanted and that was more of the same. He believed the people who flocked to the music halls and theatres to see their favourite artistes would indeed do likewise to see them on the big screen. With this in mind Blakeley continually visited the northern variety halls in search of the talent he thought would transfer well to the cinema screen. As a result, almost every picture he produced starred or featured artistes from the world of variety. It was on one of his many visits to Blackpool's summer shows that Blakeley first spotted Randle and after a brief meeting with him Randle's film career was born. Blakeley teamed Randle with Harry Korris and Robbie Vincent from the hugely popular radio show 'Happidrome', along with Dan Young forever billed as the dude comedian. Young had been used by Blakeley in the Formby films and was in fact to become a regular for Blakeley making around a dozen films with him. Blakeley's films were all shot within a matter of weeks

Dan Young eccentric 'silly ass' singer and 'dude comedian'

and always on a shoestring budget. Randle's debut picture *'Somewhere in England'* was no exception taking just over three weeks to shoot with filming commencing on May 27th 1940 at the Walton-on-Thames Studios.

In his teenage years Al Miller worked at various minor film studios and often worked with cinematographer Geoffrey Faithful. Geoff worked on five Randle films three of which were for Blakeley's Mancunian Film Corporation. Today 83-years-old Al recalled, *"When I say I worked with him, I really mean I was working at the studio and in those days as a young lad, was basically a hand rag and I used to do many jobs, some of which occasionally involved me working closely with Geoff Faithfull. I remember the Randle films simply because I was a Frank Randle fan having seen him many times on stage".* It has often been said that the director John E. Blakeley, shot his films using just the one fixed camera or static shot. This however, was true only for certain scenes which were signified on the script by the words BUS or BUSINESS. As Al Miller recalled, *"When the word 'BUS' was inserted in the script it meant that Randle was required to fill enough film time with some of his own typical humour or 'business', usually items from his stage shows. Not knowing what was actually going to take place, Geoff was unable to light the shots in the usual way or how he would have really liked and so the only way to make sure everything was captured was to light every corner and use the one wide angled camera".* However, if one looks at Randle's 'Old Hiker' from *'Somewhere in England'* it can be seen that there were numerous cut-away shots. Indeed for another scene from the same film, where Randle and his cronies are being chased by sergeant Harry Korris, three cameras were used. Having caught sight of several pretty young Land Girls sitting atop a passing hay cart private Randle starts to wave at them and walking backwards falls headlong into a ditch. To shoot this sequence two 'De Brie' cameras were used to capture the start of the scene, specifically the hay cart, Randle waving and the beginning of his fall. While an automatic 'Neuman Sinclair' camera

126

concealed in the ditch itself was used to secure the full impact of his ultimate descent.

'Somewhere in England' was made at a time when the country needed to laugh to escape from the grip of a nation at war. A fact that no doubt led to its success for laugh they did. Although devoid of any real plot, the concept was appropriate for the time. The storyline for *'Somewhere in England'* sees Korris as the stereotypical sergeant, along with new recruits Randle, Dan Young and Robbie Vincent coming to the aid of a young soldier falsely accused of theft. Throughout the film Randle shows a complete disregard for authority and army life in general and is continually back-chatting his sergeant.

Korris: *"You'll be a lot of good in the front line without any teeth".*
Randle: *"I thought I had to shoot Germans not chew 'em".*

While Korris was given top billing, Randle impressed in his first film outing presenting 'The Old Hiker', 'At the Bar' and his 'Boxing Match' routines, all of course variants from his stage shows. He also managed to throw in one of his catchphrases 'Get off my foot' not just once but a good half dozen times. As with the other stars Randle was given little opportunity to show off any acting ability that he may have possessed but his comedy interpolations were enough to carry the film, which he did admirably. There are a couple of contrived situations to take Randle away from the army base just to aid in creating some comic shenanigans. One such scene has Randle visiting a nursing home to see his wife and newborn offspring. Over excited and decidedly lost in the hospital corridors the anxious father stops a passing female and enquires, *"Are you my wife"?*
Female: *"I beg your pardon".*
Randle: *"Nay that's not right. "Do you know where my mother is"?*
Female: *"Your mother"?*
Randle: *"No. I'm all of a quiver. It's my wife – aye that's it. She's had a baby by wireless. No I mean she's had a telegram to say we've had a baby. No that's not right".*
Female: *"It doesn't seem right".* She starts to walk away.
Randle: *"No, don't go – don't get excited. Is this the eternity ward?"*
Female: *"Maternity ward. Eternity means the hereafter".*
Randle: *"Aye, that's what I'm here after. Eh, it's my wife and baby you see. I'm a Dada, eh I'm as proud as a Cock Pea, eh, eh, I'm as pea as a, eh, eh, I'm proper proud".*
Female: *"Well I think you're crackers.*
At his wife's bedside Randle asks what shall we call it. Sebastian she replies. *"Is it?"* says a startled Randle. Back at camp and on parade

Randle is ordered to stand to attention to which he replies, *"I am. It's my uniform that's at ease"*. How many recruits watching the film in 1940 would have liked to have said something like that to their sergeant? Incidentally Randle repeats the same line in his final picture *'It's a Grand Life'* in 1953

Although Blakeley's films were a phenomenal success in the north of England they fared less well in the south - though this is perhaps a little unfair as even there they played well in the smaller houses. However, with this in mind the publicity surrounding the release of *'Somewhere in England'*, which was advertised as having a 'world' premiere was perhaps pushing the boundaries of Mancunian's popularity. The premiere was held in Blackpool on Monday 19th August 1940 at the 'Palace Pictures' with personal appearances by both Harry Korris and Frank Randle. The film eventually proved to be a great hit with the working classes and those in the armed services. Judging the mood of the audiences Blakeley soon recruited the same stars for a follow up picture *'Somewhere in Camp'* with the winning combination eventually leading to a third production *'Somewhere on Leave'*. The scheduled filming on 'Camp' was delayed somewhat due to a dispute between Frank Randle and The Wilton Brothers'. Randle had the boys under contract for his shows and offered them bit parts in the films even

though they were Blakeley's productions. According to Arthur Goulding, Randle had contracts drawn up that were so blatantly one sided in the comedian's favour. Arthur recalled, *"When my brother and I went in this office of his, he said 'are you ready to sign lads. Well my brother read the contract and said, 'this says we can't leave, but you can sack us'. So we said we weren't going to sign. Well he got mad at this and came*

Korris and Randle together appeared in three 'Somewhere' army capers.

round the counter and grabbed my brother and flung him out of the office. Then Randle came back in and said 'right Arthur you sign', I said 'no, that's my brother you've just thrown out. So out I went too and we were banned from the studio for a while. We went to the Variety Artistes Federation who gave us a free solicitor who fought the case for us and won – we got a bit of back money not much and the film was restarted". In *'Somewhere in Camp'* the Wilton brothers' feature prominently in a short musical scene with Randle. Arthur is

Frank with banjolele a la Formby with the three Wilton Brothers

seen playing the piano accordion with his brothers Ron and Gordon on violin and guitar. Randle plays the banjolele while singing, a la Formby. *"Well he couldn't really play the thing"*, said Arthur, *"in fact that was very impudent, very impertinent. I think he was jealous of George Formby who was more famous than him. So he got himself a banjolele and just learnt a few chords"*. Both *'Somewhere in Camp'* and *'Somewhere on Leave'* ran the full gamut of Randle's persona. His indifference to authority is evident when in the latter film he attends pay parade. Here his Captain explains that his pay has had several stoppages deducted.

Randle: *"I expected an increase not stoppages".*
Captain: *"Increase? What for?*
Randle: *"Well my wife's had an increase sir, twins".*
Captain: *"Oh, congratulations".*
Randle: *"Thank you. Oh, don't I get the King's pardon?"*
Captain: *"Oh you mean the King's bounty. No, you get the King's bounty for three not two".*
Randle: *"Well aren't I all right for a place".*
Captain: *"I presume your wife will get the increased allowance in due course".*
Randle: *"She will and I get nowt".*

Captain: *"That's so".*
Randle: *"Do you call that Christian gratitude? She wouldn't have had the twins only for me".*
Captain: *"That's quite enough".*
Randle: *"Quite enough, twins! It's more than enough".*
Captain: (taking his wallet out of his pocket and offering a note to Randle) *"Here's a little present for you, from me, just to mark the occasion".*
Randle: *"Oh thank you sir, I'll wet the babies' heads. I'd like to give you something in return sir".*
Captain: *"Oh, and what would you like to give me"?*
Randle: Raises two fingers to the captain *"The twins sir".*
His unruly behaviour is combined with his chatting up of the opposite sex when a pretty sergeant confronts him in the ATS ranks.
Sergeant: *"What are you doing in this squad?"*
Randle: *"I'm enjoying myself – I'll warm thee".*
Sergeant: *"Who sent you here?"*
Randle: *"Sergeant Korris, misses, er miss, corporal, sergeant".*
Sergeant: *"Sergeant Korris? I'm sure he didn't".*
Randle: *"Yes he did. Well, he told me to go somewhere warm and I bet you're a bit of a hot 'un – get of my foot".*

Almost all of Blakeley's productions contained contrived situations, whereby theatrical and musical interludes could be presented and in both *'Somewhere in Camp'* and *'Somewhere on Leave',* they were featured as army camp concerts. The first sees Randle performing as a lecherous old man interviewing for a housekeeper in a sketch entitled 'Wanted a Housekeeper'. The interviewee and recipient of his amorous advances was a dragged-up Harry Korris. A similar state of affairs also faced Dan Young in *'Somewhere on Leave'* when he appeared in drag for the sketch 'Putting up the Bans' with Korris playing the vicar. Within a year of *'Somewhere on Leave'* Randle was back in the studio, this time making the first of his non-Blakeley productions, *'Somewhere in Civvies'.* Produced by T. A. Welsh and directed by Maclean Rogers, the film has often been mistaken for being a Blakeley production. It is understandable why this should be for the producers had craftily kept the 'Somewhere' prefix and with a similarly small budget it had virtually the same quality, or lack thereof.

For the first twenty minutes or so *'Somewhere in Civvies'* is more or less a continuation of the first three 'Somewhere' films as once again we see private Randle causing havoc in the ranks. The recipient of Randle's disruption and mischief is Colonel Tyldsley played by H. F.

Maltby, who gives the star every opportunity to shine in his first scene. To the sound of bagpipes, Randle enters sitting astride a donkey.

Colonel: *"What are you doing there?"*

Randle: *"I'm sat on my ass"*.

Colonel: *"Well get off your ass when you talk to me"*.

Colonel Tyldsley's temper reaches boiling point when Randle casually calls him cock. To which the Colonel blusteringly replies, *"Cock? Cock? Cock? It's Sir to me!"*

Randle: *"Sir Cock"*.

Colonel: *"Do you realise you're wearing the King's uniform"*.

Randle: *"I thought it was a poor fit"*.

There are a number of good one-liners from Randle before he goes

into his 'Medical Board' routine, another reworking from his stage shows. Unlike the Blakeley productions Gus Aubrey as Pilkington is given more opportunities in 'Civvies' to show off his comic talents, proving an amusing foil for Randle. It is while visiting the Medical Board that the pair manage to wangle their discharge from the army and from this point the story begins to unfold. Randle's late uncle has left him £50,000 in his will, which he can receive only if he is of sound mind. Unfortunately, Randle knows nothing of the bequest; however, his evil cousin, Matthews (Joss Ambler) does and wants to claim the legacy for himself. Consequently he enlists the help of George Doonan, Randle's ex-sergeant, who has wangled special leave in order to help his ailing financial brokers business. Matthews explains about the will and how if he can prove Randle unstable he could himself receive the money – and obviously make it worth while for Doonan. Together they hatch a plan to get Randle admitted to a lunatic asylum. However before this is put into motion, Doonan's office cleaner Mrs Spam (Suzette Tarri) comes across the will and realising Randle could soon be rich sets her sights on marrying him. Doonan tells Randle that he has managed to find him a job redecorating the local asylum – while at the same time arranging with the doctors to have him admitted as a patient. Once again, aided by Pilkington the comic duo creates havoc from the moment they arrive, cementing the beliefs of the doctors that the pair should remain as patients. Before long though, Randle realises the situation and together he and Pilkington make a run for it. Hiding from staff in a doctor's office they discover the disguises which they hope will

'Somewhere in Civvies' – 1943

Top: *Gus and Frank create chaos at the asylum*

Bottom: *Randle's Comedy Band*

set them free. Stepping out from the office Randle complete with teeth is immaculately dressed in suit, top hat and cravat with stethoscope and bag completing the look of a Harley Street consultant. Whereas Gus, being Gus is dressed in a nurse's outfit. Attired thus the pair manage to distract staff and escape the building. An irate Matthews learning the plan has failed confronts Doonan, who assures him that he has another scheme which this time cannot fail. Under the pretence of giving his ex-army colleague a chance to settle in civvy street, Doonan offers Randle yet another position, that of night watchman at a remote country house. Here stage illusionist 'Devante' is in residence, and has been working on his routines and props. Devante is desperate to keep the intricate secrets of his illusions away from his competitors, who will apparently stop at nothing to get them – hence the night watchman's vacancy. Having already failed in one attempt to hook Randle, Mrs Spam discovers where Randle will be working and plans to visit him at the isolated residence. When Randle arrives he told his duties by Devante who informs him that under no circumstances should he let anyone in. He also makes clear that Randle should ignore any of the unusual happenings that he may see or hear - adding that he has no need to be frightened. But frightened he becomes, indeed he is almost scared witless when the mysterious Devante proceeds with some of his tricks and illusions. Screams, crashes, bumps, flying swords and bats soon have Randle running for his life. Amidst all this thunderous noise a voice can be heard, *"Franky it's me, your bride".* He becomes even more startled when he sets his eyes on Mrs Spam, yelling, *"Blimey the place is full of 'em".* In an attempt to lose her Randle dashes off...

Mrs Spam: *"But I'm your little workers playtime.*

Randle: *"Oh it's Mrs Miniver.*

Mrs Spam: *"Franky, Franky.*

Randle: *"Get away I'd rather have a pint anytime – get away beer's my passion – I'm in enough bother already – get away.*

Mrs Spam: *"Oh Franky think of our future.*

Randle: *"I'll ruin yours if you don't hop it.*

Avoiding Mrs Spam and other hair-raising stunts Randle eventually manages to find his way outdoors. With yet another failed attempt leaving Matthew desperate, it seems that his only hope now is to get rid of Randle for good. He sees his opportunity to do this at an army camp concert. The concert had been organised by Doonan at the request of Colonel Tyldley as part of the arrangement when temporary leave was granted. In the show we see actress Mary O'Neil singing 'Somebody's Kisses' while Randle is set to appear conducting his crazy band of assorted musicians. Doonan as MC is waiting in the wings for his cue from Randle... 'I wish I could play the harp', at which point he is supposed to walk on stage with a revolver and say 'so you shall', while shooting him. But Doonan has forgotten the gun giving Matthews the chance he needs. Offering to get it for him he proceeds to replace the blank cartridges with live ammunition. Meanwhile on stage Randle again gives a flavour of his own 'Scandals' shows by presenting a version of his comedy band routine. Featured here are The Wilton Brothers', Arthur Cannon and Ernie Dale the latter giving a rendition of 'The Sergeant Major's on Parade' – Ernie was the first man ever to introduce this song to the public. While the band is keeping the audience in fits of laughter with their antics, backstage other antics are starting to unfold. Mrs Spam who had brought some flowers for 'her Franky' discovers what Matthews has done and duly informs everyone. However, as things turn out neither Matthews nor Randle obtain the money as unnoticed, a codicil had been added to the will with instructions that the money should go to Randle's niece. The niece played by Mary O'Neil had been the love interest element of the film playing opposite Colonel Tyldesley's son Ralph, acted by Grey Blake. Throughout the film there is a running gag, where we see two uniformed army personnel in constant pursuit of Randle. Attempts to accost him are foiled firstly when he leaves the army

'Somebody's Kisses' sung by Mary O'Neil in 'Somewhere in Civvies'

camp after his medical discharge, then again while dressed as a doctor fleeing the asylum and once more when he makes his escape from Devante's house. They eventually succeed in apprehending him as he takes his final bow on stage at the conclusion of his comedy band routine.

Randle: *"Gerroff"*

Officer: *"It's your civilian pension – sign that"*

Randle: *"Blimey, I can't live on that for the rest of my life, it's back to the army for me".* So, with 'the end' credit on screen we see Randle once again entering army life.

To say that the Randle films were merely popular is perhaps over simplifying the circumstances, for the records of a Macclesfield cinema illustrate significantly how well liked the films were. Their records showed that *'Somewhere in England'* was the fifth highest grossing picture they had screened in 1940. While figures for 1942 and 1943 showed that both *'Somewhere in Camp'* and *'Somewhere on Leave'* were second only to the big Hollywood productions *'Mrs Miniver'* and *'Holiday Inn'.* If this is taken as a representation of cinemas throughout the north of England one can see just how popular the films were. The films had certainly increased Randle's popularity and paid him handsomely.

Though John E. Blakeley had been busy during 1944 making his Norman Evans vehicle *'Demobbed'*, he was ready by the following year to have Randle back under contract for their fourth picture together. This film *'Home Sweet Home'* was Randle's first peacetime film and at last took him away from Army life – though even here we see him briefly back in uniform for a Home Guard get-together. The film is a somewhat episodic affair with scenes mainly set in Randle's home, his workplace and a nightclub. Randle is a happily married man awaiting the arrival of his newborn and for a short while, he is blissfully unaware that his wife has given birth to quads. Much play is made of the mix-up between this event and the arrival of four puppies belonging to his son. Of the distinctive Randle traits, the violent side is to be seen when he confronts his son, Herbert (Stan Little) with the words *"I've 'ad enough o' thee, if I get hold of you I'll spiflicate you. I'll tear your arms off and batter you over your ears with 'em. I'll pull your 'ed off and stuff it in your mouth".* Randle is a constant irritation to his employer Colonel Wright (H. F. Maltby), for whom he works initially as a commissionaire at Wright's piano factory. Incidentally Maltby who had appeared in the previous Randle film, *'Somewhere in Civvies'*, was also destined to write the story for Randle's final screen outing *'It's a Grand Life'.* After several visual and verbal interchanges Colonel Wright puts Randle to work in his warehouse. This sets up another visual slapstick routine between Randle, Ernest Arnley and Donovan & Byl. By this time one wouldn't have expected to see a Randle film in which the star wasn't involved in some drinking session and of course *'Home Sweet Home'* was no exception. Here we see Randle and Colonel Wright hitting the whisky bottle after a Reunion Concert and Randle being rather too flirtatious with the Colonel's wife. After encountering the pair somewhat worse for drink and surprised by the vision of a bedraggled and drunken Randle, Mrs Wright (Hilda Bayley) asks of her husband, *"Who is your friend?".* Before he has time to respond, Randle rudely interjects with the remark, *"Henry, who let this pin-up thing in here?",* to which the Colonel replies, *"This pin-up thing is my wife".* Getting close to Mrs Wright, Randle tells the Colonel, *"It's too late to apologise now".* A somewhat shocked Mrs Wright pleads of her husband, *"Protect me Henry".* Randle quickly responds with, *"If you pardon me madam I think it's Henry who needs protection..."* However, he is not

135

drunk enough to pass up an opportunity of flirting with a woman and continues with, *"...what are you doing tomorrow night?"*. The Colonel being the worse for drink can only counter Randle with a drunken laugh and the words, *"You wretch".* In the meantime Mrs Wright is quickly fleeing the room with a lecherous Randle in hot pursuit. *"Don't go away"* he shouts, and while passing the colonel adds, *"You'll excuse me sir".* Randle while still pleading *"Please don't go"* to Mrs Wright as she takes flight up the staircase gives up the chase and returns instead to continue his drinking binge with Colonel Wright.

'Home Sweet Home'

'Home Sweet Home' also has the usual love story woven in to the tale with Randle's lodger Jacqueline Chantrey enamoured with Colonel Wright's son, Eric (Tony Pendrell). This is much to the disapproval of Mrs Wright, who makes her feelings clear to Jacqueline. Upset by this revelation the young woman runs away and finds work in a nightclub. However it is Randle who pursues her and eventually brings her home for the usual happy ending. In bringing this about, we have more slapstick from the comedian with his impersonation of an eastern European prince. As Prince Tampoori of Amphibia, Randle gains entry to the club and we are treated to some of the comedian's dancing footwork. Before the final fade out we see Randle at home dressed in top hat and tails coining in the money by exploiting the curiosity value of his newborn quads by charging the public for admission to see them. The film also included director and producer John E. Blakeley's usual musical interlude, which on this occasion, was in the guise of a Home

136

Guard Reunion Concert. This section saw a dance routine from Arnley & Gloria, songstress Helen Hill singing 'Home Sweet Home', and international duo-pianists Rawicz and Landauer. Randle himself had filmed a piece which was not included in the released version of the film. However, this and an extended version of the Arnley & Gloria routine, as well as an unused segment by Donovan & Byl, were later released as a 'short' under the title *Randle and All That'*. In this scene, Randle plays the part of a boot and shoe repairer, Joe Higgins '82-years-old and 50-years in the business' – *"I've swallowed enough nails to last me all my life time – my belly's armoured plated"*. The short segment involves verbal exchanges between Joe and several customers. The first customer – a newcomer to the area, he'd only lived there for fifteen years – brings in a pair of boots for repair only to find that it will be quite some time before the job can be done. In conversation, the customer – quite amiable and friendly to Joe – first offers him a sweet and later when he learns that Joe has just celebrated his 82nd birthday presents him with a one-pound note for a drink. In reaction to the kindness, Joe offers a concession on the length of time it will take for the repair – now it will only take six months. However we soon learn that this gentler characterisation still has several of the usual Randle traits especially when it comes to dealing with young women.

Young Woman: *"Hello Joe, are my dancing shoes done – the ones I brought in yesterday?"*

Joe: *"They are that love, I did them straight away, before I went to the scout meeting last night".*

Young Woman: *"Oh how nice of you".*

Joe: *"Oh it's a pleasure – I wouldn't disappoint a smashing young woman like you, you know".*

Young Woman: *"They tell me you were always a ladies man".*

Joe: *"Aye, It's my sex appeal... That's what it is".*

Putting on the shoes the young woman tries them out by performing a little dance routine.

Joe: *"All my family were dancers – my grandfather died dancing... on the end of a rope".*

The film closes with Joe reminiscing to his pet budgie about his late wife. *"I'll tell you what Dickie, we'll put my wife's favourite tune on...".* To the strains of 'Auld Lang Syne' Joe continues, *"She's been gone a long time – I'll be joining her before long - worse luck, she was always a blasted nuisance".*

Although *'Randle and All That'* was short on laughs, in playing Joe, Randle showed precisely what an excellent character actor he indeed was. One cannot help but wonder why Blakeley or other film makers never gave him an opportunity to portray such a character throughout a full length film.

Again, his next film was bereft of laughter but gave him some acting opportunity. 'When you come home' was the last of the two films not to have been produced by John E. Blakeley. This 1947 production was directed and produced by John Baxter. During filming, Randle was to earn the healthy sum of £1,000 per week. However, the film itself was eventually to cost around six times more than his previous offerings. Considering the increased production costs combined with all the publicity gained from national newspapers and film magazines, one would have thought the film should have been a huge success. Yet, this was not to be. The increased costs and the fact that it was simply not funny resulted in this being the least successful of all the Randle films. All had not been well during the actual filming since Randle and Baxter just didn't get on with each other. Randle from the outset had plainly disliked the script and told Baxter he thought it totally unfunny

The film's story involves two unscrupulous businessmen, Mr Botts and Mr Parsons who along with the bogus Doctor Franklyn plan to purchase the Empire Theatre, Carnworth. The three are aware of future plans for the development of the town which will make the land on which the theatre stands worth a fortune. Mr Botts is solicitor to Lady Langfield (Hilda Bayley) owner of the theatre. Lady Langfield has only just returned from abroad and knows nothing of the plans or how business is progressing at the theatre. Consequently, Botts convinces her that the theatre is not doing well, but encouragingly says that under the guidance of the prominent stage hypnotist Dr Dormer Franklyn the theatre could be pulled round, and urges her to sell to him. However, unknown to Lady Langfield the theatre is actually surviving pretty well under the management and current lessee Mr Joshua Rynglebaum (Tony Heaton). Though the theatre is proving popular with the working-classes as a music-hall Mrs Rynglebaum (Lily Lapidus) would prefer to take it upmarket, and not knowing Dr Franklyn's ulterior motives looks to him for help. So much so is she duped by the said Doctor that she is trying now to manoeuvre a romantic liaison between him and her adopted daughter Paula (Diana Decker). However, Paula is actually in love with local journalist Mike O'Flaherty (Fred Conyngham). Mike through his paper has organised a charity concert in which Dr Franklyn (Jack Melford) has decided to appear and prove his ability as a professional hypnotist – there are many people including Mike who have had their suspicions about the Doctor and think him a charlatan. So where does Randle figure in all this? Well Frank, under his own name, is employed by Rynglebaum as the theatre's odd job man and

138

'When you come home' was the most expensive of Randle's films

the person chosen by the local paper to be Dr Franklyn's hypnosis subject during the charity concert – until now the Doctor had always used the same individual his stooge Delia (Lesley Osmond). Before this though, we see Frank tidying the dressing rooms and collecting the empty beer bottles – the deposits from these provide him with a little beer money of his own. However, in one dressing room he gets somewhat of a surprise. In a rather bizarre situation we see a ventriloquist dummy seemingly coming to life and talking to Randle. The dummy has a serious message for Frank and urges him to assert himself and not to be so downtrodden – not just at work but also in his home life. At home Frank lives with his wife (Rene Sibley-Grant) and her parents who moved in over ten years earlier and have refused to budge since. As the dummy's words are repeated in his mind, Randle subsequently becomes a changed character. With a new determination he finds the courage to throw the in-laws out into the street, much to the delight and enjoyment of his wife. Then again, thanks to the dummy's echoing words he finally exposes Dr Franklyn for the fraud he is. This disclosure is made at a party held by theatre owner Lady Langfield who had her own suspicions about the Doctor. Mr Botts and Mr Parsons are seen sneaking away as Lady Langfield reveals to Randle that she herself was an ex-chorus girl and loved the theatre. She thanks him for preventing her from selling the lease, for exposing Dr Franklyn and for saving the jobs of those who work at the theatre. Inviting everyone to join in a toast to Mr Randle she turns to see him slowly walking away. This in effect is the end of the film's plot, a film which to a degree showed Randle could act even though the script restricted him. *'When you come home'* was unlike Randle's other films and perhaps suffered from having too much of a storyline. He obviously did not have the same freedom as his other films and was hampered by a script that handicapped him completely. On the plus side the film did show Randle's excellent portrayal of 'Grandpa' in a specially adopted version of 'Grandpa's Birthday'. This is the film's opening and closing scenes with the main plot being revealed in flashback, as told by Randle to those gathered at his party. Randle is credited on the film as having written additional scenes and comic dialogue – he obviously was responsible for the Grandpa scenes though whether he contributed more is unknown – the film is certainly short on laughs.

Also featured in *' When you come home'* were Gus Aubrey who for a few minutes revels in an effeminate performance alongside Randle and Rynglebaum. He later returns for fleeting appearances, as too does Ernie Dale who in one scene joins Randle, while he is shaving Rynglebaum, in a short rendition of 'The Barber of Seville'. 'The Two Leslies' Sarony and Holmes are also given ample opportunity to show off their musical talents.   The pair were very popular with British audiences through regular radio performances, stage appearances and

Randle as 'Grandpa' with Rene Sibley-Grant as 'Grandma' in 'When you come home'

recordings with the Jack Hylton Band. Diana Decker who played Paula Rynglebaum had arrived in England from her native America in 1939 making her film debut in 1943. She continued her career mainly as a singer and is perhaps best remembered as a recording artist, her biggest hit being 'Poppa Piccolino'. There were others and her version of 'Rock-a-Boogie Baby' is classed as a rock 'n' roll gem. Diana also appeared on the London stage and had many TV appearances to her credit one as foil for Arthur Askey in 'Before Your Very Eyes'. Pat Williams had a very brief appearance as 'Grandpa's' father in the film's opening scene.

It seems strange that while Randle's films were often shown abroad they never reached the screens of London's West End. Dubbed or sub-titled *'When you come home'* was released in various countries including Finland and Belgium where it was known as *'Un Fameux Loustic'* ('A Famous Guy'). Strangely enough, even some of his wartime efforts were eventually released in post-war Germany including *'Somewhere in Civvies'*, which in 1952 was released as *'Franky wird Zivilist'* (Franky becomes a Civilian) with the tag line 'The world champion of humour presents the first English military comedy'.

Both 'When you come home' (left) and 'Somewhere in Civvies' had foreign releases.

However, Frank Randle 'movie star' was to reach national coverage through the pages of the picture comic 'Film Fun'. His appearances in this weekly favourite were inspired by the 1947 Butchers film release of

141

'*When You Come Home*'. Undoubtedly all the publicity surrounding the film had had some good outcome with Randle first appearing in their pages under the heading of Frank Randle - Famous Star of Butcher's Films. The artist who ably caricatured the comedian was Harry Parlett (1881-1971) a long-time illustrator and comic strip artist with the Amalgamated Press and father of George and Reg Parlett who followed in the family tradition at

Frank Randle appeared in the British comic Film Fun from 1947 - 1955

the same firm. Although if only in cartoon form, Randle's emergence in this popular British comic, where he appeared alongside favourites like, Laurel and Hardy, Red Skelton, Abbott & Costello and others, seemed to seal him as a family favourite. The Frank Randle strip continued to run under the subtitle 'Famous Star of Mancunian Films' continuously in 'Film Fun' until 1955 two years after Randle had made his last film and just two years before his death.

Randle's film career had two distinct phases, the first being the London period that ended with John Baxter's production '*When you come home*'. The second phase comprised the films produced in the Manchester studio of John E. Blakeley. Although up to this point all of Blakeley's films had been shot at London studios, they had all been conceived and planned in his Manchester based office. It had long been Blakeley's ambition to open a studio in Manchester and when it became increasingly more difficult to obtain studio space in London he made his dream a reality. Having purchased an old church on the outskirts of the city centre and after much money had been spent on its conversion into a working studio it was officially opened on May 12th 1947. Having already formed a company board of directors consisting of important local theatre and cinema owners, Blakeley was soon to acquire another addition in the form of Frank Randle.

Randle had experienced troubles on his last film '*When you come home*' and the relationship between him and producer/director John Baxter had been strained to say the least. Each swore never to work with the other again. Of course Randle had never been a saint when filming for Blakeley but they did at least have a decent working relationship. Consequently Randle offered himself up to Blakeley as a board member. It was a sensible move for both parties concerned. On

Randle's part he would be paid for his films and also receive a salary and profits as a board member. For Blakeley by accepting Randle as a company director and knowing he was still a box-office attraction also secured the comedian for use solely in his own productions. Together they worked side by side from 1947 to 1953 producing *'Holidays with Pay', 'Somewhere in Politics', 'School for Randle'* and finally *'It's a Grand Life'*. A real love/hate relationship was to develop between the two

Film producer John E. Blakeley

during the lifetime of the studio. For Randle not having the same restrictions imposed upon him as when he had filmed in London often took liberties much to Blakeley's annoyance. There were the occasions when after a few late night drinking bouts he could arrive late for filming or cause havoc on the set or simply refuse to leave his dressing room. Arthur Mertz jnr., son of Blakeley's late scriptwriting partner Arthur snr., also worked in the studio and it was his job to make sure all the artistes were on set whenever they were required. Arthur found most of the stars quite amiable even when woken at their hotels for early morning shoots. Randle however, was different. Getting him on to the set was a particular trial especially if there had been any friction between him and Blakeley the night before. After Mertz eventually got Randle to the studio he found he could still be quite obstreperous about coming out of his dressing room. *"I could see Blakeley walking up and down, getting very impatient"*, recalled Arthur, *"Eventually he'd say, 'Arthur, for God's sake go and get Frank will you?'. Of course I had to be careful how I treated him, after all he was a director of the company. Anyway I would go into his dressing room to try and talk him onto the set, and he'd say 'have a drink'. So I'd join him and have an easy chat and eventually I'd say are you coming on the set Frank? He'd say, 'alright then Arthur', and he'd come down onto the set"*. As Arthur recalled, this was then the time for Blakeley to exercise some form of retribution, for the very moment Frank walked on the set Blakeley would call for a break.

Randle had always been the energetic type and enjoyed daily exercise – many an early dog walker could often catch sight of him in

Blackpool's Stanley Park doing his morning workouts. At the Manchester studio Frank had a punch-ball installed in his dressing room along with chest expanders and weights, all of which were constantly in use.

There were times when Randle, annoyed by Blakeley, would retreat to his dressing room and the punch-ball and would then, as Arthur Mertz recalled, *"knock hell out of it".* Arthur's wife Wynne who was the pay-clerk at the studio recalled hearing him swearing and name calling Blakeley while thumping away at the punch-ball. *"I caught him on a few occasions",* Said Wynne, *"I thought there must have been someone in with him when I could hear him talking and punching away. But when I'd knock at the door and enter there'd be no one else there, just him and a swinging ball. He'd say 'oh I'm just having a go he's got me all worked up again".* As Arthur also pointed out Frank wasn't always as bad as he was painted. *"We were actually very close friends and got on extremely well together. Of course he liked a drink and indeed I joined him many times. I wasn't a boozer but I could hold my own. Frank was a most generous man. Whenever I took Wynne or my mother back stage to see him at a theatre he was always the most perfect and charming of gentlemen".* Gentleman Frank disliked people swearing in the presence of women and would berate them severely if they did so. Wynne recalled, *"He would say, 'do you mind there are Ladies in this room'".* He also had an aversion to women smoking and felt it quite un-lady like.

Actor Gerry George appeared as a child extra in three of Randle's films and admits to seeing nothing of Randle's sinister side. Although his first meetings with Randle was as a child, Gerry still clearly recalled Frank Randle as being a very, very smart and dapper looking man in spats, vicuna overcoat with astrakhan fur collar. *"He was forever making us laugh with tricks like the one in which he would flip open his platinum cigarette case, flick a Woodbine into the air, and catch it in his mouth. We kids used to revel in it because he was like a magician or a combination of Father Christmas and the Wizard of Oz. He had a lot of time for kids and he liked to encourage them and give them a hand, he was very magnanimous like that."* Gerry also recalled that Randle was a good source for *"newly-minted half-crowns, which he used to dispense to us with great regularity, whenever he turned up on location or at the studio".*

Having his own studio Blakeley was not now restricted to time and this was evident with Randle's first Manchester produced picture *'Holidays with Pay'.* The film took around ten weeks to film as opposed to his first

144

London film, completed in just three weeks. Blakeley as a film producer knew what he and his audiences wanted and that was laughter – good old northern humour. However, Randle did not like to be directed and basically wanted to do things his own way and despite the direction, he was given plenty of scope to do this. With the scripts being thin on storyline it was up to Frank to inject enough visual gags to keep audiences happy. This was of course fine with Blakeley and indeed, what he had planned for as proven by the script pages carrying the words BUS or BUSINESS.

Randle having used his influence with Blakeley to have Sally Barnes featured in *'Holidays with Pay'* had now taken the opportunity to continue his interest in her. This secret affair was not as secret as the two would have liked, for most of the studio staff were aware of it while others guessed or sensed something was going on. Frank of course, stayed in his caravan with Sally during the course of filming; only returning to Queenie at the weekend.

When Wynne Mertz paid out the weekly wages by cheque to the actors on the Friday, Frank Randle always left enough cash to be handed to his manager Jim Munro. This was to enable Jim to collect two large bouquets of flowers from the local florist, as ordered by Randle. Returning with the said blooms, Jim would sit with Wynne Mertz in her office while he wrote out the cards for Frank. One read, *'To my darling Queenie - With all my love'.* The other read, *'To my darling Sally...Love you forever'.* Jim said to Wynne one Friday, 'My God Wynne if ever I get these cards mixed up there'd be a riot'.

Of the ten Frank Randle films perhaps *'Holidays with Pay'* more than any other typifies the audience for whom it was made. Randle played the part of Jack Rogers with Tessie O'Shea as his wife Pansy. Together with their two daughters Joyanne (Joyanne Bracewell) and Pam (Sally

Fun on Blackpool beach with Frank Randle in 'Holidays with pay'

145

Barnes), they live somewhat overcrowded with Randle's brother Randolph (Dan Young) in a terraced house in a typical Lancashire neighbourhood. In the film, the Rogers family like many thousands of others from the cotton and mining towns of northern England, take their annual wakes week holiday in the workers paradise of Blackpool. One of the first things these holidaymakers would have done on their arrival was to book tickets to one of the summer shows, which on numerous occasions would be to see Frank Randle. It was no wonder they laughed at his antics for they knew exactly where he was coming from – he was one of them. Down to earth no nonsense characters like Randle could be found in every northern street, cotton mill and public house, the people knew him and he knew them. This feeling certainly shows through in the Blackpool location shots for 'Holidays with Pay'. For here we have Randle joining in the fun mixing with the genuine holidaymakers at the swimming pool and on the pier.

Most of Randle's films usually contained a romance for the juvenile leads and 'Holidays with Pay' was no exception. When the family car breaks down en-route to the resort, Pam Rogers meets up with Michael Sandiford (Sonny Burke) and a relationship begins. As the plot unfolds it is revealed that one of Michael's ancestors was murdered on July 7th 1592. Now centuries later, in order to retain the family estate, Michael must spend the night of the anniversary in the family home or forfeit it to the next in line, his cousin Jasper (Peter Lily). Legend has it that ghosts return to the house on this night in order to re-enact the fateful crime. The Rogers family having been forced to leave their boarding house join Michael at the mansion. Jasper, in an attempt to claim the estate, has plans to kill Michael but first needs to frighten away the Rogers'. This he hopes to achieve by installing in the house several bogus spooks, skeletons and even an Egyptian mummy. However, after a night of mayhem and confusion Randle and company reveal the truth and foil Jasper's plans. Before they finally leave the house however, a genuine ghost (Frank Randle) makes an appearance.
Tessie O'Shea: *"Oh what a grand old man".*
Randle: *"I've come to cut your water off"*
Dan Young: *"Who are you?"*
Randle: *"I'm a spectre from the past".*
Dan Young: *"An inspector from the gas?"*
Randle: *"No, I'm one of these here ghostssssss. I was murdered in 1592 – I've never been the same fellow since".*
Tessie O'Shea: *"What have you come back for dad?"*
Randle: *"My ration card, aye, aye".* Looking at Tessie O'Shea he adds, *"That's a fine boiler. Mmm, aye, if I wasn't an old spook I'd take a fancy to thee".* In classic Randle fashion the ghost begins to strut his

feet. The scene finally ends with the ghost informing them, *"I think I'll fade away – goodneet – Boyee".*

With Michael retaining the family estate and winning Pam's hand in marriage the film ends happily for all, with Frank Randle complete with false teeth appearing dapper in his formal wedding outfit. Josef Locke made his film debut in this production, but purely in a singing role, appearing in an end of pier show in a scene set in a Wild West saloon. Although everyone was dressed in western attire there was only one song in keeping with the setting, 'Moonlight and a Prairie Sky'. Locke's other song being 'I'll Take You Home Again Kathleen'. The Rogers family also appeared, with Randle dressed as a western gambler while Tessie O'Shea sang 'He's not much to Look at' and 'Strolling by the Seaside'. Sonny Burke and Sally Barnes joined together to sing 'A Natural thing to Do'.

Sally Barnes had often been invited on to Randle's yacht the 'Namoura' though for differing reasons than most of his other guests. Randle was no sailor; he had only bought his vessel so he could impress his showbusiness colleagues. Two of whom, Syd and Max Harrison, were to join Randle on board during a break in filming Randle's next film *'Somewhere in Politics'.* Filming had begun at the Manchester studio for *'Somewhere in Politics'* on April 5th 1948 and was completed by June. Unlike most of Randle's films this one actually had a storyline. Randle and Tessie O'Shea play husband and wife Joe and Daisy Smart who are about to move into their new home with their son, bank clerk Reggie (Sonny Burke). Arriving by public transport – a number 129 Manchester Corporation bus - Joe just manages to pronounce *"What a beautiful domicile"* before he falls headlong into the garden. After picking himself up he adds in his poshest of voices, *"I've got a gobful of grit".* Noticing that his wife Daisy is carrying a new hatbox he enquires, *"What's that?".* Somewhat sheepishly she replies, *"It's my new hat",* but is reluctant to let him see it. He snatches the box and opening it finds that it actually contains a chamber pot. After a tussle in trying to retrieve it Daisy drops it and to the sound of porcelain shattering Joe says, *"Ee, you've broken your new hat".* Trouble is soon with them when they discover that the house has mistakenly also been let to Martha Parker (Bunty Meadows) and her brothers Tony and Arthur (Syd and Max Harrison). At the suggestion of the estate agent (Sally Barnes), the two families agree to share the large house, especially as the two women discover that they both belong to the same local Women's Freedom Guild. There is a good deal of slapstick from Syd & Max Harrison and Frank Randle as two lots of furniture is brought into the house. One scene has Joe hiding from his wife in a wardrobe. Tony and Arthur (Syd & Max) then take the wardrobe upstairs by turning it over and over all the way to the top. When they finally reach the summit the wardrobe is accidentally dropped over the rails coming to rest with a crash back where it started. With the door hanging off its hinges, Joe, bruised and bewildered, staggers from inside the wardrobe. After eventually settling in their new home, the comic trio manage to gain work as radio engineers and are employed by Councillor Willoughby (Josef Locke) at his Radio and Music shop. Daisy persuades her husband that he should stand against Willoughby at the upcoming local election and so the campaigning begins. Councillor Willoughby also owns the 'Blue Moon Hotel Ballroom' where he regularly entertains audiences with some popular songs. It is here that Willoughby is holding one of his campaign rallies. This is of course another contrivance by producer John E. Blakeley to include his usual 'variety show' interlude. Here as Willoughby, Josef Locke sings 'Oft in the Stilly Night', 'Machushla' and his famous 'Violetta'. Joe and Daisy soon arrive uninvited, supported by Martha in the company of her Women Freedom Guild members and Tony and Arthur. More fun erupts as Daisy (Tessie O'Shea) gains the stage and gives a song of her own with the comical 'Spade and Bucket' before going into an outrageous and chaotic dance with Joe (Randle). In a bid to force Joe out of the election Willoughby's store manager, Howard (Anthony Oakley) frames Joe as a forger of five-pound notes. However, the plot is foiled by eagle eyed bank

clerk Reggie Smart who also happens to be in love with Willoughby's daughter Marjorie (Sally Barnes). The film ends with Joe being cleared of any wrongdoing and narrowly winning the election. Willoughby, magnanimous in defeat, invites everyone to the 'Blue Moon Hotel Ballroom' where Joe in typical Randle fashion has a good deal too much to drink.

On the final day of shooting with the last scenes finally captured everyone was relieved as the heat in the studio had been unbearable – indeed Manchester itself was basking in hot summer sunshine. As the cameras stopped rolling the large steel studio doors were flung open to let in what cool air there was. There were still a number of props lying around including several musical instruments that had been used in the Radio & Music shop scenes. Randle picked up a banjo and started to play. Josef Locke picked a drum and banging away commenced to sing. Soon Syd & Max Harrison had selected instruments for themselves and were quickly followed by other cast members. As if leading a street parade Jo Locke and Frank Randle guided the motley assortment of 'musicians' through the huge doors out into the streets of suburban Manchester stopping traffic as they went. By the time they had marched all the way to the top of the Road and turned to march all the way back again the footpaths had filled with people. Many had come out of their houses, buses stopped as their passengers were glued to the windows, the local shops emptied as Randle danced and skipped his way down the street. It is perhaps not surprising that the studio was known locally as 'Jollywood'. Breaks in filming had given Frank Randle more opportunity to visit his yacht and the personal invitation he had extended to Syd & Max Harrison had been given on proviso that if they accepted then they were to attend wearing full naval uniform. Randle loved to play the role of captain. Not the 'old sea dog' of his alter ego, the 'Old Boatman', but smartly attired in slacks, blazer and cap. For the visit of Syd and Max Harrison he also wanted them in suitable apparel. In going to such lengths to get his appearance accurate it was a pity he hadn't done the same with his navigation. For in attempting to sail up to the central pier he misjudged the tides and as it turned he ran the boat aground. Unfortunately, today *Somewhere in Politics* is classed as 'lost' as no known print survives – though hopefully one will surface one day. However, a 'short' extract from the film entitled *Full House* does exist.

Life on the set of Randle's films was so unpredictable for everyone, depending on the man's mood, which could change so dramatically. For a while he could be cheerful and friendly with all he came into contact with then, for no apparent reason, his character would be totally different. He would pull people up for the slightest of things; argue with people even though he was in the wrong. At one point on the set of *School for Randle*, the next in the Randle canon of films, when everything seemed to be going well Frank suddenly demanded to speak to Blakeley regarding Fred Harries, the film's Musical Director. Randle had decided that he wanted Harries off the film. He was convinced that the talented musician was continually giving him the wrong note for a musical sequence. It is possible that Harries may have given him the wrong note once but for him to have continually done so as implied by Randle seemed unlikely. Harries was no amateur, he was a well-respected musician and musical director with years of experience behind him. He had been Musical Director for the Palace Theatre, Manchester and had been responsible for organising the orchestra to play at the studio. He had become a popular performer on the Manchester dance scene and had broadcast countless times for the BBC. All of which counted for nothing as far as Randle was concerned, he was the star and Harries was incompetent and had to go. Blakeley conceded and Randle had his way, with Billy Butler soon replacing Harries. There were smiles and quite a few frowns on the faces of those who witnessed Butler and Randle's first run through of 'Sweet and Low', for Butler gave the very same intro note as that previously given by Harries. Ironically the number performed by Randle never saw the light of day in the finished feature film.

End of filming on 'School for Randle'.

Left:
Producer/Director John E. Blakeley.
Assistant Director Tom Blakeley.
Frank Randle with member of production crew

The story line to *'School for Randle'* has Frank playing the part of a school caretaker, nicknamed 'Flatfoot' by the pupils. Unbeknown to pupil Betty Andrews (Terry Randall), Randle is her real father and has taken the position at the school just to be near her. When Betty runs away from her adoptive parents it is Randle who follows her and returns her safely home. Reading thus far one would wonder where the Randle comedy is to be discovered. However, true to Blakeley's productions the comedy is not to be found in the plot line but in the Randle peripheries. One incident has Randle, Dan Young and Alec Pleon performing on stage as the 'Three Who Flungs' incompetent Chinese magicians. Another scene, deleted from the original release but issued as a 'short' subject was 'Bella's Birthday' which included the 'Sweet and Low' number performed by Randle.

It was four years later before Randle was to walk through the doors of Blakeley's studio again and on this occasion he was a different man. For during the intervening years his career and personal life had deteriorated somewhat. He had appeared in court on numerous occasions, he was drinking more heavily – if that was possible, his health was worsening, he was not the box office draw that he used to be and had even talked of quitting the variety stage. John E. Blakeley too had undergone a downturn in fortunes. He had hoped to put Randle into a new army caper called *'Shoulder Arms'* but found funding for it difficult to obtain. Instead, to secure any form of financial backing, the studio had made the decision to turn to different types of productions under the guidance of John E. Blakeley's son Tom. By the summer of 1953 the studio, which had been silent for around twelve months, sprang back into life with Blakeley's long awaited Randle vehicle. Obviously the wily filmmaker had found funding from some source

and there is strong indication that Randle himself may have put more of his own money into this film. If Randle's career was in decline then that of his co-star was still in its ascendancy and destined for far greater things. Indeed, Diana Dors would soon be a national favourite. Though, after signing a £1,000 contract she then began to have last minute thoughts believing that appearing with Frank Randle might not be a good career move for her at that time. However, after being threatened with legal action for breach of contract it was soon off to Manchester for the Blonde Bombshell.

Off to Manchester for the Blonde Bombshell

Randle soon learned of Diana Dors' reluctance of appearing with him and was somewhat taken aback. One can almost imagine him saying in the tones of a Shakespearian actor – 'does not want to appear with me, the greatest comic character actor in the country'. Consequently on her arrival at the studio Randle's aversion of her was already evident and he was ready to bring her down a peg or two. Tom Blakeley, when talking with Jeff Nuttall for his book 'King Twist' recalled that Randle soon got her drunk on tumblers full of spirits leading to her absence from set for three days. This southern beauty would be firmly put in her place. There has been much said about Randle and Dors during the filming of 'It's a Grand Life' – of drinking sessions together and of sexual activities. Stories of Randle chasing her around the studio brandishing his manhood and also of a naked Diana Dors being drunk and locked in her dressing room by the comedian. The two, it has also been said, hired a plane to fly around the Fylde coastline while blissfully drinking the afternoon away. There is no doubt that Diana Dors enjoyed her drinking sessions though perhaps not to the same extent as Randle. Though she certainly liked her parties and was indeed quite a character. So it was that Randle may have begun with some inner hatred but it wasn't too long before the pair had formed some sort of unlikely platonic alliance.

Of the many studio workers that we spoke with in the course of writing this and our previous book most had heard these stories. All agreed that the pair did indeed get drunk together but were uncertain whether anything else was going on. Most however, didn't believe the stories of them indulging in sexual acts and couldn't even imagine how they could ever have been thought of as true - Though again no one was willing to offer any assurances of this. There was of course the fact that Diana's then-husband, Denis Hamilton, was often near to hand, which surely would have dampened the ardour of any man. Randle obviously knew of Hamilton's reputation and would not have wanted to get involved in that way with Diana. If there ever had been anything or not between the pair, Diana in later years, was to distance herself from the comedian when she described him as a 'disgusting, dirty old drunk' and that she had hated working with him. The late Bob Monkhouse, having provided us with a foreword for one book and helped with research on another, had told us in the past of his love of the comedian. Knowing this we contacted him again to see if he could provide any anecdotes of the great man. We were however; somewhat surprised at what he did have to say, "Oh the stories of Dors and Randle were once well known in showbusiness circles. Though to my mind any fling between them would have been a definite non-starter. Knowing Diana as I did, Randle, even at his most immaculate best and he certainly could be elegant with oodles of charm, would not have appealed to her. It is well known now that I had my own sexual dalliance with Diana. The experience only took place because I thought her gangster-like husband was thousands of

152

Diana and husband Dennis Hamilton

miles away in America. Make no mistake, he was a real hardened criminal well known to the police (though I don't think he was ever convicted as such) and to members of the underworld. If you valued your life you would never, and I mean never ever cross him. I believe he'd think nothing of killing, certainly nothing of causing unspeakable bodily harm, if not personally then by other hands". Even though Randle had possession of a gun, which he certainly fired on occasions and with threats to kill people – they were of course all empty threats. Most were carried out in drunken rants with all shots being fired into the air – no one was ever hurt in these instances. Hamilton's threats would have been seriously meant. Randle had of course been a boxer, he knew boxers and wrestlers and people who could handle themselves. Recent illness had perhaps made him not as strong and physical as he had once been but no doubt if in any trouble would still be able look after himself. Taking all this into consideration it still seems unlikely that he would have risked displeasing Hamilton who perhaps not always at hand did often show up at the studio. However, being the drinkers and party-type of people they were, Hamilton would have thought little of his wife and Randle enjoying that same privilege together.

Randle, if not with Dors, certainly had 'girlfriend' problems at this point. Diana Dors in a 1972 radio show, recalled his girlfriend at the time, *"He'd roped her in to manage the wardrobe and the costumes for this film. Everything would be all right until they'd have a quarrel and then he'd throw her out bag and baggage. All the actors would then be poodling around at 7.00 in the morning looking for their clothes – nobody could find them it was utter chaos"*. Studio receptionist Eileen Mackleston had good reason to recall another incident concerning one of Randle 'girlfriends'. One day while the actors were on set filming, a young woman arrived at the studio to see Frank Randle. Eileen explained to her that studio procedure barred admissions on set while the red light was showing. Several times she had to make clear that when filming was taking place no one at all could be admitted – eventually and somewhat angrily the young woman left. The following day Eileen was summoned to the office of studio manager Bud Kelly – to whom Randle's friend had vigorousiy complained. Having recounted the events to the satisfaction of Bud Kelly this then seemed to be an end of the matter. However, later that day while chatting in the studio canteen Randle suddenly burst into the room enraged and yelling. Eileen recalled, *"He looked at me while shouting at the top of his voice 'I want you'. He was going raving mad and everyone just sat there and never moved. He kept shouting, 'I want you'. He was effing and blinding with every other word"*. Luckily, one of the nearby studio hands calmed him down and managed to persuade him to return to his dressing room. Eileen continued, *"Shortly after this, I heard bangs - gun shots. It was Randle again. He was firing his gun and shouting 'where is she I'm going to kill her'. So Arthur my husband went to see him and calm him down.* In what may have been a follow-up to the same incident later that day or possibly just a similar one is unclear, however Dorothy Stimson recalled, *"I suddenly heard the bang, bang, of a gun going off, and I didn't know what to think. I was obviously in a slight panic not knowing what was going on. Well I'm not sure who shouted I think it was probably one of the boys from the paint shop. He shouted 'get back, get back, it's Frank he's got a gun. There he was with this Lugar letting loose. I did manage to stop him in the end, I was shouting Frank, Frank, and eventually stopped him and asked him' whatever are you doing'. It was not one of his better days. He was shocking, he used to do such outrageous things".*

The disruption caused by Randle was also evident during the actual filming of 'It's a Grand Life'; one prank however backfired on him to his annoyance. Winifred Atwell the coloured pianist and popular entertainer of the period was to be featured in a musical interlude playing several toe tapping tunes including 'Dixie Boogie' and 'Britannia Rag'. Randle thought it would be a huge joke if he stole the scene by blacking-up in similar fashion to the 'Black and White Minstrels' - that is to say black face, white eyes and lips and white gloves. However, an astute Blakeley had discovered Randle's intentions. So, besides having the main camera on Winifred Atwell he also focused the second camera on her instead of Randle. Even though Blakeley had thwarted Randle's plans Atwell was still not happy with the whole affair believing his antics to be crass and ill-mannered.

On another occasion the disruptive Randle did cause filming to stop after taking a dislike to Bert Marrotta the assistant director. Part of

Bert's duties was to get the actors on set and if they were late he had to go out to get them. On more than one occasion he had to call on Randle – something that Randle wasn't pleased with at all. In retaliation Randle confronted Blakeley and demanded he sack Marrotta. Blakeley, as he had done before, bowed to Randle's wishes and consequently dismissed him. However, this did not go down well with the technical crew who insisted that Marrotta be reinstated or they would take strike action. Dot Stimson recalled, *"They all came to me complaining that if Marrotta didn't come back they would not finish the picture. I was like a shop steward we had a real dispute. The only filming they were prepared to do was just little bits, nothing big involving the stars; we had a three day break because of their actions"*. Blakeley, realising the consequences, could do nothing more than ask Marrotta to return, something which at first Marrotta refused to do. Eventually he had a change of mind bringing an end to the enforced lay off. Having caused the three-day disruption, Randle himself had taken the opportunity to go off on one of his benders. Diana Dors too finding herself with time on her hands took a trip to Blackpool with husband Dennis. This was to end in them hitting the headlines of the national press when they were arrested for breaking into a friend's house and stealing an amount of alcohol. When filming recommenced Randle never said a word regarding Marrotta or the dispute. However, after the filming of the last scene in full view of the crew and cast, Randle approached Marrotta and warmly shoot his hand and said 'I'm sorry for being an absolute bastard'.

As it turned out *'It's a Grand Life'* was to be Randle's final film offering and with it his movie career had come full circle as the film had him back in the army once again. However, on this occasion his uniform was a much better fit, which was about the only thing that differed from his previous army outings. The action takes place at the 29th Army Training Camp and the main story centres on Corporal Paula Clements (Diana Dors) and the two men trying to woo her. The first is Sergeant Major O'Reilly (Michael Brennan) who tries to blackmail his way into her affections only to have Paula constantly rebuffing his unwanted advances. The second is private Phil Greene (John Blythe) who eventually wins her heart. As expected from the private Randle of old, the same disregard for authority runs right through *'It's a Grand Life'*, he turns parade ground drills into comic shambles, he smokes on parade and has a roving eye for the girls... any girl. Throughout the film Randle's opportunities for conjuring up laughable moments are many and varied. One is a typical piece of Randle humour often used in his stage shows and was his play on the word 'thwart'. Randle of course pronounced it not in the usual way as if it rhymed with 'nought',

Diana and Frank in 'It's a Grand Life'

but with the Lancashire twang as if it rhymed with 'part' or more correctly 'fart' which is what Randle intended and what all his audiences realised. On stage after Gus Aubrey explains that he's been thwarted, Randle offers to open a window. In the film the use of the word has been somewhat sanitised yet its mispronunciation is still used to good effect.

New recruit Charlie Entwistle having been interviewed by Randle asks, *"Why fling thy thwarts at me?"*
Randle: *"Thwarts? Why fling thy thwarts in thy face? I've never flung a thwart in anybody's face."*
Entwistle (to Dan Young): *"You know his thwarts have a powerful sting.* Young: *Do they?"*
Randle (to Dan Young): *"I didst not know I'd stung him with my thwarts".*
Entwistle: *"Why, can't you tell when you're going to thwart me".*
Randle: *"Thou must let me know thee next time I thwart thee – But surely you wouldst not stop me from thwarting thee, wouldst thou?"*
Entwistle: *"No, thwart away if it makes thee happy".*
Randle: *"So be it. To thwart or not to thwart that is thee question?"*
Several of Randle's friends from the wrestling fraternity made appearances in the film and were seen giving him a pre-match massage

156

and rub down. The bout in question sees well-known and popular wrestler Jack Pye face up against private 'Homicide' Randle. With a little help from Diana Dors, Randle is soon victorious. The usual musical interlude is again present and comes from the popular recording artiste of the time pianist Winifred Atwell, who plays several toe-tapping numbers at Paula's 21st Birthday/Engagement party. This event had only been possible after Randle had rescued Paula from drowning for which he was promoted to Sergeant-Major. Randle's final scene sees him in full Scottish regalia addressing the party guests as he would his theatre audiences thanking them for coming along to see him. The film's ultimate fade out, which has Randle complete with shining teeth smiling happily to camera, was as it turned out, his last ever screen appearance. Randle never again set foot in front of the cameras for by the time the film went on general release, Blakeley's Manchester studios had closed, eventually being sold to the BBC.

Trade advert for 'It's a Grand Life' - 1953

One of Randle's biggest regrets was that his personal pet project for producing his own film never came to fruition. It had been one of his strongest hopes and aspirations to bring to the screen his own screenplay 'Wigan Peer' (not pier) which he also intended to direct. His one time manager Jim Munro once recalled, "*Together we typed the script, often working for eighteen hours a day weeks on end, and it would, I am convinced, have been an epic. He had even selected the people he wanted for the parts, in fact some parts were written for particular artistes*".

Chapter Six.

Basta, Basta.

After completing filming on *'It's a Grand Life'* and having no 1953 summer season booked, Randle again returned to touring. Appearing in Liverpool in July he spoke of his disappointment regarding the play *'The Devil a Saint'*, only one theatre in Ireland, had shown an interest. He said, *"I can have bookings galore for variety, revue or pantomime. Quite likely I'll be forced to take over a theatre so that no one except myself runs a risk. I certainly take this as a challenge. I will get my teeth further into straight acting. In the past I have always found that when people have dissuaded me from doing something, my course was best in the end. The fact that everyone has said, 'Give it up' and 'You're making a mistake' has given me an incentive to stage the play. I am prepared to risk practically everything - but I can't do it if I don't have the theatres".* Unfortunately Frank never did get the theatre booking he so desperately wanted, to them he was a variety act, and although an exceptional character comedian they did not look upon him as an actor.

After Liverpool, the tour continued with an itinerary that trod familiar ground with appearances at Wigan, Cardiff and Derby before a three week September visit to London taking in Chiswick, Hackney and Brixton Empires. After this the company moved northwards to the Midlands finishing the month at Leicester. September also saw an addition being made to the bill with the arrival of ex-boxer Jack Doyle, once regarded by many as a legend and certainly a colourful character. Earlier in his life Doyle had left his Irish homeland to join the Irish Guards where his pugilistic talents were soon spotted and encouraged. After initially boxing for the army he eventually turned professional and before long became a sensation within the sport. By his early twenties he had already become a British phenomenon the likes of which the nation had never seen before. He once attracted 90,000 people to a fight at London's White City. In a boxing career which lasted ten years (1932-42) he lost only six of his twenty-three fights (two by disqualification). One of these defeats cost him the British Heavyweight crown. All, apart from four of his seventeen victories, were by knockouts with the first ten being won within two rounds. A talented singer Doyle, made the first of eleven gramophone recordings in 1933 and he also made guest appearances at the London Palladium and had

Jack Doyle

minor success in a few British films. A spell in America saw him losing a fight in the first round to Buddy Baer. Doyle stayed on in the US and attempted to break into Hollywood. Although unsuccessful in finding film stardom he nonetheless found close friends within the industry eventually marrying film starlet Judith Allen. After the breakdown of the marriage and subsequent divorce he then married another Hollywood beauty, Mexican born Movita. Jack Doyle revelled in the high life throughout the 1930s and 40s with his and Movita's popularity being on a par with that of Richard Burton and Elizabeth Taylor. The pair also toured extensively around the British theatres to packed and enthusiastic houses. There is no denying that Frank Randle like the proverbial Aristotle was 'a bugger for the bottle' yet in comparison to Jack Doyle he was a mere lightweight. By the age of thirty, Doyle's thirst and zest for pleasure had seen him fritter away three-quarters of a million pounds on his booze fuelled playboy lifestyle. Throughout his life he was quite insistent that he was the one responsible for discovering the great Irish tenor Josef Locke while the singer was still a member of the Royal Ulster Constabulary. However, Locke was equally emphatic that there was no truth in this as the pair had first met when Doyle paid a return visit to the Irish Guards at a time when Locke was part of their ranks. They did undeniably know each other quite well and both being lovers of a certain Irish stout had many a boozy session together, usually with Doyle getting the better of his pal. One can only imagine the drinking sessions Doyle and Randle would have been involved in after their shows together. It was not unknown for Locke to drop on Randle for an impromptu booze-up and if this happened while Doyle was also on the scene all hell would no doubt have broken loose. In 1953 having appeared in the London Bankruptcy Court, the now divorced Jack Doyle – Movita had married Marlon Brando – was trying to make a living with his lilting voice. He had just literally celebrated his fortieth birthday as he joined the 'Randle's Scandals' tour. The mass adoration and high life he once enjoyed must now have seemed a million miles away.

The show continued with several North Country dates which included Southport and Morecambe. *"Out with those teeth and let the braces dangle. When Frank Randle comes to town inhibitions take a fast train out".* So wrote the Manchester Evening News of the October 26th visit to the Manchester Hippodrome. Travelling across the breadth of the country on Sunday November 1st the show opened the following day at the Hippodrome, Ipswich. It was here that another addition to the company was made with the inclusion of the Norman Teal Trio, a musical and comedy act. Norman Teal was a well-known and much loved figure in theatre circles and the act had just finished a tour of his own show 'Happiness Ahead'. Alongside Norman were the multi-talented Marjorie Kendall and a young man who in later years was to become one of the country's best-loved top line entertainers, Roy Castle. Today, Marjorie still has vivid memories of her time spent

The Norman Teal Trio:
Left to right, Norman, Roy Castle and Marjorie Kendall

working alongside Randle and she told us, *"Working with Frank was a real experience, we had just finished 'Happiness Ahead' and the 'Scandals' was totally different to our happy show... We never knew what would happen next".* One of the first things Marjorie had to come to terms with were the meetings to which Randle would summon all his company. *"We would all sit in the front stalls while Frank sat on the edge of the stage with a pint of beer in his hand",* she recalled. *"He would often lecture us using the bluest of language - what a character".* Within weeks of joining the show Marjorie witnessed first hand the side of Randle's character that often attracted newspaper headlines. The show had opened for a week at the Wood Green Empire on Monday November 23rd. During the first house on Thursday evening Frank introduced for the first time a male vocalist Walter Kavan. The singer had been with Frank for just one week and was a little nervous about his debut. To try and ease him in and settle his nerves, Randle ordered that a recording by Lawrence Tibbett of the 'Barber of Seville' be played, to which he himself would light-heartedly mime. Part way through this he invited Walter Kavan on stage to join him and finish the song straight. Being satisfied with the outcome of this, Randle believed that Kavan was confident enough to sing the piece alone during the second-house performance. Unfortunately, not being fully aware of the situation a stagehand again started the record just as Mr Kavan began to sing. Now singing in a different key to the recording the resulting sound was a little off-putting, nonetheless the singer continued with his rendition. Although the record was eventually stopped the audience by this time had taken against Mr Kavan and began shouting and stamping their feet. Randle did not take the reaction well and in defence of the artiste he stormed on stage and began to verbally attack them. In no uncertain terms he told them just what he thought of them, 'bastards', being his word of choice. The theatre management hastily ordered the curtain to be rung down to bring an abrupt end to the show - and Randle's outburst. Mr Hoare, the theatre manager insisted this was the end of the show's week-long engagement and instructed Randle's company to collect their costumes and props the following day. *"I could not have Mr Randle using bad language to the audience so I rang the curtain down, that's really all there is to say",* Mr Hoare told reporters when questioned. His decision had also been influenced by the fact that members of the local council had been in the audience and he was afraid the theatre might lose its license if Randle's behaviour had been allowed to continue. Defending himself to Mr Hoare Randle said, *"Me, swear on stage? What am I supposed to have said".* Mr Hoare told him. *"You called the audience bastards".* To which Randle responded, *"Nothing of the sort - they were cheering so much I said basta, basta, - enough, enough".* However, a different story, again from Randle, appeared in the press - when he admitted to using some naughty words to the audience. Giving the Daily Mail its headline 'Naughty Words' - put sudden ban on show'. Randle did add however, that these were words he had used many times before in his act. Over the years the countless retelling of this tale has seen its location switched to the Finsbury Park Empire with many additions to Randle's vocabulary. However, facts clearly show that the story refers to the incidents as they took place at the Wood Green Empire.

As Frank Randle and his company returned to the Wood Green Empire on Friday to retrieve their belongings the situation developed into what would probably be best described as pandemonium. The management had acquired an injunction preventing Randle from stepping onto the stage with the presence of a police constable to enforce it if need be. Almost fifty of Randle's company were milling about backstage trying to retrieve their make-up, props and clothes and occupying the dressing rooms into which members of the hastily booked replacement show

Frank giving a dressing room explanation to journalists on events at the Wood Green Empire

were also trying to gain access. Yet, Randle was still insistent no one should leave until he said so. Randle himself was still residing in the star dressing room and had invited the press to hear his version of events. Dressed informally in pyjama jacket and clutching a glass of beer he said, *"A couple of people in the audience stood up and I back-chatted like I always do. "Then I used some words which I have used in the act many times before - and the curtain was rung down."* While Randle was chatting to the press another attempt to dislodge him was made by the management to which Randle's curt response was, *"Shut up - go away!"*. Roy Castle once told our acquaintance Mike Craig of his recollection of that time. Roy and Norman had returned, like the rest of the company, to retrieve their belongings and had found that a juggler was already ensconced in their dressing room fully attired and made-up in readiness for the new show. The juggler who travelled with a dog for company, explained, that under no circumstances should the dog be let out of the dressing room. Having duly collected their instruments and sundry items the pair on departing 'accidentally' left the door open. Roy told Mike... *"The dog shot out like it was on a piece of elastic. We could hear 'The Sabre Dance' on the Tannoy so we knew the juggler was doing his spot. Suddenly we hear the dog*

162

barking, followed by laughter, followed by the tail wagging dog trotting back to the dressing room - a juggler's club between its teeth!"

This was not a good time for Frank Randle. The week following the Wood Green incident and trouble was still simmering in nearby Chelsea at the Palace. Randle was constantly over running, causing problems and he was often the worse for wear through drink. The latter, probably exacerbated by the news that his booking for the following week at the Hippodrome, Dudley, had been cancelled. Randle insisted the cancellation was nothing to do with the Wood Green events and was simply due to *"disagreements over the contract"*. One would have hoped that by the time the show opened for their scheduled appearance at the Theatre Royal, Barnsley, on Monday December 14th things would have settled down somewhat.

Although this was an ever-increasing traumatic time for Randle, his depression often placed him in rather troublesome situations, fuelled by his ceaseless drink intake. More than ever before, he was becoming a Jekyll and Hyde character. For the majority of the time on stage in front of an appreciative audience he remained his brilliant comic-self, the laughter he raised veiled many of his problems. The laughter of an audience it seemed could transport him to another world and he enjoyed every passing moment so much so he never knew when to say goodnight to his responsive audience. Time and again his act would over run much to the delight of his watching fans. However, this action on occasion could also bring him back to reality. Such was the case when the show was at Barnsley. Having overrun almost every night, Frank was presented with a bill on the final evening for the overtime incurred by the musicians and also for their numerous taxi fares home. Randle said at the time, *"Other stoppages of a like character included about £25 for removal of properties in and out of the theatre"*. In total his bill amounted to around £70 which Randle thought excessive. During the interval a meeting was held to try and resolve the problem and took place between Randle and theatre manager Dorothy Francis. However, this soon erupted into a full-blown argument. Although Randle was used to such confrontations and was at his argumentative best, Francis stood her ground. This resulted in Randle taking the only action he thought the situation deserved. He brought the show to a close. He ordered a member of his own company to make the announcement to the audience, who of course were blissfully unaware of the backstage hostilities, that owing to a disagreement the show would not continue and money would be refunded. This was followed by a second announcement from the theatre management explaining that there was no reason why the show could not continue and that if anyone did want their money back they were advised to seek out Mr Randle himself. This obviously implied that any disruption was down to the temperamental comedian and not the Theatre.

There was of course not much time to dwell on this or even to unwind as on the Sunday he and most of the company were travelling to Middlesbrough for the Christmas season. After one dress rehearsal on Monday, the pantomime *'Cinderella'* opened on Tuesday December 22nd at the Empire Theatre. Aided by his usual troupe, with Gus Aubrey as 'The Baroness', Randle took on his familiar 'Buttons' role to great success. With healthy bookings everything looked to be set for a good run. This production saw Randle showing off his benevolent nature by way of giving a young 16-years-old singer, Wendy Edwards, an opportunity to further her show business career. Wendy's dreams had taken a knock when her double act partner had fallen ill forcing them to pull out of a pantomime at Barrow. Informed of her talent, Randle agreed to her auditioning for him. Her performance so impressed Randle that he immediately offered her the part of understudy to Jackie Herrick's 'Cinderella', with the promise of at least one appearance in the role. Although the show had been fully cast he also created a special part for her adding that if she made it a success he would invite her to join his next 'Scandals' tour. Wendy was eventually given the opportunity to play the title role in the pantomime at a performance during the final week for which she gained praise and a standing ovation. However, her success was somewhat tainted by the reaction of Jackie Herrick. Apparently unaware of Wendy's impending public appearance Jackie had dressed as usual for the part and was somewhat disgruntled. It is unknown

GUS AUBREY

Seasonal
Greetings
to All

"Baroness"
in
"Cinderella"
at
Empire Theatre
Middlesbrough

Seasonal cheer for Gus and the rest of the cast would soon be in short supply

whether this was simply a lack of communication between Randle and Herrick or if he had actually engineered the event to get back at Herrick. For she and other members of his company had threatened Randle during the week with strike action over matinee payments.

Although there had been matinee performances for the first three weeks none were planned for the final week and Randle had accordingly said their payments would be adjusted. A walkout was averted by the intervention of the theatre management who stepped in to cover the payments. Randle's reaction to this was that if they were going to be paid for a matinee then they would perform a matinee. Compelled to wear full costumes and makeup it must have been quite strange for the cast to appear before an audience of just ten people – the only advertising for the performance had been a board outside the theatre. The orchestra pit was bereft of musicians apart from the sole figure sat at the piano. The company presented the whole show on one set, with no scenery transformations, all very confusing for the tiny audience, when it came to location changes.

So, once again Randle had encountered trouble, and it seemed to be following him wherever he was booked to play. On this occasion it was a situation that was to end on a rather sad note, one that would bring an end to friendships of many years standing. The plain fact was that after the pantomime came to the end of its run, the 'Scandals' company said they were parting from Randle and his shows. He countered by saying they had been sacked.

Perhaps at another time matters may have been resolved more amicably. However, at this time Randle was a man with worries. The taxman was pursuing him, he was dreadfully disillusioned with the way the theatre business was heading, and he was beginning to feel increasingly under the weather. Although hard work, variety had been his life and until recent times had been enjoyable for him. Now the growing appearances of girlie type shows and male orientated revues depressed him - he had always championed the family show. Theatre and to some extent his own career, had reached a nadir and uncertainties about the future troubled him. He still held thoughts of presenting northern comic plays. His mind no doubt was in turmoil and he admitted, *"Physically I am fit, but mentally I am not taking to the work as I did formally".* Although he had alcohol as the great reliever, things were evidently getting on top of him. The situation with his 'Scandals' Company over the matinee payments just brought matters to a head. Randle was not one to be dictated too and his former colleagues of sixteen years standing should have known this - so, sacked they were and sacked they would remain. Before leaving Middlesbrough, Randle said that he hoped his new company, which he would shortly assemble, would also perform straight plays to variety audiences. In order to bring back the family show once again to the stage he also indicated that he would be willing to take over any music hall in the country and provide everything in its entirety from the show itself to the staff and orchestra.

Inevitably after breaking away from Randle, the 'sacked company' held a meeting where a collective decision to remain together was made. Rather than all go their own ways in seeking bookings it was thought they could use the situation to their advantage. After all, together they already had a show albeit without a star name. Using the *'The Unemployed Scandals'* as the name for their show it was hoped they could build on the recent press coverage of events at Middlesbrough. Sonny Roy was elected to be the spokesman for the troupe with Brad Arnott as their manager, the pair also provided financial backing for the venture. Seeing an opportunity for at least a successful short-term tour for the company, Bolton based agent Bernard Wooley started to arrange dates for them. Acting quickly he soon announced that he had a proposed seven-week tour starting at the Hippodrome, Accrington on January 25th 1954. On hearing this news Frank Randle immediately instructed his solicitors to write to Mr Wooley threatening legal action should *'The Unemployed Scandals'* use any of his material for their shows.

On the first night at Accrington, the enthusiasm of the new company shone through as each member was introduced during the opening song 'Smile, Damn you, Smile' - rather aptly the song's first line continued, 'Things are never as bad as they are painted'. The audience could still sense their bond of camaraderie right into the finale suitably titled 'Side-by-Side'. None of the cast seemed to have any regrets about leaving Randle and starting up their new endeavour. Gus Aubrey said, *"Never since I first went on stage at the age of nine have I felt such a warm feeling of companionship, a sense of all being in it together"*. But how did Randle himself react?

Faced with a number of bookings without his team - the first being at Blackpool's Queen's Theatre where he was to open on January 25th - he quickly had to assemble a new troupe of entertainers. Advertisements had been placed with the theatrical press and numerous telephone calls were made to fellow performers and friends. One of the first to respond was 73-year-old Arthur White, another favourite Lancashire character comedian. He came out of retirement to *"help my old mate Frank"*. Just three days before the Blackpool show was due to open Randle had engaged twenty-two artistes but there had been little rehearsal and time was running out. Another obstacle in Randle's way was the none-arrival from Middlesbrough of his props and

166

The Leigh and District Lending Society, Ltd. 13 Cannon St. Preston

TELEPHONE 2362

£10 to £1,000 Without Security

Telegrams: "BESTERMS"

For a Practical Job at Reasonable Charges
Try E. BROWN
LADIES' and CHILDRENS' DRESSMAKER and COSTUMIER
Carlton Chambers, 79 High Street, Preston.
OWN MATERIAL MADE UP

For Morning Coffee or a Good Cup of Tea
CALL AT
TERRY'S SNACK BAR
116, LANCASTER ROAD
Soups — Soft Drinks — Sweets Etc.
Open Saturdays until 11 p.m.

Everything for the Home Decorator
PAINTS, VARNISHES, DISTEMPERS
WALL PAPERS and REQUISITES
S. & E. WALLPAPERS
267, NORTH ROAD, PRESTON.

THE SURGICAL STORES
For all Surgical Appliances and Rubber Wear
TRY OUR POSTAL SERVICE
5, BUTLER STREET PRESTON (Near Station)

STANLEY CARWIN LTD.
MILLER ARCADE
Tel. 2190 ∴ Tel. 2619
FOR
THE BEST IN
RADIO, ELECTRICAL, TELEVISION

OVERTURE—The Palace Orchestra will play popular melodies—M.D. James White

1 **MEET THE SCANDALS** Entire Company will introduce themselves

2 **NEWSPAPERS** News in Brief

3 **JEAN CHADWICK** A-la Gracie Fields

4 **ON THE BALL** Football Gone Mad

5 **FLORENCE WHITELEY'S FAMOUS** "ZIO ANGELS"

6 **KAY SOTHERN** A Smile and a Song

7 **GUS AUBREY** The "Lady" they all talk about

8 **KENTUCKY** Entire Company bring you memories old and new

INTERVAL—" The Pirates of Penzance " by A. Sullivan
Played by the Palace Orchestra—M.D. James White

9 **RIDING ON A RAINBOW** Entire Company

10 **JACKIE HERRICK AND SONNY ROY** Boy meets Girl

11 **ARTHUR CANNON** Maestro of the Banjo

12 **THE PETERS BROS.** Variety's Mother and Son

13 **ERNIE DALE AND BOB HULME** Brilliant Entertainers in their latest successes

14 **SONNY ROY** The Funny Boy will make you all laugh

15 **FLORENCE WHITELEY'S FAMOUS** "ZIO ANGELS"

16 **SIDE BY SIDE** Entire Company will say Goodnight

GOD SAVE THE QUEEN

Programme Subject to Alteration

Company Manager .... BRAD ARNOTT
Choreography .... KAY SOTHERN
For The Unemployed Scandals

Extra comedy material by Sonny Roy. Gus Aubrey's gowns designed and executed by Arthur Forster of Darlington.

Self-Drive Car Hire Service
173 NORTH ROAD, PRESTON
Hire a Car and Drive Yourself

It's is yards from this Theatre visit the
TEMPERANCE HALL NORTH RD.
Inspect the most selective stock of Tile Fireplaces in Town
Finest, sizes and designs to please everyone at
NEWERA FIREPLACES

Visit **THE CAFE ROYAL** TITHEBARN STREET, PRESTON.
A GOOD MEAL

KINGSALE IN NIP-SIZE BOTTLES
LION BREWERY, BLACKBURN.

Lion Ales

L.B. AND I.P.A. IN HALF-PINT BOTTLES
OBTAINABLE AT THEATRE BARS

All Children must be paid for.
Responsibility is disclaimed for the unavoidable absence of any Artiste mentioned to appear.

TO PATRONS BOOKING SEATS. Booked Seats will only be available for the Performance they are booked for.

MONDAY NIGHT IS OLD AGE PENSIONERS' NIGHT.
ANY UNBOOKED SEAT 1/-

THE PRESTON
PALACE THEATRE
Vicarage and Tithebarn Street.
Box Office Phone 51171 Preston
Advance Box Office Open Mon. to Fri. 10-10 to 12-30, 2-0 to 4-0, 5-45 to 9-15.
Saturday 10-30 to 12-30, 2-0 to 9-0
Proprietor: PERCY B. BROADHEAD (Manchester)
Licensee & Manager: Percy B. Broadhead, Jun.
Sec. M. Avril Broadhead.
Trustees: Arthur Chapman. Acting Manager Bert Moore.

Week Commencing Monday, February 15th, 1954
6-15 TWICE NIGHTLY 8-25
THE MOST TALKED ABOUT SHOW OF THE YEAR
THE UNEMPLOYED SCANDALS
" THE GOOD COMPANIONS OF 1954 "
You've read about them in your Daily and Sunday Papers
Now see them in your own Theatre

Theatre programme for
'The Unemployed Scandals',
The Palace Theatre, Preston,
February 15th 1954

SEATS BOOKED BY TELEPHONE MUST BE CLAIMED BY 6-0 AND 8-10 OR THEY WILL BE SOLD.
PROGRAMME ——— PRICE TWOPENCE

scenery. However, under rehearsed and with just the theatre's own curtains and backcloths, the show opened with two pistol shots and Randle's voice saying, *"By Gum, We'll get this show off to a cracking start"*. While acts performed on stage, a flurry of activity was taking place in the wings as the missing props and scenery eventually arrived. At the show's finale Randle addressed the audience, *"We might not have had every bit of the scenery here in time for tonight's performance but I think you'll agree with me that we have had the people here who matter most the artistes and musicians"*.

Over at Accrington, at the end of the first house performance of *'The Unemployed Scandals'*, theatre manager Mr Ross Jones also went on stage to speak to the audience. He made a promise to them, that having brought them this new company he would now bring Randle himself - the very next week. It was another ploy in his quest to build up audience numbers at the theatre, which had been threatened with closure on several occasions during the past year. Soon after leaving the stage Mr Jones was speeding his way to Blackpool, arriving just before the curtain rang down on Randle's second house performance. The following day Randle announced that he and Mr Jones had held talks - *"Mr Jones had asked if I was prepared to appear at Accrington - it was his own idea entirely - we were actually booked for Rochdale, but I agreed - I owe him a date anyway - we will re-arrange Rochdale"*. Randle went on to read to a Northern Daily Telegraph reporter an open letter to his former 'Scandals' colleagues - which appeared in print on Tuesday morning.

"Dear lads, and lassies,
"At this stage of the proceedings I do in all sincerity wish you good fortune. I admire your guts as always, and I still retain a liking for you as I have always had. And now that you have all flown from the edge of the nest, I do trust that the storms you may weather may not be too inclement.

"If there is anything I can do, please let me because, in the words of a mental giant, in my humble opinion. I only pass once this way. On this occasion I will pass after you. The first shall be the last, and the last shall be first. I know Accrington will not let you down. Accrington has never let me down; therefore, naturally it is beyond the realms of possibility that it should happen in your case.

"Forgive Father - Mother Carey for following in the wake of his-her chickens. I do hope you have left me enough scratching ground. Naturally the mother always allows her chickens to have the first

pickings of the food and will be content to have what is left, which, in my humble opinion will more than suffice for the nonce.

"Good luck to you all and may you not have to plough the hard furrow that your mentor has had to in the past.
"Perhaps one day I may have the pleasure of working for you.

"Yours most sincerely.
Frank Randle."

This prompted a reply in which Sonny Roy on behalf of *'The Unemployed Scandals'* said, *"This is a fine and welcome gesture. We are very pleased to hear it. There was no enmity between us. We reciprocate Mr Randle's fine gesture and wish him good luck - particularly in his forthcoming venture of putting on straight plays".* All the company shared this opinion

By the time *'Randle's Scandals of 1954'* opened at the Hippodrome, Accrington, Frank had put together what would be his new touring company. Dick Carlton had joined him to replace Arthur White who had helped Randle out with his Blackpool show. Dick Carlton perhaps is

---

PROGRAMME
subject to alteration

1. Overture. Up with the Curtain.
2. Introducing the Company.
3. HAL & WINNIE MACK
   The dancing Demons.
4. **FRANK RANDLE** shows you what a good actor he is.
5. WAL & EDDIE REID and their Banjos.
6. DICK CARLTON.
7. 6 WHIRLWINDS.
8. MAJOR'S REFLECTION with **FRANK RANDLE** & DICK CARLTON.
9. THE MANDALAY SINGERS with Don Carlos, John McCullum, James Edgar.

---- INTERVAL ----

10. WENDY EDWARDS goes to a party.
11. The famous WAZZAN TROUPE.
12. MARIE JOY Personality Girl.
13. NORMAN TEAL TRIO.
14. **FRANK RANDLE** as the old Hiker.
15. FINALE.

GOD SAVE THE QUEEN.

General Manager —	FRANK RANDLE
Manager ----	NORMAN TEAL
Production & Technical Adviser	NINA RATHBONE
Assistant Manager —	PAT ASTELL

NEXT WEEK:

Snow White and the Seven Dwarfs

Hippodrome Accrington, Week Commencing February 1st 1954, Ross Jones Proudly Presents the Starring Engagement of Frank Randle and His New Company.

best remembered today as one of the stooges to comedian Jimmy James, a similar position that Roy Castle would hold at a future date. Castle and Marjorie Kendall had returned at Accrington as part of the Norman Teal Trio. Teal himself would once more act as manager for Randle's show, the position he held during December of 1953. Also on the bill were Wendy Edwards whom Randle had introduced in the Middlesbrough pantomime, Wal and Eddie Reid - and their Banjos and Hal and Winnie Mack. Randle appeared in three sketches, the first being his oft performed 'showing what a good actor he is', secondly he presented a new sketch 'The Major's Reflection' and finished with 'The Old Hiker' as the climax. 'The Major's Refection' featured Dick Carlton with Randle playing a drunken Major looking into a full sized mirror - with Carlton as his reflection. Marjorie Kendall recalled, *"This was a very good routine and their timing was excellent. "The two of them really worked well on this and it was so funny the audience loved it".*

After a successful week at Accrington the show moved to the Oldham Empire. Here however, Randle faced a dilemma, for due to a mix-up between agents and the theatre management another show was also booked to appear. Ken Frith, pianist from the BBC's Al Read radio show, was due to top a variety bill. Randle insisted that both shows would go ahead and taking control he attempted to present an amalgamation of the two under the heading of 'Highlights of Variety'. However, from the moment the curtain rose for the first house performance it was to be total chaos both on and off stage. The members of each show had no idea as to what the running order was. When acts were given an opportunity to perform they were rushed on stage and before they could get into their stride just as quickly hastened off again. Original bill topper Ken Frith even had his piano whisked away from him in mid act and he didn't appear at all for the second house. A total of seventeen acts managed to perform in the first house, which lasted for over three hours. The second was no different. Almost without warning the Norman Teal Trio were ordered on stage. Marjorie Kendall remembered, *"I had to dash up to the dressing room to get my trumpet, Roy too. The xylophone*

Roy had to dash to get his trumpet

170

was brought on and we did a little of our act. The poor orchestra were totally confused; they had the band parts but had no idea who was coming on stage until they actually saw them". As act after act took to the stage the night wore on and several people began to leave the theatre for their last buses home. Reluctant to close the show and, as if appealing for the audience to remain, Randle took to the stage. Marjorie Kendall recalled, *"He came forward down to the footlights and said, 'You haven't seen Hal and Winnie Mack yet!'"* The pair then made a quick entrance and ran through an abridged dance routine. Amongst the evening's confusion Randle obviously still found the time to perform 'The Major's Reflection' with Dick Carlton and 'The Old Hiker'. It was well after midnight when those members of the audience who had remained finally left the theatre. The following day Randle called both companies in for a rehearsal. He had worked out a schedule whereby his show would be presented with the addition of the variety acts from the other company. To make the extended show possible it was deemed necessary for the remainder of the week that there would be just one performance nightly commencing at 7pm. After such a hectic week some form of normality returned - if such a thing was ever possible with a Randle show - as *'Randal's Scandals'* moved on to Barrow-in-Furness and then Doncaster. At Doncaster the audience were given a bonus as Randle also included a revival of his sketch 'Anymore for Sailing'. Even though both first and second houses overran on the opening night, the capacity crowds remained in their seats until the end - a situation that was repeated throughout the week.

Although Frank Randle was still drinking heavily during the weeks he had been on the road with his new company, any major confrontations between them seemed to have been averted. There had of course been the occasional choice words between him and his troupe but as most realised this was just Randle being ... Randle. However, towards the end of the week's run at Rochdale, where they had opened on March 1st, events unfolded which culminated in a public display of his temperament. Prior to Rochdale the dates played had on the whole been good, but the visit to the Lancashire mill town resulted in Randle reconsidering how his future shows should be staged. The week had opened to poor houses and never really improved, with both audience numbers and takings down. A persistently under the weather Randle, whose money problems had not improved since the tour began, became disconsolate and more depressed each passing day. For the 'Scandals' shows to be viable they had to attract far bigger turnouts than were being given by the Rochdale public that particular week. Knowing him to be so depressed and angry his company did their utmost to avoid upsetting him any further during those miserable six days, especially witnessing the amount of his drink intake. Randle had always been a stickler when it came to spotlights and disliked careless operators, his lighting had to be perfect and he would not settle for anything less. So the incompetence of one spotlight operator at Rochdale brought matters to a head. While performing his 'Sewing on a Button' routine the light failed to follow him as he crossed from one side of the stage to the other. Consequently Randle in a rage stormed off into the wings. He returned a few minutes later and began verbally assaulting the operator from the stage using several choice expletives. Nina Rathbone when speaking to a journalist two years earlier, recalled how as Randle's stage director she had witnessed similar outbursts. The spotlight had to follow his every movements precisely, *"On the first night of a run he was fairly tolerant of mistakes"*, she remarked. If mistakes continued for a second night Randle became irritable, should the operator fail in the third evening he would receive a curt note and if not rectified by Thursday he'd feel the wrath of Randle as he vocally reprimanded him. On one occasion while Randle was on stage, the spotlight failed. Nina recalled that a generator had broken down and panicking she rushed to the operator to see if he could fix it. Being told there was nothing he could do, she feared the worst. Entering Randle's dressing room, she expected the inevitable dressing-down. 'I'm very sorry' she began, but was cut short, as Randle interrupting said, 'That's all right, don't let that worry you'. Nina was amazed even though she had come to expect the unexpected as far as he was concerned. *"He's the most unpredictable man I've ever met"*, she said. As the Rochdale week was grinding to its conclusion, and continuing in his depressed mood, Randle on the Friday of the week contacted the local newspaper 'The Rochdale Observer'. He informed them that at 10.30pm on Saturday the curtain would fall for the very last time on his 'Randle's Scandals' shows, as he had decided to bring them to an end once and for all. In explaining his reasoning behind such a move he told the local reporter, *"The expense of carrying big shows round to small places is too much when the response of the public is so lukewarm, it gives you no chance at all"*. He also went on to say how he intended to keep most of his 35-strong company and to rely on their individual talents rather than on expensively staged shows. If this was to be the end of the 'Scandals' shows he intended them to go out in a blaze of glory... literally. During Friday afternoon, he and members of his company packed their scenery on to a lorry ready for transportation to the nearby cattle market. Here it was stacked in readiness for a Saturday night bonfire, which, if he received permission, Frank himself hoped to ignite. However, he was deprived the opportunity of carrying out his plan when the council informed him that the market was a smoke free zone. Not wishing to bring about any more trouble with 'authority' Randle dismissed the idea. The disappointment felt by many of the locals who had gathered to watch the fire was soon overcome as many helped themselves to 'souvenirs' from the pile of costumes and props. A few youngsters even attempted to start the fire themselves and although at one-stage flames, not of Randle's making, were seen, the fire never really got a hold. These facts are quite different to the distorted tales widely told in which, Randle in a mad rage, supposedly dragged his scenery out into the street and set them ablaze. Or that while in a drunken stupor he ordered the stagehands to take the scenery out and burn it - Then on the following day, having sobered up, had no recollection of the event.

The rapid decline in popularity of live theatre and variety in general was still something Frank Randle felt quite strongly about. He had already expressed his thoughts on the situation and offered what he thought were suitable remedies. His main point, which he again reiterated during March, was centred on the old tradition of having twice-nightly shows. He thought that this was now outdated and believed the time was right to introduce once nightly shows commencing around 7pm. This was already something he had tried himself once at Oldham during 1951 and, albeit for different reasons, the concept now remained the same. In order for the audience to be at the theatre for the 6.15pm first house overture they had to dart home from work jostling through heavy rush hour traffic, have a hurried meal, change their clothes and quickly dash out again. It would be far better, Randle thought, to have one performance at a slightly later start time with two shows on Saturday. There could be a standard closing time of 9.30pm, which would still allow the workingman time for a drink and the opportunity to catch the last bus home. Randle had said on more than one occasion that variety was fighting for its life. Now he was adding, *"that if it was to survive there must be a general and immediate overhaul, and all who hope to get jam and bread out of it have got to roll up their sleeves and work as they have never needed to before".*

He was discontented with the way the theatres were relying more and more upon nude shows and moving away from general entertainment. He had already indicated that he was personally willing to take on the running of any theatre in an attempt to provide family entertainment. He was aware that the Hippodrome at Accrington was being threatened yet again with closure. On three occasions in the course of the past year the theatre had almost been forced to close. However, after playing a week there himself and knowing how the *'Unemployed*

Scandals' show had been received Randle thought he could well revive the theatre's fortunes.

While he was playing Rochdale he noted that once again the *'Unemployed Scandals'* were having a decent run with a return visit to the Accrington Hippodrome. On journeying back northward on Sunday March 21st after ending a week in Bedford, Randle had the Accrington theatre firmly on his mind. Not just for the week he was booked for - from Monday March 22nd - but for his deliberation on whether or not he should take over the running of the theatre. By the end of the week's performances he had made up his mind and consequently made a statement saying that he would take over the lease of the theatre for a twelve month period from Monday March 29th. Everything however, did not go as planned and by 4.00pm on the Monday evening, Randle had still not signed the lease. Incumbent manager Ross Jones not knowing what the situation was had a decision to make - did he close the theatre or try to put together a show albeit at very short notice. With the generosity of a number of artistes who agreed to perform without a fee, Mr Jones managed to fulfil his wish of keeping the theatre open. Since the artistes had agreed to perform for nothing the manager offered free admission to the public. The very fact that only one in every five seats were occupied should have given any new owner serious doubts regarding the theatre's future. While it seems that the efforts of Mr Jones to keep the theatre opened should be commended, the man had however, for some time been swindling the then owners. Why he should have remained in his position as manager while his trial was taking place is unsure; however by mid-April he had been found guilty of the theft of £300 and sentenced to a twelve months gaol term.

As had been the case on many occasions while travelling the country with his road shows Frank stayed in his caravan. With his March appearance at Accrington he had settled locally at Green Haworth and with a good deal of work involved in the take over of the theatre this is where, for a few weeks at least, he remained. One perhaps would wonder why with all his personal problems Randle would want to add more stress and worry to his life. Probably the simple answer was that this was something he felt quite strongly about and he genuinely thought he could help. Gordon Duckett a reporter at the time with the Northern Daily Telegraph met up with Randle at his caravan and over a pot of tea at breakfast time was told of his plans for the Hippodrome. *"I shall devote every energy to it and so will the people around me"*, Randle explained. *"I will try to create a good atmosphere,"* However, he warningly added, *"This is positively the last throw for Accrington's live theatre*". Incidentally, years later Mr Duckett revealed that at the time of the interview - early in the morning - Randle was still in his pyjamas and drinking whisky.

Leasing the theatre from owners Terence Byron Ltd, Randle installed Mr Jack Curry as new resident manager and with a temporary licence granted he could at least start things moving. His plans included a change of name to the New Queens - though this never materialised - and the introduction of his much-vaunted idea of once nightly shows. Speaking again to the Northern Daily Telegraph, he explained that he had booked an attractive once nightly variety show to commence from Monday April 5th. However, we cannot say for sure if this show went ahead as there was no advertising or review for it within the pages of the local press. There was a similar lack of advertising for the following weeks commencing April 12th and April 19th. However, it is a certain fact that the latter show did take place opening on Easter Monday and not without a touch of trouble for Randle. Among the crowd bustling around the box office that day was a representative from the Inland Revenue. He had observed that tickets for the two-shilling seats were being issued without entertainment stamps. Randle explained that he would take full responsibility and it was his intention to rectify the matter later. Being Easter Monday, the local Post Office was closed and he had been unable to obtain the necessary stamps. At a court hearing later in the year Randle was fined for committing the offence.

The Hippodrome, Accrington, turned into a white elephant for Frank Randle

The first show to be advertised in the local press was the one starring Phil Kelly due to commence on Monday April 26th. In reviewing the entertainment, the paper had nothing but praise for the performers but also added, "The only thing missing from this show is an audience to give it the applause it deserves". Although not billed to appear, Frank Randle did make an appearance on the opening night as Phil Kelly remembered, "The old bugger caught me off guard again when he suddenly came on stage. After my initial shock and with him having done this to me before, I knew how to react. We sang the duet, as we had in Blackpool... he had his hiker's gear on and the audience, what there was of it, loved it".

Frank catches Phil Kelly off guard at Accrington

Meanwhile Randle had mid-week been granted the full transfer of the licence for the theatre at the local magistrates court where he was also reminded that there were several repairs that needed to be carried out as ordered by the County Architect.

Back now touring with his own shows Randle was constantly kept informed by manager Jack Curry of events at Accrington. This in the main was frequently bad news and may have been inadvertently to blame for Randle's bad attitude when ending his week at Newcastle. Performances had gone fairly well at the Palace Theatre and Randle and his company had even been invited to perform at a charity event to be held at the local Town Hall. Randle was always happy to help with good causes and soon agreed that members of his show would attend later in the evening after their last Palace Theatre show had ended. However, this arrangement did not go down too well with some of Randle's fellow artistes. They didn't relish the prospect of tackling a third performance at a time when they should have been back in their lodgings, relaxing and tucking into their much needed evening meal. Happily Randle had anticipated this and had only agreed to freely attend providing a substantial repast was provided for his colleagues. So, everyone was happy and on the night, several artistes including the Wazzan Troupe and Hal and Winnie Mack, all presented shortened versions of their acts. Dick Carlton in assisting Frank Randle then brought the proceedings to a close. It was at this point that the exhausted performers were ushered out to the Mayor's parlour where they were to receive their culinary delights. Before casting his eyes on what had been prepared for them, Randle was taken aback by the newspapers which had been strategically placed over the luxurious and elegant carpet. This, thought Randle, was what one did when training pet animals not entertaining guests. However, his blood really began to boil when he noticed the table on which was placed a tea urn with an assortment of mismatched mugs and a small number of plates with sandwiches, sausage rolls and cup cakes. This clearly was intended to be their substantial supper meal. Randle ignored the nearby poor council employee, who he in no way blamed, and headed instead to the fountain head. Accosting the Mayor, he was informed that refreshments had been provided as requested and that the paper was to prevent there being any mishaps. Frank now felt as though they were attending a Salvation Army soup kitchen rather than the prestigious Town Hall. Realising the cost of the food couldn't have been more than a few pounds Randle quickly removed a five pound note from his wallet and presented it to the Mayor. Thus, having purchased the measly collation, he commenced to throw it at the walls with much contempt. This was not quite as indiscriminate as one may think, for the walls were adorned with magnificent portraits of past Mayor's and Frank was taking careful aim. When his ammunition had run out he stormed out of the room quickly followed by his fellow artistes.

The latest news from Accrington was not good. The recent show starring Phil Kelly had cost around £275 with the eventual takings amounting to just £85 and there had been one week where takings came to a mere £55. Obviously this was not a good situation. Commencing Monday May 3rd, another of Randle's theatrical colleagues, ex-boxer Jack Doyle was booked to head a bill which included Terry O'Neil with his song and comedy act and the acrobatic routines of the Roberto's. However, by Thursday a notice was displayed at the theatre, which explained, that unless returns improved the Accrington Hippodrome would have to close. While the artistes for the following week were attending the morning band call on Monday May 10th, Frank Randle telephoned Jack Curry and informed him to cancel all performances. The few patrons who attended for the first evening performance were greeted by a notice, which simply said, 'Sorry there will be no show tonight'. Frank Randle's explanation was that the theatre had to close temporarily while necessary renovations took place.

Frank was certainly finding the going tough at Accrington and was even having problems locating artistes of calibre willing to appear - certainly there were none prepared to work on a percentage deal. Yet without decent pulling power the people would simply stay at home. There were also many problems with the fabric of the building and a good deal of money was needed for restoration, repairs and decoration. At the start of the second week of closure, Randle had an open letter to the people of Accrington published in the local paper. Here he explained how he was disappointed at not having received encouragement from the people. How he had already spent a good deal of money on urgent repairs and of his strategy and thoughts for the future of the theatre. Included in his suggestions were ideas to, *"Level the bottom floor after removing the seats of course, and make a dance floor, have cabaret on the stage, boxing nights, wrestling nights, roller skating, old time dancing, dinner dances, fancy dress balls, lengthen the bars and perhaps have a small whippet racing track, along with other amenities, while still retaining the element of the theatre".* He admitted that he had taken on the theatre *"at the worst possible time"* but that he intended writing to many of his theatrical friends to see if they would *"give both Accrington and myself a break".* True to his word a letter appeared shortly after in the theatrical trade paper 'The Stage' in which he wrote:

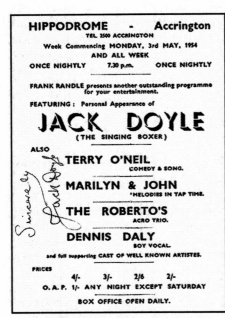

As things turned out the show starring Jack Doyle was the last presented by Randle at the Accrington Hippodrome, May 1954.

Dear Folks,
As you realise the business is in a far from inevitable position, and theatres are in a somewhat perilous state - especially the Hippodrome, Accrington. Well, I do not like to be licked so easily, so having had experience of the sportsmanship of pros on the whole when they have been appealed too, I have the temerity now to appeal to all from the biggest to smallest members of show business, and ask you to have a go with me at the above Theatre, just to spare one week of the 52 - to

see if we can beat this so-called slump. If you can draw at all, let me hear from you, I do not want to make anything out of it, you will not either, but you will feel that you have done something worthwhile, and if it works here it will work elsewhere in other lame theatres, so let Mr Butler whistle for his tax for one week. If I only get one favourable reply from any of the big fish I will be satisfied. My name happens to be Randle - not 'Nuffield' so I cannot offer you more than five or six hundred for the week for each act. I now sit and wait the influx of letters telling me what to do with the theatre. Anyway here's wishing the best of luck to you all.

Yours, so frantically,
Frank Randle.

PS: I have had £1,373 here on an ordinary week and not so long ago. FR.

Randle's appeals to the locals and artistes brought little response and by July he brought the curtain down on the venture. He explained, *"I would dearly have loved to make a go of it. I have done my best to do so. In fact I would still have a go if anyone would take a bit of weight. But I see no alternative to closing down"*.

The lack of support for local theatre was not something that could be directed solely at the people of Accrington for the same was happening in many towns throughout the country. During June and July Randle himself was experiencing both good and not so good weeks, which could be said of almost anyone in the business at this time. His dates throughout these two months however, did indicate once more that Randle had a countrywide audience and not just a northern based one. Towns on the tour included Leeds, Folkestone, Scunthorpe and Luton.

Just what financially the involvement with the Accrington Hippodrome had cost Randle is unknown but it is believed that in July the Inland Revenue were taking a very close look at his financial affairs. While he had been touring and with his Accrington commitments, this is one trouble he may well have dismissed for a while. Nonetheless, it was now looming ahead larger than ever.

As intended, Frank had laid his 'Scandals' shows to rest and since Rochdale, his touring appearances had him as the headliner on variety bills or being advertised as 'Frank Randle and Supporting Company'.

179

ALMA THEATRE
LUTON 5780/81

THIS WEEK
TWICE NIGHTLY — **MURDER ON THE NILE**

NEXT WEEK — 6.10 Comm. MONDAY. 28th JUNE 8.20
TWICE NIGHTLY

PERSONAL APPEARANCE !
OF THE FAMOUS STAGE. RADIO AND SCREEN STAR

FRANK RANDLE
AND FULL SUPPORTING COMPANY

No more 'Scandals'

During his appearance at the Alma Theatre, Luton where he opened on June 28th, Randle had a surprise call from Jack Taylor. The producer's Blackpool summer season show *'She's Funny that Way'*, at the South Pier Theatre was doing dreadful business. It had opened to poor houses and takings were in free-fall. Drastic action was needed to save it. Many people had perhaps harshly judged Randle as being an unsafe proposition for a Blackpool season - too many risks involved. In the past Randle seemed to be a magnet for attracting trouble at the resort and there was no guarantee that trouble couldn't still follow him. Yet, Taylor knew the comedian's name on a Blackpool bill could almost be an assurance of full houses. By the end of the run at Luton, Randle had already cancelled the following week at Brighton and all remaining dates to take up Taylor's offer. Frank Randle was not to headline the South Pier show but was billed as guest artiste - confined only to performing his 'Old Hiker' sketch. The saying 'there's no business like show business' proved itself correct as a summer which had initially started without a Blackpool show for Randle actually ended with him having two. Not only had this so called bad boy been installed in the pier theatre to boost takings, he also found himself topping the bill at the resort's Hippodrome Theatre. Fellow Lancastrian George Formby had been headlining with his own show *'Turned out Nice Again'* until being taken ill with gastro-enteritis. Although having missed some performances, Formby was expected to appear on Thursday August 19th. However, this didn't materialise as the performer thought a return to the stage may endanger his heart. Jack Taylor, in acknowledging Formby's health should come first, released him from his contract. On doing so the producer then turned to Randle to fill the gap. This was no easy task but Randle relished the opportunity of appearing before four different audiences, in two different shows, in

George Formby

two different theatres. Those people taking in the night air along the pier would have been surprised to see a toothless octogenarian defying his years by quickly running the length of the pier swerving to avoid anyone in his way. With every increasing stride his naked bony knees

180

protruded through a half buttoned rain coat. Cheeky youngsters tried in vain to run along side him but the aging sprinter left them in their wake. As if on cue, pedestrians passing by the pier entrance seemed to stop leaving a clear path for the darting figure to pass and almost dive full length into the back seat of a waiting taxi. Seconds later, amid the cheers of the on looking crowd the vehicle sped off into the night. This of course was Frank Randle, still in his Hiker make-up and costume making what was to be a nightly dash to the Hippodrome. Needless to say after the performance the same mad run had to be done in reverse and then repeated yet again later in the evening. For two weeks Randle performed this feat and as if that wasn't tiring enough, for one night he added something extra to his hectic itinerary. Being a boxing fan, Frank agreed to appear in a fund raising event which was to be held at the Central Working Men's Club. This necessitated yet another rush to squeeze in a fifteen minute cabaret performance on behalf of the Blackpool Sporting and Athletic Centre. Yet again by appearing at this event Randle showed how he could often go out of his way to help people - something which sadly people hardly ever mention when they describe the man. Randle continued as replacement for Formby until the last scheduled show on September 4th with his own show 'She's Funny That Way' finishing one week later on September 11th.

With the end of the 1954 summer season Randle hadn't really time to recharge his batteries before he began the run up to Christmas by heading variety shows in various towns including a significant appearance at the Theatre Royal Oldham in November. These shows saw the return of Gus Aubrey who, since the dispute with Randle at the end of 1953, had worked with the 'Unemployed Scandals' and undertaken several solo dates. This short tour concluded in December with shows at the Empire Theatre, York from the 6th followed by a week at the Palace Theatre, Grimsby. It appears that Randle may not always have been on top form as contrasting reviews from the shows at York and Grimsby testify. The local reviewer at York reported, "A rather disappointing Randle..." Whilst Grimsby's local press proclaimed "Brilliant Randle at the Palace". Both papers however, agreed that the supporting artistes gave excellent performances. These acts included the skating Lucerne's, Ernie Dale, Bob Hulme, Kitty Masters and singer Phil Kelly. It is Phil that we have to thank for clarifying a mystery surrounding an often repeated story regarding Randle and the bombing of Blackpool with toilet rolls. The reasons, dates and discrepancies of this bombardment are varied. This is due no doubt, to the 'Chinese whisper' syndrome, all of which meant that this tale had its foundations firmly in hearsay. However, Phil Kelly finally shone light on the whole subject when he told us of the true happenings. "As you know there *are lots of tales regarding this event, but I know the truth behind it because I was there. We were at home in Blackpool over the week-end before going to York for a December week in 1954. I was having a drink with my friend Dr Magellan at the 'Kite Club' over at Blackpool airport when Frank Randle who was also there came over to me. He told me he had hired a plane to take him to York and that I could travel with him".* Phil went on to explain that when he arrived at the airfield on the following morning Randle was standing at the side of his car chatting to his chauffer. It was to become evident that this was no idle chatter for as Phil was soon to discover, Randle was plotting. After warmly greeting Phil he then requested a favour of him, asking him to accompany his chauffer in the car to a nearby chemist and obtain a number of toilet rolls. Bemused by this request Phil asked the obvious question...why? Randle perhaps, not so much in a rage but more a fervour, answered, 'I'm going to fucking throw them on the Accrington Hippodrome', a smiling Phil recalled. On Phil's return from his trip to the chemist he and the chauffer were walking around the car when he noticed Randle in deep conversation with the pilot. Incidentally according to Phil the pilot was a typical RAF stereotype very upper-crust complete with handlebar moustache. *"I could overhear Randle talking to this toffee-nosed pilot who had such a snobby, private school accent. The pilot said, 'I'm afraid old chap we're not going via Accrington, it's a chartered flight and so we're going all the way to York, flight plans can't just be altered on a whim you know'".* Imagining the comedian's response we asked Phil if Randle appeared disturbed by this. *"What! He was furious; absolutely mad he was. When I asked him just what we were going to do now, all he kept saying was how he wanted to bomb Accrington with the toilet rolls. He wanted to get his own back because they hadn't appreciated what he'd tried to do for their town and theatre".* To Randle this would have been a clear form of retribution. Throughout the whole Accrington Hippodrome saga there had been many whom Randle believed had stood in his way by setting up insurmountable barriers and demands. It is also possible that he held a grievance against the townspeople of Accrington as a whole for their negative response in support of his costly venture. As Phil recalled, *"Randle tried vainly to run that big damn theatre, a rough looking place down a little street it was, but he was wasting his time with it the poor old bugger. Of course it didn't work and it cost him a lot of money".* Thus, to have dropped toilet rolls on the town would not just have given Randle a feeling of satisfaction but, as he hoped, would also have brought a good deal of embarrassment to the people. So, thanks to Phil Kelly we are enlightened to the fact that it was Accrington and not Blackpool that was the target of Randle's intended toilet roll bombing raid. Knowing now that Randle couldn't fly over

Accrington and bearing in mind all the hearsay about bombing Blackpool, we suggested to Phil that perhaps the rolls as unwanted cargo were simply jettisoned from the plane as it flew over the resort. *"No, no".* Insisted Phil emphatically, *"He wouldn't have done that, not to Blackpool".* Therefore it appears this story like so many others over the years has with its retelling strayed so far from the truth.

The Theatre Royal, Oldham where Randle had enjoyed a recent visit was actually experiencing turbulent times. The theatre had closed early in 1954 at the conclusion of its pantomime season. Since then and up to autumn of 1954, three different owners had tried unsuccessfully to resurrect its fortunes. Around October a Manchester builder James Bowers, who had gained some success as a band promoter, bought the theatre and by booking in some top name artistes, including Frank Randle from November 1st, was making a valiant attempt at keeping the theatre open. Mr Bowers appointed Mr W. Cedric Bailey as the bookings manager and the pair soon began looking for a Christmas show. After his November appearance, Randle was approached by Bailey with an offer for him to appear in their as yet un-named Christmas pantomime. Being so late in the year Mr Bailey found it difficult to obtain a suitable script, however good fortune came his way and he was able to acquire a version of *'Aladdin'.* With the script and Randle secured all looked well particularly as three other performers from his show, Kay Sothern, Ernie Dale and Gus Aubrey, were all available after the conclusion of their December 18th week at Grimsby.

The pantomime, which unfortunately was destined to be an ill-fated venture, was planned to open on Thursday December 23rd, which would have been some sort of achievement, even had everything run easily. For Mr Bowers however, things ran anything but smoothly. His next job after finding the cast and script was to find appropriate scenery. Further time elapsed before this was finally accomplished. However, on its arrival at the theatre it was found to be up to 20 foot too wide and 4 foot too high for the Royal's stage. Mr Mike Barnes, the theatre stage manager and his staff had the unenviable chore of cutting it down to size, *"We did in three days what would normally take a month",* he said. More disaster followed when all the band parts were lost. The only part available was a piano copy from which a harassed musical director, Mr Harry Bostock, set about transcribing parts for all the other instruments - a monumental task. Three days before the show was due to open, someone made the discovery that there was no chorus! Mr Bowers, again building up the theatre telephone bill, contacted numerous agents who managed to gather together a group of six girls. When the cast had arrived for their first rehearsal they found it impossible to even get onto the stage. With a lack of stage plans there was no indication as to where the scenery should be placed for each individual set, so the recently cut down scenery had all simply been abandoned in the centre of the stage. Consequently as opening night fast approached there hadn't even been time for reasonable rehearsals. As can be imagined the first performance was a total disaster and anything that could go wrong did go wrong. The orchestra wasn't in time with the singers and didn't play at all for the dancers; their accompaniment was the sound of humming off stage. The orchestra seemed totally lost, not knowing what to play next. Backcloths through some obstruction failed to drop properly. Lights went off... on... and off again, with no clear reason why. The cast didn't know what positions to take up on stage and at one point were falling over dogs that were still running about from a previous scene. A local reviewer made no reference to Randle or for that matter any of the company, with the exception of Abanazer played by Harry Duke who ironically was the director and as such should have been responsible for the smooth running of the show. The reviewer said, *"The curtain started to go up, and there was Aladdin (Kay Sothern) in the cave and, standing chatting to him, was Abanazer (Harry Duke). In the cave? Surely he should be outside. Suddenly Abanazer threw a startled glance at the audience and dashed up the steps leading to the cave entrance, threw himself through the opening, and then peered back into the cave to say, 'I'm waiting, Aladdin. Get the lamp'...and so the pantomime limped on to its pathetic finale".*

After the final curtain had gone down on the opening night several of the female artistes were in tears. Everyone knew that something had to be done to change things around or there would be no pantomime. During the inquest that followed it was somehow decided that Randle would take control. He proceeded to arrange for a rehearsal early the next morning. If the first night had been a disaster then this rehearsal was to be a total fiasco. Two separate events were to unfold both leading to the same conclusion... Frank Randle would leave the pantomime. The first of these was the actual rehearsal, which did not go as expected. In hindsight it was probably a mistake to let Randle take charge because he, of course handled

Kay Sothern had played 'Aladdin' in Frank Randle pantomimes on several occasions

184

this task in his own inimitable way. He took a seat in the stalls from where he directed proceedings using a select choice of bad language. Obviously this did not go down well with some of the cast members and when Joy Zandra who was cast as Princess Luvlee made a complaint to Randle he reduced her to tears. To Kay Sothern, Ernie Dale and Gus Aubrey an attitude like this from Randle was perhaps unsurprising, even predictable. They may not have liked his way of behaving but they knew how to handle it, or perhaps ignore it, but one thing they agreed upon was that Randle knew his job. For the rest of the cast however, Randle's way of doing things would have come as a total shock. They were far from happy especially at the blue language directed at them. At one point blows were practically exchanged as they felt Randle was attacking their professionalism. Someone from the cast even threatened to call in the police. The theatre management intervened but several of the cast were adamant that as a result of Randle's behaviour towards them they would no longer work with him.

The second event to unfold was also during the ill-fated rehearsal. Gus Aubrey asked Randle if the routines they were working on had been passed by the 'Lord Chamberlain's Office'. Being fully aware of the consequences, Gus didn't want any more trouble with the authorities and he certainly knew Randle would think the same. In view of Aubrey's remark and knowing that he had already handed in a script for his own material to the theatre management, Randle sought reassurances that all was in order. Failing to gain a satisfactory answer as to when the script had been sent for approval he made it known that he was not prepared to risk trouble again and would not go on stage without such assurance. With no such guarantee forthcoming and with all the problems surrounding the production of the show, Randle said that he'd had enough of the whole affair and was going home to Blackpool. He ultimately announced that he was not just quitting the show but quitting show business altogether, *"I have finished with show business after this"*, he said, *"I have done my best for it, and this is the end"*. Speaking of the pantomime he went on to say that he had been in the show on a percentage basis, adding, *"It was my name on the bills that brought in all the advance bookings and I shall see none of that money now"*. Mr Bowers, having the last word said that it was he who had sacked Mr Randle, ordering him from the theatre. Following Randle's departure Gus Aubrey was given top billing. But the loss of its star saw the following performances playing to very poor houses; the Oldham public it appeared wanted Frank Randle. With future bookings also looking unhealthy the pantomime run was cut short with the curtain coming down for the last time on Saturday January 8th.

Chapter Seven.

All Change at Crewe.

Unexpectedly back home for the New Year celebrations, Randle tried to overcome the misery of the past few weeks. A family holiday was planned on the continent somewhere, anywhere, it didn't matter much to Randle. The one thought was to get away from everything, no hassles, no worries, a need to recharge the batteries – just what the doctor ordered. With time on his hands soaking up the sun, Randle's creative mind began to work. Ideas flashed in and out again, with one, the thought of him working on TV due to linger. Back home, the April showers turned into a downpour bringing a rejuvenated Randle back down to earth with the news that the Inland Revenue, who had been looking in to his affairs, were about to close in. Undaunted, Randle got on with his life, a visit to his local pub 'The Farmers Arms' just a brisk walk from 'Craig Royston', a few drinks and things wouldn't seem so bad. Drinking and conversation with Ben and Eveline Bannister, a joke or two, and somehow the topic turns to an old phonograph owned by Mr Bannister. Randle was enthusiastic about this informing Ben that it would be an ideal prop for his idea for a TV show he was hoping to pitch to the BBC.

The pitch however, would have to wait as the dark clouds over Randle's head were turning decidedly gloomier. His illness was now starting to affect him further. Unknown to everyone Randle had been diagnosed a few years earlier as having the TB infection. Although the biggest proportion of people with the TB germ did not go on to develop the actual TB disease, Randle's doctor no doubt informed him that there would be around a 10% chance of that possibility. Though Randle was carrying the TB infection it did not mean he was contagious to others as his own immune system was capable of fighting it and there would no outward signs of illness. However, it seemed now as though the time had come when Randle's body could no longer contain the germs and he was becoming sick as a result. Randle was now experiencing typical symptoms of the TB disease, prolonged coughing, chest pains, weight loss and tiredness, all of which he was doing his best to hide from everyone. On top of all this came more worries with the Income Tax problems. Very soon a tired, sick and deeply depressed Randle would heartbreakingly be forced to put his beloved 'Craig Royston' on the market. With a need for income Randle, still hiding his illness, amazingly drew strength from somewhere and with a fighting quality, was by July taking to the road once again. However, with the dreaded taxman having had his pound of flesh this had left Randle without the finance to mount his own shows. This was to be taken on by Jack Gillam a producer of pantomimes, variety shows and ironically girlie revues, of which Randle had so condemned in the past. As if to place the 'Scandals' title truly in the past, the show was given the somewhat optimistic title *'I'm a Good Boy Now'*. The actual concept of the show was nothing new; it was Randle assisted by Gus Aubrey in several sketches and a bill made up of variety acts. The tour started on July 4th with a week at the Liverpool Pavilion and from the moment Randle walked on stage he must have felt overwhelmed by the reception he received. The rapturous welcome proved that the public still held him in such high esteem and were delighted to see him back on stage where he belonged. This to Randle was better than any medication prescribed by his doctor. Randle repaid the enthusiastic audiences by presenting 'In the Jungle/The Medical Board', 'An excerpt from Pantomime' and for a finale 'The Old Hiker'. At the end when the spontaneous applause had reached a crescendo Randle spoke softly to the audience thanking them for their kind support. Despite a summer heat wave in the city, the theatre was packed for every performance giving the tour a more than encouraging start. It was a similar story

the next week at Wigan and the week after at Bolton's Grand Theatre, where audience figures increased nightly culminating on Saturday with hundreds of people unable to gain admission. The tour then proceeded on to the Midlands, first to Aston and then Wolverhampton - where the show was held over for a second week - before moving on to Halifax, Preston and Hull. In Preston, Randle gave one local fan, Mr G. F. Chattell a moment to remember for the rest of his life. As Randle made his entrance as the 'Old Hiker', Mr Chattell could not contain his laughter, and although this became infectious with others in the audience, Randle had spotted the originator and descended the few steps from the stage making a beeline for him. Mr Chattell recalled, *"In the glare of the huge spotlight*

Congratulatory letter from Jack Gillam - With hopes for a few drinks at Wigan

which enveloped us both, and amongst great laughter from the audience he demanded to know why I had started to laugh without his permission before his act had even started. There were a few more minutes of banter before he went back on stage - An unforgettable experience".

So far on this tour Randle had been trying hard to live up to the show's title. Although by now he was beginning to feel the strain and there were days because of his illness that it would seem unlikely that he would be able to appear. But appear he did. Unlike on a previous scheduled date at Preston. Mr Chattel said, "I was in the audience that particular night when we were saddened to hear the announcement which said 'Mr Randle had been held up due to fog' and would not be appearing. Rumour surrounded the town next day that rather than being held up he was tanked up at the 'Green Man' public house in nearby Broughton".

Frank and Gus turn a page from pantomime

Needless to say Randle was of course drinking during the run of *'I'm a Good Boy Now',* though his usual intake of beer and whisky was now supplemented with even more of the spirit....'purely for medicinal purposes'. No doubt there was also still the occasional choice cross word with members of the company. But, at this stage he had never let anyone down by not appearing, there had been no destruction of dressing rooms nor had he got into any headline making trouble. I'm a Good Boy Now... well perhaps, compared with the not too distant past. The reviews for the shows had all been excellent, as indeed had the audience responses. Tom Moreland, reviewer with theatrical paper 'The Performer' and the man who originally crowned Randle the 'Stormy Petrel of Show business', saw the show in Newcastle and wrote, *"As a performer I thought his work second to none. Earthy, yes, but as comedy characterisation, brilliant. Here I would say how much is due to the feeding of Gus Aubrey, but Frank Randle on his own is surely our outstanding character comedian, if only for his Old Hiker, a character he lives - not acts".*

Randle's health was increasingly becoming a genuine concern for many of the company. When, during October the tour played Doncaster and Middlesbrough the fact that Randle was often seen in prayer was a frequent topic of conversation. His coughing spells and difficulties in catching his breath were now getting worse and it was often after a bad bout that he seemingly would go into prayer. If any member of the troupe accidentally interrupted him, Randle would hit the roof calling them every foul name imaginable. One poor 'call boy' rapping on the dressing door with a cheerful 'curtain up in two minutes Mr Randle', was told in no uncertain terms, 'Fuck off, I'm praying!'

On a lighter note on the arrival at Blackpool, the whole company had received an invitation to attend a civic reception at the Town Hall. Randle arranged for his troupe to meet up at the Queen's Theatre, where the show was to open on October 31st, and travel the short distance from there to the Town Hall. Ronné Coyles, who was present at time remembered, *"That day Frank was wearing a sort of check jacket with silver grey trousers. He was sporting gloves which he carried in one hand with his silver topped cane in the other, with his glasses shining he looked absolutely dapper. He turned to me smiling and said come on laddie into the car, lets go".* Aware that Randle was due to arrive at the Town Hall a small but eager crowd of onlookers had gathered, while the awaiting dignitaries lined the steps leading to the entrance. All had one thought in common, how would Randle conduct himself. Would he be sober and polite or in a drunken and uncontrollable frame of mind - after all they knew of Randle's past antics. The moment of truth arrived as at the sight of his speeding car approaching, those assembled on the footpath began to cheer while the Mayoral party thought the worst as the car screeched to a halt. Apprehensively they waited, the car door opened and out stepped the immaculately attired Randle. After standing for a moment to survey all around him he walked slowly towards the steps. Ronné Coyles takes up the story; "As we made our approach we could hear people saying 'isn't he grand, isn't he lovely' and the like. On the steps the Mayor stepped forward to greet him and said, 'Mr Randle how delighted we are that you honour us with your presence this afternoon'. When Frank was in the mood he had a very good speaking voice and it was in this vein that he replied, 'Not at all, not at all. The pleasure is entirely mine and I speak for the whole of my company in thanking you for your kind invitation". At this point it was as though a collective sigh of relief overcame all those present, for they now knew there was to be no trouble this day. Consequently, everyone slowly began to make their entrances, when, as Ronné again recalled, "As they approached the doors the Mayor casually turned to Frank and with a gesture said 'By the way Mr Randle, this is my wife'. Eyeing her up and down Frank turned and - under his breath but loud enough to be heard - replied, 'Aye, well that's your fucking fault".

A reporter from the local paper reviewed the Blackpool opening night's performance of 'I'm A Good Boy Now', and though he got his actual diagnosis wrong, it is clear that he thought Randle was unwell. He wrote, "Few of the audience, laughing uncontrollably at his antics, realised they were watching a sick man. Only a slight cough and an occasional gasp for breath betrayed the fact that he was suffering from bronchial asthma. But even this did not hamper the skill of this artist, who, together with Gus Aubrey, presented old favourites such as his famous Army sketch". The concerns Randle's company were having about his health were to be proved well founded as news reached them the following day that he had been taken seriously ill. Gathering at the theatre they were informed of Randle's condition and that he would no longer be able to continue. Consequently, all remaining tour dates would be cancelled. Although all deeply saddened by the news, the show from their point of view had to go on, for that night at least. Perhaps the person most affected by the news was Gus Aubrey, who, fighting back the tears, had to face the audience and inform them of Randle's absence. "It was one of the saddest moments of my life", he once recalled. The complete disintegration of Randle's physical condition was now such that his doctor was urgently recommending he be admitted to the Devonshire Road Sanatorium in Blackpool. As arrangements were being made for his admittance, Randle moved into a house at Rossall Beach, Cleveleys, rather than into the family home now at Bispham Road, Blackpool. It was thought that this would give him the rest and isolation needed to help his recovery. With his eventual admission to the sanatorium it became public knowledge that Frank Randle was suffering from Tuberculosis. He was to remain there for several months on a special diet and undergoing complete rest and on controlled medication.

Actor Keith Clifford based his one-man stage play 'Scandals - the Life & Liver of Frank Randle' on this phase of Randle's life. Clifford portrayed Randle as a sick man who took to talking to a clown doll with which he reminisced about his past life - the highs and the lows. It has been said that during the last two years of his life, Frank Randle turned to religion and was welcomed into the Catholic faith. When exactly this event occurred is unknown. It is a fact that he was often observed praying during his *'I'm A Good Boy Now'* tour, which indicates he may at that time already have embraced the faith. If not then, it is more than likely it happened during his enforced confinement in the sanatorium. Certainly at this time, his beliefs were reinforced by regular visits from Father Moulding of St. Cuthbert's Roman Catholic Church, South Shore. The two men were to remain very close friends for the rest of Randle's life. Whilst hospitalised, Randle wrote a piece for the local Blackpool newspaper in which he said, *"I know it sounds crazy but I am terribly sincere when I say that I honestly believe that it is almost worth going through this illness for the grand change in body and mind I personally have experienced"*. Drawing strength from his new found beliefs and with renewed fortitude he vowed to return to the stage for as long as time and God would allow. With this in mind, much of his time in the sanatorium was spent writing new material and sketches as he wanted nothing more but to prove wrong all the miserable individuals who said he would never come out. With his renewed vigour, come out he did and on returning home, though still on medication and with the words of his doctor 'not to perform again' still ringing in his ears, he endeavoured to adjust his life. It is impossible to know precisely the state of health of Randle at this time. To help discover a little more about Tuberculosis we spoke with Stephen H. Gillespie, professor of Medical Microbiology, who without having Randle's medical records could obviously only speak in general terms of how TB could affect people. One major fact that would have related to Randle is that alcohol is one of the risk factors of TB, people who drink in excess as did Randle are more likely to develop the disease. The medication that Frank would have been on after being released from the sanatorium would probably have been streptomycin. This was a drug which had only been introduced in 1948 and by the early 1950s was the most commonly used drug. Yet this and others like PAS were still in reality only experimental and somewhat restricted. Whichever drugs Randle was taking they would certainly have been prescribed and as with streptomycin would have been administered through injection.

After walking the dogs, Patsy and Fifi, on the morning of Thursday March 29th Frank returned to 'Oakdene', his Bispham Road home, and sitting down with a mug of tea, he began two-finger typing his business letters on his trusty old Remington typewriter. One letter in particular was addressed to Ben and Eveline Bannister with further references to the old-fashioned phonograph which they owned. Having recently contacted the BBC regarding his idea for a TV show he thought it expedient while awaiting their reply to enquire of the Bannister's whether or not they still had the phonograph in their possession as the machine was a vital part of what he had in mind. Randle's rough plans for the TV show had him playing the part of the 'old cock', a sprightly ninety-two-year-old. Surrounded by a large number of grandchildren, he would play to them a selection of music on the old phonograph. As each selection played it would become the introduction to a sketch or dialogue performed by Randle, which would clearly be inspired by the music. Obviously, today with no extant scripts it is impossible to say if Randle's TV concept had any merit or promise. David Bannister, son of Ben and Eveline, informed us that Randle visited their home, *"I was about six years-old"*, he said, *"when, according to mother, he came to our house to see the old gramophone and apparently spoke to me"*. *He was working on the idea of having me in the show as one of the children"*. Eveline Bannister is, as we write, herself 'a sprightly ninety-two-year-old' who recalls that Randle was quite excited about the whole idea. It is not known whether Frank Randle ever did get a response from the BBC but unfortunately he never made the television appearances he so desired. It is criminal that such a talented character actor was never given the opportunity. Just why one of the country's greatest visual comedians was overlooked in this way remains a mystery. Writer C. V. Curtis, in the regular 'Television Topics' column of Playgoer Magazine posed the same question in a 1950 issue when he said, *"Frank Randle, for 20 years comic*

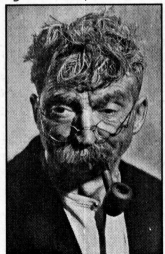

Randle sadly overlooked as a talented character actor

Cock of the North and *Midlands. His mobile features are ideal for television. Why hasn't some astute producer snapped him up? [Frank Randle's] mugging and superb sense of comedy would be a gift for TV"*. Taking this a step further, why did no film producer other than the shoe-string variety step forward with a suitable vehicle for his talent. Journalist Keith Ellis wrote of Randle in 1952, *"...that if he accepted a well-written character part in a first feature he would achieve the national acclaim which has so far eluded him.*

While continuing to convalesce, Randle put more wheels in motion for yet another project. He had the vision of taking on fee paying pupils and instructing them in the art of comedy. To this end Frank placed an advertisement in the local press which read; 'Would you like to be a comedian, either character, red-nosed, light, knockabout, silent or clown? - 'Would you like to do an act?'. With his vast knowledge of theatre and his experience of performing as a clown, comic acrobat, comedian and character comic Randle was willing to tutor others in the myriad forms of mirth making. Unfortunately, this venture proved too slow in its progression and reaped little monetary success.

Although at the back of his mind Randle knew the possibility of dying from Tuberculosis was still a real threat, the recuperation and use of Streptomycin had for the moment made him feel as if he could again tackle theatre work. Consequently, Randle made the decision to return to the stage, with producer Jack Gillam once again putting the show together. Randle suggested to Gillam that he engage comedian Billy Rhodes to act as his foil. Frank and Billy had worked together in the past and had been friends for many years. Billy had effectively retired as he and his wife Chika Lane had been running a boarding house in Blackpool. However, Rhodes not only agreed to join the show but also took on the role of tour manager. Notably absent from this production however, was Gus Aubrey whose appearances with Randle now seemed to be over. Instead it was down to impressionist Ronné Coyles and newcomer vocalist Joe Lee to aid the comedian in his sketches, as well as having their own spots in the programme. The show titled *'Let's Be Frank'* opened at the Pavilion Theatre, Liverpool on May 28th 1956 with the Liverpool Echo stating, *"This show... marks the comeback of one of the shining lights of the music hall – Frank Randle. He is right back in form with all his old salty humour and down-to-earth innuendo".*

At this time most touring shows were facing great difficulties and Randle's was no exception. He was still a popular entertainer however, and could draw decent houses albeit more often than not in the smaller theatres. Up and down the country, many theatres were closing down,

193

FRANK RANDLE

PAVILION, LIVERPOOL. Frank Rings the Bell for the third time. Business as Last Visit—Terrific—in

LET'S BE FRANK

Sincere thanks once again to my friend JAMES BRENNAN for his confidence; To JACK GILLAM for the continuence of our happy association; To JAMES LOVELACE (The Manager of the Pavilion, Liverpool) for his many kindnesses; To BILLY RHODES for being such a great trouper and grand comedian; To THE LASSIES AND LADS of the company for their grand support; and last, but by no means least, to my many FRIENDS for their letters and telegrams of good wishes and congratulations

All business communications :— JACK GILLAM (ENTERTAINMENTS) LTD.
PANTOMIME HOUSE, UPPER MEDLOCK STREET, MANCHESTER 15.

'Let's Be Frank' opened at the Pavilion Theatre, Liverpool – May 1956

making it difficult for the smaller productions and lesser names to find venues in which to stage their shows. Variety itself was also changing. Many people looked upon Randle's shows and those in similar vein as being from a bygone age... Music Hall. Times, as well as peoples tastes, were changing. New entertainers were breaking through; many already firm favourites with the public thanks to television appearances. Television itself was proving to be huge competition for shows such as Randle's and was a major factor in the dwindling audiences, especially in the smaller towns. *'Let's Be Frank'* however, was facing mixed fortunes and whereby in some theatres, audience numbers were small, others could just as easily have been a full house. In all cases though, those who did turn out were fully behind Randle and appreciative of what he was doing. From Liverpool, the show moved on to Preston before arriving at The Hulme Hippodrome, Manchester, where he had always enjoyed performing and where the crowds always seemed to turn out. The Manchester Evening News reviewed the show and admitted that although some of the old Randle lustre was missing, his typical bawdy sense of humour was still as strong as ever. *"The Randle style of comedy may not go down well in the best circles but sketches like "The Camel" and "The Old Cock" are the type of thing that has made this comedian with the flashing gums a northern favourite and how they lapped it up..."*. 'The Camel' and 'The Old Cock' - sometimes performed as 'Samson and Delilah' and '92 today' - were both written during Randle's enforced stay in the Blackpool sanatorium and were proving to be great laughter making sketches. Centre stage is the beautiful Delilah resplendent in all her finery turning left and right in search of Samson. *"Oh Samson, where are you? Oh where is my Samson"?* Suddenly there is a tremendous drum roll and the spotlight hits stage right and there, standing proud and magnificent, is our hero Samson...Randle. He says nothing, just stands proud in his grandeur while wielding a huge sword in his hand - the audience is convulsed. Eventually the laughter subsides. The sighing Delilah steps back and proclaims, *"Oh verily Samson I have never seen such a weapon before!"*. Of course, Randle's response once more sends the audience

Week Commencing MONDAY, AUGUST 6th, 1956
6-15—TWICE NIGHTLY—8-20

JACK GILLAM (Entertainments) LIMITED
(in association with Frank Randle Productions)
present

FRANK RANDLE
in
LET'S BE FRANK
A New Variety Road Show

I—THE LYNBAHRY GIRLS
Lovely and lively

II—RONNIE COYLES
Never the same chap twice

III—FRANK RANDLE
is introduced by Billy Rhodes, and the fun starts

IV—VICKERS TWINS
Masters of Music

V—FRANK RANDLE
with Billy Rhodes and the Camel

VI—THE SIX DYNAMITES
Britain's Greatest Acrobatic Team

— INTERVAL —
Time for Refreshment! Our attendants will be pleased to supply
Ices and Soft Drinks
We also have Four Fully Licensed Bars : Stalls, Pit Stalls,
Side Circle and Dress Circle

VII—BRIGHT AND GAY
Yours and Mime

VIII—THE LYNBAHRY GIRLS
Rhythm is their business

IX—FRANK RANDLE
with Billy Rhodes at the Palm Court

X—THE LYNBAHRY GIRLS
Lovely to look at

XI—JOE LEE
The New Vocal Star

XII—FRANK RANDLE
The Old Cock

XIII—LES SAPPHIRES
A Study in Silver

XIV—FINALE
We wish you all " Good Night "

HER MAJESTY THE QUEEN

Programme and tickets for 'Let's be Frank', Grand Theatre, Bolton - 1956

into raptures, *"Aye. Aye I know love - That's what they all say".* Over the years there had been countless people who objected to Randle's humour and complained quite strongly at his vulgarity and use of double-entendres. These people had always been there as a constant irritation. Now just two weeks after appearing at Manchester, Randle was again faced with yet more criticism of his show's content. It was at nearby Salford that the local Churches had spoken out about Randle's material. From the stage of the city's Windsor Theatre, Randle with tongue firmly in cheek apologised. *"We're sorry - if we offend anyone and if we do, just ask for your money back. Then try to get it".* The Manchester Evening News wrote that while indeed Randle's material did come across as being somewhat crude, his homespun humour was generally less offensive than much of the suggestive innuendo that many revue comedians peddled. They continued, *"And if every audience this week is as wholeheartedly behind him as last night's, Mr Randle will undoubtedly leave the city a happy man."*

While he had been performing at Hulme, Frank Randle had been staying in his caravan. Although the use of the caravan when touring had once been a regular occurrence, at this point in his career it had not been used for some time. Nonetheless, it was used to full extent

195

during his appearances at Hulme. On this occasion the van was parked as usual on derelict land on the corner of Clopton Street and Preston Street facing the theatre. During the week Josef Locke paid a visit to his old pal. The pair, in the company of Ronné Coyles, made full use of the vehicle for a full blown drinking session. Ronné - who was not really a drinker - sat and watched as Randle and Locke downed their drinks. As time wore on the pair were obviously becoming more drunken in their behaviour and things got out of hand. As they became more aggressive towards each other, Ronné recalled, *"I thought my God what's happening here"*. Soon a row had broken out and the pair began smashing things, *"I thought my God I'd better get out of here quick"*. However, before he could even reach the door *"All Hell broke loose as they started to smash the bloody place to pieces"*. The pair certainly made a proper demolition job on the caravan for it was totally wrecked and never used again. There have been many varied tales told about this incident including the shooting of a pistol culminating in a caravan with a perforated roof.

What's a soft drink Ronné?

Although being advised to curtail his drink intake Frank found that this was virtually impossible to do and continued to drink to excess. Actor Keith Clifford's first experience of Randle was seeing a drunken performance on stage at the Palace Theatre, Halifax where the show had opened on July 2nd. Keith once recalled, *"...one night my dad said, 'Get your coat on. I'll take you to see the funniest man alive"*. However, as Ronné Coyles straightforwardly put it, *"there were times that week when he was plainly drunk - yes indeed"*. While some performers filled in for him others tried as best they could to sober him up. By the time he made his entrance he was about five or six acts late. Keith Clifford continued. *"It was a disaster. He was almost unintelligible. I kept looking at dad thinking 'what was he on about?' He was practically in tears - his idol was dying on his feet in front of him. We went home in silence and it was some days before dad spoke"*.

Performances at Blackburn, Hull, West Bromwich, and Bolton amongst others passed off without incident with the next venue being in Huddersfield. Randle was always generous to the waiters, chambermaids and all those who looked after him at the hotels where he stayed while on tour. A ritual he performed every Sunday morning, prior to breakfast, was to carefully place the gratuities into envelopes all neatly inscribed with the names of the recipients. At the end of a rather uneventful week at Huddersfield, Randle was in his hotel attempting to carry out his usual practice. The hotel was a quaint old-fashioned place full of Victorian style and décor and somewhat dimly lit. Consequently Randle said to a waitress, *"I can't see here love, this bloody light... have you got a stronger bulb?"*. Somewhat apologetic, she tried to explain, *"Well Mr Randle you see it goes with the décor it has to be...."* Before she could finish her sentence Randle abruptly shouted, *"Well fuck that, go and buy a bulb, I'll fucking pay for it."*. With his writing tasks eventually completed, Randle turned to Ronné Coyles, *"Now for some breakfast and then we'll be on our way."*. At the end of the meal, throughout which he had continually complained of the poor light, he pushed his teacup to one side and decided it was time for a stronger drink. Unfortunately, being a Sunday the hotel bar was not due to open until noon, still a good couple of hours away. Being refused service by a waiter he demanded to see the manager, who did himself no favours by keeping him waiting for around twenty minutes. The manager explained that the licensing laws dictated that the bar could not be opened until twelve o'clock. To which a less than pleased Randle snapped, *"Fuck the licensing laws and fuck you. You say you are the manager. I say you are a cunt. Now open the fucking bar."* Needless to say Frank Randle got his wish and after about three drinks it was time for the drive to Northampton.

During Randle's previous *'I'm a Good Boy Now'* tour, people of course knew he was unwell but were ignorant to the exact severity of his illness. However, since his enforced confinement at the sanatorium, his fellow performers were now fully aware of his condition, yet it was still something to which he would not openly talk about. Ronné Coyles perhaps more than anyone in these latter years spent most time with Frank Randle. Together they drove the roads of Britain between venues and the conversations were many and varied. But Ronné found Frank kept most things to himself and always appeared as if everything was all right. *"I tried on a couple of occasions when talking to get really underneath him"*, said Ronné. *"We used to chat and I was asking questions and he'd look at me as if to say 'How far is this guy going'. I just wanted to know about him and his health, but he'd just stop at certain things and wouldn't let me continue. He'd say 'another time'".*

A youthful Ronné Coyles as he would have looked when appearing in 'Let's Be Frank'

It is well known that over the years there were times when Randle, holed-up in some pub or other full of drink, could miss a show altogether. So many times have stagehands been sent round to drag him out and get him on stage. So many times have people laughed at these tales and antics. Yet, now it appeared he was happy for people to think the worst of him for his non-appearances. Rather than admitting his illness had got such a hold on him rendering him incapable of performing he would simply vanish - leaving people to assume the usual. By the time *'Let's Be Frank'* was nearing the completion of its run, Frank was apparently in pain. Although TB was not usually painful it was not uncommon for some people to suffer some amount of pain. Of course, there are many forms of pain, not just physical. People have said that while on this tour Randle had been secretly injecting himself. The only secrecy here was that he was keeping the full facts of his illness to himself. He had not explained to anyone about his disease or the medication he was taking. When he was observed injecting himself, it was with his prescribed medication Streptomycin. However, it was not normal practice for the patient to administer the drug themselves. By doing so Frank could have suffered serious consequences. Not only was he in danger of overdosing, uncontrolled, the drug could have caused renal failure, dizziness or even destroyed his middle-ear. Being away from home and constantly on the move it does seem likely that Randle would have been shown by his own doctor how to inject himself properly. Obtaining supplies of Streptomycin while travelling would also not have been easy and Randle had probably made arrangements with private doctors in various towns. Unfortunately, medication and drink wasn't enough to get him on stage at Reading.

Ronné and Frank had travelled down from Morecambe by car as usual and arrived in Reading on the Sunday evening. Ronné was dropped off at his theatrical digs while Frank went to his hotel. On the Monday morning, October 15th, all the artistes assembled at the Palace Theatre for the band call. Except for Frank as he failed to appear. Nor did he turn up for the first night performance. Ronné again recalled the Randle of this period, *"You know, this was a very, very sad time. I quite honestly think Frank knew he didn't have long left - to me he was a man who was rapidly going downhill, very sad indeed".* The first night went on without him and by the start of Tuesday's performance people still had not heard from him - but to quote the old cliché 'the shows must go on'. It seems quite repetitive to say that Randle was bolstering his medication with alcohol and using it as a mask for any discomfort - yet it was indeed a fact. Unfortunately, as had always been the case, too much alcohol brought with it, if not complications, then certainly embarrassing moments.

As the Tuesday performance of *'Let's be Frank'* was underway, Frank arrived just in time to walk out for his first spot. He instantly brought the house down. One over enthusiastic member of the audience shouted out to him *'hey Frank it's good to have you here'.* Frank was stopped in his tracks and turned and said *'ehh, you, you cunt you'.* Meanwhile Ronné Coyles was situated behind the curtains making preparations for the next sketch. Luckily in those days the only microphones were at the front of the stage and so unheard by the audience Ronné, from behind the curtains, tried to speak to Frank. Ronné recalled, *"As I heard him, I thought 'Oh my God' and rushed to the tabs and said 'Frank, Frank'".* As the audience sat stunned, Frank stepped backwards towards Ronné and said 'What!'. *"I'm behind the tabs talking to him and I say, 'the man said it's great to have you here'. And Frank says, 'Oh aye, aye'. Then he went forward and the cleverness of the guy... he went on and said, 'please ladies and gentlemen my apologies ... and he apologised and apologised and before a minute or so he was getting applause and laughs".* A few minutes later and the audience were believing he was not the one to blame and as if to prove this he said, 'Ladies and Gentlemen I cannot continue if that man is still in the audience' and he sent for the manager who promptly had him ejected from the theatre. He then carried on with the show and he won over the audience completely. The rest of the week was uneventful, though by the time it was completed, Frank was looking decidedly tired.

The car journey from Reading to Wigan, the last date of the tour, was a fairly long one. One on which Ronné was expecting several stops.

However, the pair was only about half an hour away from their destination when Frank spotted a pub and decided it was time to pull in for a drink. The protests from Ronné that their journey was almost completed were to no avail.

The room was quite busy as they approached the bar and they could hear the whispers from the lunchtime revellers ... 'look it's Frank Randle'. Frank was like a king walking among his subjects. 'What you having Ronné?' he asked. Not being a drinker Ronné settled for lemonade while Frank ordered a pint and a short. *"The room had a real buzz about it"*, Said Ronné. *"I don't know if it was always like that... I doubt it"*. Frank was really the centre of attention and everyone seemed to want to talk to him. It was as though he was meeting up with old friends he hadn't seen for some time, 'what you drinking Frank?' were the all too familiar words which filled the air. With each drink that went down the atmosphere seemed to rise as the bar became increasingly livelier. The landlord could hardly believe what was happening. The fact that Frank had reached a stage where he was so intoxicated he ended up on the floor behind the bar was of little concern to the landlord. *"We had only been in there just over an hour before the drink had gotten a hold. I thought my God, 'No Please'"*. As Frank lay flat out on the floor, and with closing time fast approaching Ronné Coyles was becoming a worried man. *"I didn't drive then and I thought what do I do?"*. With the closing of the pub and people making their way home to tell of their afternoon spent in such illustrious company, Ronné Coyles stood alone. Gathering his thoughts he decided to telephone the theatre, in those days it wasn't uncommon for someone to be working there on Sunday. Upon hearing of his predicament it was soon arranged for transport to come out and pick up the performers and drive them on to Wigan. It was over a couple of hours later before Ronné Coyles arrived safely at his digs - Randle had been left at his hotel with someone to take care of him. *"I saw him next day at the Theatre, but there was no mention of the incident what-so-ever"*, added Ronné.

The show in Randle's birth town of Wigan opened and several performances went just as they should, pleasing both audience and company. Then at one performance for reasons known only to him, if indeed he actually knew a reason, Randle's unpredictability came to the fore. It was impossible to say why the events that transpired actually happened. As usual one could suggest things that may have made a contribution, his illness, medication, drink, state of mind or quite simply his temper. One could add the fact that many thought he was actually going mad - was there a full moon when this latest incident occurred?

On stage it's the '92 Today/Old Cock' sketch and the scene is set outside a public house. The landlord's son, Ronné Coyles dressed as a boy scout, is wiping down a tabletop, while several drinkers are sitting at the other nearby tables. A young female walks passed and takes the eye. Laughter soon fills the auditorium as Randle, who has swept into view in a wheel chair, follows her every step, *"By gum she's a hot un - aye, aye"*. Turning to Ronné Coyles Randle says, *"Is that your whistle dangling young man?"*. *"Yes it is Grandad"*, replies Coyles. To which Randle's rejoinder is, *"eh you're lucky then aren't you young un, aye"*. More laughter fills the air as he adds, *"I'm ninety-two, aye... and I want a drink"*. The Coyles Boy Scout answers *"All right Grandad"* as he briefly exits to return with two pints of beer. Placing the drinks on the table he puts his hands down at the side of the glasses, *"There you are Grandad"*. At this point Randle's inner demons take control, *"Take your hands off the table"*, he whispers. *"What?"* an amazed Coyles whispers back. A second time Randle repeats the command only to be told by an increasingly nervy Coyles that this is how it had been rehearsed. Randle's audible reply stunned the audience into silence and Coyles into a sense of fear, *"Take your fucking hands off the table you little bastard!"*. Scared and shaking, Coyles was at a loss as to what to do next as Randle's remarks had totally thrown him - should he continue as rehearsed and suffer more outbursts - he had no idea what Randle would do or say next. In what seemed like an eternity, but in reality was only seconds, Coyles without thinking blurted out one word 'no'. Randle immediately picked up one of the drinks and poured it over a bemused Coyles. The audience now thinking this was part of the routine once more began to laugh. As if part of a well rehearsed act, Coyles reacted on impulse by throwing beer all over Randle. At the immediate point of impact, with the liquid dripping from his face and clothing, Randle just about saw a speedy Coyles exit from the stage. *"I ran so bloody quick you couldn't believe it. I ran upstairs and locked myself in the dressing room and I thought Oh my God what have I done, what have I done"*. Any thoughts that the dressing room would provide a safe haven would soon be erased. For through the loud speaker he knew that Billy Rhodes was on stage - which indicated that Randle wasn't. No sooner had the thought registered with a cowering Coyles that he broke into a cold sweat as what sounded like a herd of elephants stopped outside the door. Accompanying the thumping and kicking which the door was receiving, came the volatile tones of Randle, *"Come out you little bastard"*. The door could take no more ill treatment a final bang resulted in its surrender to its attacker. Eyeing his prey, once more Randle repeated, *"You fucking little bastard"*. In a forlorn attempt yet again to explain that he had only done what had been rehearsed, Ronné said, "*But Frank I only...*" "*He said, 'don't you call me Frank you call me Mr Randle'. And then I said, 'Oh, Mr Randle, it was...' 'Don't call me Mr Randle call me Frank you fucking little bastard - I wouldn't care but I like you'*". Coyles couldn't believe his ears, "*you what -you've got a funny way of showing it Frank*". A missile flung by Randle whistled across the room shattering the mirror as he said, '*don't fucking answer me back*', and yet in the instant the glass was hitting the floor ne cooled. Ronné was of course thinking the worst as Randle went very thoughtful before beckoning him to come closer. "*I thought he was going to hit me. He put his hands on

Several years down the line and Ronné Coyles still had vivid memories of Frank Randle – just as he does today

my shoulders and said 'Ronné tell me do you believe in God'. I said 'yes I do' and he said 'so do I' and he said 'Ronné nobody needs him more than I do now'. I said 'bless you Frank' and I knew he was hurting inside*". Singer Joe Lee had only come to know Randle since joining the tour. However in that time, Joe could see that Frank was a sad man. "*He was very miserable, I think he had depression*", said Joe. "*The thing was I think he was poorly and working while poorly. I did see the other side of him when he was in a good mood and when he was, you could see his face light up and he was happy. Unfortunately, I think the man was in pain and suffering inwardly and I think this is what made him like he was.*

As the final curtain came down at the Wigan Hippodrome on Saturday October 27th 1956, it brought to an end the twenty-two week tour. As the company departed the stage there could hardly have anyone who was not thinking that this would be the end of Randle's career. Throughout its run the show had played to appreciative audiences if not always capacity houses and as with most of Randle's tours this one had certainly been one roller coaster ride for many of his fellow performers and back stage staff. The dressing room talk amongst the artistes that Saturday night was all about Randle, how working with him had been a chore for some while for others it had indeed been a pleasure. The one thing everyone agreed upon was that life with the great man had been unpredictable. During the run of 'Let's be Frank', Ronné Coyles more than anyone had perhaps come closer to Randle, even so, Ronné had still been unable to really penetrate beneath the surface of Frank Randle, always feeling that there was something hidden deep inside the man. If Ronné hadn't already known that Frank was married to Queenie he would never have found this out from Randle, he never once mentioned her name. In fact, in all their conversations Randle never spoke at all about anything regarding his private life and certainly not about his illness. Throughout all the time spent with Randle both off and on stage Ronné always had the constant and overwhelming feeling that here was a man who was genuinely suffering inwardly. Severe pain, sadness and loneliness were emotions that he felt Randle was going through while being unable, or incapable of talking to anyone about it. As Ronné was saying his goodbyes, shaking Randle's hand and looking him directly in the face, he had one thought on his mind, this being that he was leaving a man who had very little time left upon this earth.

With the tour completed a tired Randle rested at home and tried to put his illness behind him. There was now time for visits from family and friends and plans were made on how to spend Christmas. Obviously, over the years due to work there had been too few family Christmas's at home. Throughout this period however, Frank could not resist thoughts of appearing on stage once more. Finally, and to the surprise of those close to him these thoughts were to become reality as Randle announced that he was hoping to embark on yet another tour. Although deciding to carry on it is significant that what turned out to be the final Frank Randle shows should have

A work of art from Arthur Delaney – Frank happy with Grandchild

been tagged as his 'Farewell Tour'. Indeed Frank was personally acknowledging the fact that his career was undeniably nearing its end and was quoted at the time as saying, *"My present tour will cover a wide area and I shall be carrying on for a while but I have not been enjoying good health and one has to get ready to finish sometime".*

Randle, defying his illness, showed great determination in undertaking his last public performances, not only in drawing the strength to actually perform on stage, but also in securing the bookings. Britain of 1957 saw theatres in the doldrums; houses were constantly closing at a rapid pace. Promoters who at one time would have jumped at the chance to mount a Randle Road Show were now turning their backs on the one time money spinner. They were now only interested in sure things - if such things existed. Given a choice between a now older and visibly ill and tired Randle or a current star from radio or TV, they had no option. Entertainment in general was undergoing change; musical trends such as Skiffle were now the rage and being introduced more and more into surviving theatres. With no chance of getting on the major circuits he was at the mercy of any small independently run theatres who were willing to book him as a solo act and build their own show around him. Of the few theatres which did engage Randle, all advertised their shows quite differently. At Ashton-under-Lyne, the posters and press advertising boldly stated *'Frank Randle & Co'* with the added tagline *'On his farewell tour – for old times sake'.* At Luton it was billed as *'The Frank Randle Road Show',* while at Blackpool it was simply *'Frank Randle'.* In the hope that more dates would be added, Randle opened for the first time on January 14th at Ashton's, Theatre Royal. Sadly, this was a theatre which, having been brought back from the dead just four months previously, was to close for the final time after Randle's week in residence. The theatre had on previous occasions been a happy and receptive venue for him and this final time was no exception. The reviewer from the local press wrote, *"In this final production Frank Randle shows sparks of the spicy humour that has made his name synonymous with buffoonery. He had two spots on the bill; one as a solo act and the other with two "henchmen". Both have the audience rocking with laughter".* Ashtonian Darren Kirk holds fond memories both of the Theatre Royal and Frank Randle. *"The times I have sat reading the adverts on the fire curtain at the Theatre Royal, and now I can't remember a single one. I saw Randle in his 'Farwell Tour' and laughed so much I wet myself".* In Darren's case this was not just a figure of speech it actually did happen. Enter stage left, Frank Randle wearing a straw boater and striped blazer - which was long enough to have the audience wondering if he was wearing shorts or not. It appears to have been the womenfolk that were the first to burst into giggles, which were soon drowned by the full-bodied hearty laughs of the male contingent, which of course included Darren Kirk. After what seemed an eternity of giggles and laughter, the master

THEATRE ROYAL
ASHTON-UNDER-LYNE

Lessees: MILES BYRNE (West End Theatres) Ltd
Managing Director and Licensee - J. ROWLAND SALES
Chairman. MILES BYRNE: Theatre Manager. ALAN WALLIS

Twice Nightly 6-30 and 8-30
Monday, January 14th and All Week
SPECIAL WELCOME VISIT OF

FRANK RANDLE
AND CO.

ON HIS FAREWELL TOUR FOR
OLD TIME SAKE
also FULL SUPPORTING CAST
Don't Miss This Grand Comedian Old Age Pensioners
Welcome Monday 1/-

The beginning of the end

spoke. *'I was walking down't street and this lad sez, 'eh mister yer gobs open'.* Randle's quip sent a tidal wave around the audience, when it settled with stays straining and corsets near to bursting Randle added, *'Aye I know lad it were me that op-end it'.* At that moment poor Darren Kirk could do nothing as his bladder gave way – nothing, that was, except laugh. Another Ashton resident was Gerald Nicholas a former child film extra and youthful entertainer. In later life Gerry turned to a career in journalism before returning to his love of acting in 1981 as 'Gerry George'. Although slightly wrong with the date - Gerry recalled it as October 1956 - he does remember seeing the final show, *"On the last night it was really sad because he came out to do his curtain speech as he often did, and in the grand style he said, 'this here's a lovely little theatre with a grand little band and I'm very, very sorry that it's closing especially on my farewell tour'".* After the show Gerry spoke to Randle in his dressing room, *"I had been an extra in several of his films and chatted to him about them. He was by this time a very sick man who could barely breathe, yet he was exceptionally kind-hearted and considerate, and was almost amused at the thought of a young teenager, such as me, having any time for him when Rock 'n' Roll seemed to be the in-thing. I explained that I was, to my mind at least, an aspiring impressionist, and even though my mother had desires that I get a proper job, I was at heart a theatrical. Handing him my fountain pen for an autograph he said, 'so, you're an*

205

impressionist, now, are you, son? - Well you won't make much of an impression with this pen; it's got no ink in it! After giving it a good shake, he managed to get the pen flowing and duly wrote, Cheerio, Gerry - always try to make a good impression - Frank Randle".

Throughout his career Randle had always been sure of a great audience reception in his hometown of Blackpool – this again proved to be true when, after a week at the Grand Theatre, Luton, he opened at Blackpool's Queen's Theatre on February 4th. The review from the Blackpool Evening Gazette read, *"Frank Randle the comic who needs no introduction in any town in the country returned last night to the Queens Theatre, where he was taken seriously ill a year ago. At that time it was thought that his stage days were over, but this week he is at the top of his form and as funny as ever".* It went on to say that his appearance though, may well be his last in the resort.

Although Randle's performances had been good throughout and audiences had found him to be as funny as ever, the simple fact remained that the work was not forthcoming. It was now certainly obvious to Randle that to stage a full scale 'farewell tour' was a non-starter, a fact that evidently saddened and troubled him. Just why Randle didn't retire there and then is difficult to assess, as he obviously knew he couldn't carry on much longer. Perhaps, as with many performers before and since, Randle drew strength from actually going out on stage - take that away and you in effect take away their life.

With only a few weeks work behind him since the start of the year, a dejected Randle was now spending most days at home brooding over past events in his life and in the business, the friends and enemies he had made. More so the enemies. He firmly believed that there were those who were now deliberately out to stop him from obtaining work. Rightly or wrongly, these very thoughts eating away at him on a daily basis were not helping Randle. His health was deteriorating rapidly yet perhaps, if he had not held such a fervent desire to work, he may have succumbed to his illness even more rapidly.

His longing to work and the thoughts that people 'had it in for him' were evident in the words he used in a letter sent to his old friend Alex Munro in April 1957. In this, he asks Munro's advice on the situation within the business, the state of theatres and what people were being paid, *"I mean the real truth without any codology in any way",* he wrote. For even after his recent setbacks, he was still admitting he'd like to put on a show. Although he does also say at one point that perhaps he should give up the business completely and advises Munro should do the same. This train of thought being sparked by the fact that Randle believed he was the victim of a smear campaign and was asking Munro if he could throw any light on it. It transpired that Alex Munro had once warned Randle that people were out for his blood in regards his position in the business. Randle wrote that he had heard recently that there was a block on his work, *"Perhaps if you were to tell me of what I'm accused of from every angle and if possible who the accusers are, I would know exactly how to react"* he wrote. He acknowledges that theatres are in a bad state and that that the poor performers either have to work for a percentage of small houses or for a meagre salary... *"When he can get it, don't forget the supply is FAR greater than the demand, it has developed into a rat race"*. Randle showed no liking for promoters or agents, these being the ones who were still managing to make money.

Long time friend, Alex Munro

It is obvious that his friend Alex had suggested an idea combining Randle's 'Old Cock' with a Scottish equivalent played by Munro. Randle had obviously given it some thought and was suggesting that perhaps it might simply be along the lines of Randle up in Scotland with Munro trying to teach him Scottish dialect and accents so that he could perform as a Scottish comic. *"But how do you propose getting it on the BBC"*, he asks, *"They won't stand for threats as I believe they have their own protection society and if you mention my name to them you're liable to a term of not less than five years. Still it might come off and it is nice to know that a couple of weeks on the BBC will keep us for the rest of the twelve months"*. So, in a three page letter we learn what Randle thinks of the state of the business and theatres and that work when available is for a pittance. He mentions very little of his health except to say that he is not at his best in the mornings. Despite all this and still believing people are blocking his progress, he nonetheless feels he would like to put on another show but was adamant that he would not beg, *"I will NOT bow the knee Alex"*.

207

We have been unable to ascertain how much work, if any, Randle managed to secure during April and May 1957, however, he was booked to appear at the New Theatre, Crewe from May 3rd. His digs at

Dressing room reflections

Crewe were at a public house just a short walk from the theatre, where for much of that week he had been drinking heavily. He hardly had any contact with the other performers on the mediocre bill preferring instead to lock himself away in his dressing room with a just bottle of whisky for company. As he took his final bow on Saturday June 8th 1957 the small but enthusiastic last house audience were unaware that this was to be the end for one of the country's greatest ever comedians. The Old Hiker was still funny, Randle despite his ill health was still funny and this undoubtedly acknowledged by the Crewe audience. The other seasoned performers on the show, Harry Jerome - a comedy magician, jugglers Idris and Belle and specialist entertainers Eddie Fox and Beryl, mattered little to most of them. Nor did newcomers 'The Crescents' skiffle group and singer Fay Smith, although both had their supporters. The group certainly mattered little to Randle who throughout the week had referred to them quite derogatively as 'the piffle group'. It was in fact a sad end for Frank Randle to finish his career with such a third-rate show. Far better if he could have been in the company of his Scandals team or with his greatest of stooges Gus Aubrey. But at least he made his final bow before a laughing audience, which is just what he would have wanted. Frank had once recalled a sad story about an ageing comedian who, having failed to make his audience laugh, turned to them and said, *"ladies and gentlemen, I can't make you laugh, so I'll dance"*. Added Randle, "*This is the most pathetic thing I've heard - I hope I die in harness like Tommy Handley or Sid Field"*. The desire within Randle to perform for as long as he could clearly kept him going for months if not years. Unfortunately that desire died at Crewe.

For the next three weeks a dark cloud hung over the Randle household. It was a sad and difficult time for Queenie as there was no getting

208

away from the fact that her husband was dying. As the news spread via the show business grapevine, many performers who lived in Blackpool came to visit him. Several impresarios, agents and a few of his old 'Scandals' team took it upon themselves to call. Arthur Goulding heard from his brother, a near neighbour of Randle's, just how near to death's door he was. Although Arthur had personal reasons for disliking the character and behaviour of the man, he still felt he had to go and visit his former employer, *"I held no animosity"*, he told us. *"It felt strange, quiet; the three of them were sitting there, Randle, Queenie and his mother who was looking after him"*. Randle explained how he had TB in his lungs, but Arthur at the time thought it was cancer. *"I thought it was cancer because of his heavy smoking, he was a Woodbines man all his life"*. Goulding added, *"His temper over the years must have raised his blood pressure hellishly which wouldn't have helped his condition"*. Randle was glad to see Arthur and for a short time the two remembered past times. Other than the family, Arthur had been one of the last people to see Randle alive; sadly he would also be one of the first to see him after his death.

When talking with Jeff Nuttall (for his book 'King Twist'), Queenie recalled how during this time Randle had been reminiscing about his old pal Gus Aubrey. One thing which remained planted in Jeff's mind was how on the morning of his death, Frank was still thinking of Gus, saying to Queenie how he was worried about his old pal's future. After a lifetime of drinking, smoking and years battling with TB which had ravaged his lungs his immune system could no longer cope. Sadly on July 7th 1957 Arthur McEvoy, alias Frank Randle passed away at his Bispham Road home with the actual cause of death being stated as gastro-enteritis.

To enable people to pay their last respects Queenie had arranged for her husband's body to be laid out in their living room the day before the funeral. Throughout that day a constant stream of visitors called including family friends and neighbours and of course, many of Randle's show business colleagues. Arthur Goulding was amongst the first to call and offer his condolences to Queenie and Rhoda. *"Queenie took me into the front room. Randle was laid out there and he looked quite peaceful for once, poor soul"*, said Arthur. *"As you would expect Queenie herself didn't look too well"*. This was an opinion echoed by Bob Monkouse, *"There were no other visitors when I arrived or any who called during my short stay but Mrs Randle told me she was staggered by the number of people who had dropped by. "She looked very tired and worn out besides quite naturally being emotionally upset"*. The way Bob Monkouse explained it to us we gained the impression that he had felt somewhat guilty about being there, as if perhaps he was adding to Queenie's grief. Though as he added, *"Being in Blackpool for the summer season I simply felt as though I had to say goodbye to one of the greatest".* From America came a hand written letter of sympathy and words of comfort from fellow Lancastrian and funny man Stan Laurel. Randle's old pal from Wigan and accomplice in his boy hood 'sand dance', Tom Hall and his wife Florence also called to pay their condolences. Yet, even on this sad day the gloom-laden face of Arthur Delaney briefly sported a huge grin. For in a brief respite from visitors at the house, a worried Queenie showed Arthur all the weapons, the firearms and guns Randle had accumulated over the years, asking Arthur if he knew which, if any, were legal and what she could do with them. In the twilight of the day Randle's body was transported to the Holy Family Roman Catholic Church, North Shore, where at least sixty people were waiting to pay their respects. The general public turned out in force the following day when a crowd of around two hundred gathered outside the church as the mourners arrived. The chief mourners were obviously led by Queenie and Rhoda and included close relatives Mrs B. Melling, Mr & Mrs A. Melling. Arthur Delaney, along with Queenie's long-time companion Mrs Kitty Risk, were also present, as were Alex Munro and Gus Aubrey. Other mourners included a number of show business stars, promoters, managers and executives. Producer Jack Taylor who had mounted many of Randle's shows and John Blakeley jnr from the company that had made most of his films sat side by side surrounded by the laughter makers wearing the saddest of faces, such as Jimmy Clitheroe, Sonny Roy, Dave Morris along with Kay Sothern and Mabel and Wilfred Pickles. All sat in silence as Randle's close friend Father W. Moulding of St. Cuthbert's Church, South Shore, said the Requiem Mass. An even bigger crowd had gathered outside and when the congregation made their exit, hundreds of people lined the church drive as Randle made his last curtain call before his fans, a journey to his final resting place, Carlton cemetery. One hundred and fifty people assembled at the cemetery with many bringing floral tributes to add to those which already made a huge blanket over the grave with a four foot long floral cross from Queenie being the most prominent. The inscription on his headstone included a stanza which Queenie had originally found jotted on a scrap of paper tucked inside Randle's wallet.

I got nothing that I asked for
But everything I had hoped for
Despite myself my prayers were answered
I was among all men richly blessed

Last resting place – Carlton Cemetery, Blackpool.
Frank Randle (Arthur McEvoy) 1901-1957

Epilogue:

Shortly after Randle's death, Queenie returned to her London roots settling in New Cross where she had been brought up and eventually remarried. Rhoda continued to live in Blackpool until her death in 1965. When details of Randle's will were released, the comedian had left a gross amount of £3,799 and a net amount of just £2,096. Of all Randle's professional friends and work colleagues the one most affected by his death was Gus Aubrey. Although Gus had been expecting the worst for some time, when he heard that Frank had passed away he was absolutely devastated. The two had worked closely together since 1939 and although they had their differences – people lost count how many times Randle fired him – the relationship between them both and the esteem they had for one another was indeed special. Speaking of Frank shortly after his death Gus said, *"As an artiste he was a genius. Many people never got to know the real Frank Randle, he was human, a very generous man"*. It took some time for Gus to get over Randle's death, however, being the trouper he was he obviously carried on, though things were tough with bookings harder to find. In the 1960s Gus appeared with two old friends from the Randle era, a pantomime with Ronné Coyles and a show with the

Gus Aubrey

diminutive Jimmy Clitheroe. He also performed with Danny La Rue, another drag artiste who, like Gus, portrayed a glamorous 'lady'. Indeed, Aubrey actually gave tips and advice to Danny on how to dress and walk. However, the gaps between jobs were starting to get longer, adverts in The Stage brought no offers and eventually, and somewhat reluctantly, he decided to bring his time in show business to an end. After taking this step, Gus took up employment in one of Manchester's top departmental stores at Kendal's working in their menswear department. He moved to a house in Haslingdon in rural Lancashire, just eighteen miles from Manchester city centre. Here he settled down with his long-time partner Arthur Cragges Forster. The pair kept a low profile in the community, keeping themselves to themselves and never publicising their relationship or their theatrical past. Gus Aubrey, alias Edward Brown died on April 26th 1975.

Randle Filmography

Somewhere in England – 1940
Offered to the BBFC for classification at a running time of 79m 13s
The classification of '**A**' granted on 30th July was only achievable through cuts to the film.
Production Company: Butcher-Mancunian.
Distribution: Butchers Film Services.
Studio: Walton-on-Thames
RCA Photophone Sound System
Producer: John E. Blakeley
Director: John E. Blakeley.
Story: Roney Parsons
Screen Adaptation: Anthony Toner
Cinematographer: Geoffrey Faithfull.
Art Director: R. Holmes Paul
Editor: E. Richards
Production Manager: C. Sanderson
Sound: Hal Fuller
Assistant Director: Cecil Dixon
Musical Director: Percival Mackey
Music: Albert W. Stanbury
Lyrics: Arthur Mertz
Orchestrations: Hal Bevan & Oscar Naylor
Cast: Harry Korris, Frank Randle, Winki Turner, Dan Young, Robbie Vincent, Harry Kemble, John Singer, Sidney Monkton, Stanley King, 8 Master Singers, Percival Mackey's Orchestra.

Archive Status: Held at NFTVA/Blakeley Films/NWFA

Incomplete 35mm copy held at NFTVA. 16mm copy in private hands Blakeley Films and NWFA have digibeta copy from this.

Somewhere in Camp – 1942
Offered to the BBFC for classification at a running time of 88m 19s
The classification of '**U**' granted on 27th January was achieved with no cuts to the film.
Production Company: Butcher-Mancunian.
Distribution: Butchers Film Service
Studio: Riverside Studios.
RCA Photophone Sound System
Producer: John E. Blakeley
Director: John E. Blakeley

Story: Roney Parsons and Anthony Toner.
Cinematographer: Stephen Dade.
Art Director: W. Hemsley.
Editor: A. C. Knott.
Production Manager: E. S. Laurie.
Sound: George Burgess.
Ass Director: W. Boyle.
Lyrics: Arthur Mertz.
Music: A. W. Stanbury.
Percival Mackey and his Orchestra.
Cast: Harry Korris, Frank Randle, Robbie Vincent, Dan Young, Tonie Lupino, John Singer, *(Peggy Novak, Clifford Buckton, Gus Aubrey, Betty Wheatly, Eve Carcroft).*

Archive Status: Held at BBC*
The BBC copy is purportedly 35mm film.

Somewhere on Leave – 1942
Offered to the BBFC for classification at a running time of 96m 07s
The classification of **'U'** granted on 14th October was achieved with no cuts to the film.
Production Company: Butcher-Mancunian.
Distribution: Butchers Film Service
Studio: Riverside Studios.
RCA Photophone Sound System
Producer: John E. Blakeley
Director: John E. Blakeley
Story: Roney Parsons and Anthony Toner.
Cinematographer: Geoffrey Faithfull.
Art Director: W. J. Hemsley.
Editor: E. Richards
Production Manager: E. S. Laurie.
Sound: George Burgess and S. Jolly.
Ass Director: D. Weeks.
Lyrics: Arthur Mertz.
Percival Mackey and his Orchestra.
Cast: Frank Randle, Harry Korris, Dan Young, Robbie Vincent, Tonie Lupino, Pat McGrath, Tonie Edgar Bruce. *(Noel Dainton, Gus Aubrey).*

Archive Status: Held at BBC*
BBC copy is VT acquired from Channel Four who held previous licence for the film.

Somewhere in Civvies - 1943
Offered to the BBFC for classification at a running time of 87m 43s
The classification of '**U**' granted on 30th July was achieved with no cuts to the film
Production Company: Butcher-Empire Production
Distribution: Butchers Film Service
Studio: Riverside Studios, Hammersmith, London
Producer: T.A. Welsh
RCA Photophone Sound System
Produced by Butcher's Film Service Ltd (Managing Director – FW Baker)
Director: Maclean Rogers
Photography: Geoffrey Faithfull
Recording: G Burgess & S Jolly
Assistant Director: Donald Weeks
Production Manager: E S Laurie
Art Director: Jim Carter
Camera Work: A Mason
Editor: Ted Richards
Story & Dialogue: Con West
Musical Director: Percival Mackey
Gags: Frank Randle
Cast Joss Ambler, Gus Aubrey, Grey Blake, George Donnan, H.F. Maltby, Nancy O'Neil, Frank Randle, Suzette Tarri & Frank Randle's Band.
Archive Status: 16mm prints in private hands.
NWFA/Blakeley's hold digibeta copies from one of these.

Home Sweet Home - 1945
Offered to the BBFC for classification at a running time of 93m 31s
The classification of '**A**' granted on 11th July was only achievable through cuts to the film.
Production Company: Butcher-Mancunian.
Distribution: Butchers Film Service
Studio: Riverside Studios
RCA Photophone Sound System
Producer: John E. Blakeley.
Director: John E. Blakeley.
Story: Roney Parsons and Anthony Toner.
Comedy scenes devised & arranged by Arthur Mertz
Cinematographer: Geoffrey Faithfull.
Camera: A. Mason
Art Director: Jim Carter
Editor V Sagovsky
Sound: G. Burgess & L. Clark

Production Manager: E. S. Laurie
Assistant Director: Don Weeks
Musical Director: Percival Mackey
Starring Frank Randle. Introducing as Guest Artistes Rawicz & Landauer. With Nicolette Roeg, Tony Pendrell, H.F. Maltby, Hilda Bayley, Cecil Frederick, Stan Little, Donovan & Byl, Arnley & Gloria, Bunty Meadows. Special Musical Ensembles by Percival Mackey – Soloist Helen Hill

Archive Status: Held at NFTVA/BBC*
BBC retain VT mastered from surviving16mm film which has now been donated to NFTVA

When You Come Home - 1947
Offered to the BBFC for classification at a running time of 93m 23s
The classification of **'U'** granted on 5th March was achieved with no cuts to the film
Production Company: F.W. Baker-Butcher.
Distribution: Butchers Film Services.
Film Studio: Nettlefold – Walton-on-Thames
Producer: John Baxter
Director: John Baxter
Screenplay: Geoffrey Orme, David Evans
Additional Scenes & Comedy Dialogue: Frank Randle
Cinematographer: Geoffrey Faithfull
Art Director: C. H. Gilbert
Editor: Ted Richards
Production Manager: E. S. Laurie
Assistant Director: Don Weeks
Musical Director: Percival Mackey
Camera: Arthur Grant
Continuity: Marion Ward
Make-up: Harry Webber
Original Songs, Written, Composed and Sung by: Leslie Sarony & Leslie Holmes
Choreography: Fred Conyngham, Hazel Gee
CAST; Frank Randle, Leslie Sarony & Leslie Holmes, Diana Decker, Fred Conyngham, Linda Parker, Jack Melford, Tony Heaton, Hilda Bayley, Lily Lapidus, Lesley Osmond, Gus Aubrey, Ernest Dale, Rene Sibley-Grant.

Archive Status: BBC
BBC acquired a slightly worn 16mm 'collectors' print from which they managed to re-master a tape suitable for broadcast. The original film may have been donated to the NFTVA.

Holiday's with Pay - 1948
Offered to the BBFC for classification at a running time of 113m 45s
The classification of '**A**' granted on 1st March was achieved with no cuts to the film.
Production Company: Film Studios (Manchester) Ltd
Distribution: The Mancunian Film Corporation
Studio: Film Studios Manchester
Marconi Visatone Sound System
Producer: John E. Blakeley
Director: John E. Blakeley
Story: Anthony Toner
Screen Adaptation: Harry Jackson and Mavis Compston
Cinematographer: Ben Hart
Camera: Gerald Pullen, John E. Blakeley Jnr
Sound: Kenneth Ross
Editor: Dorothy Stimson
Continuity: Joyce Bedale
Art Director: Joseph Gomersall
Production Manager: Bernard Kelly
Make-up: Victor Arnley
Hair Stylist: Ann Reynolds
Casting Director: Arthur Mertz Jr
Assistant Director: Thomas Blakeley
Lyrics: Albert W. Stanbury
Musical Director: Fred Harris
Furnishings by Pauldens Ltd Manchester
Cast: Frank Randle, Tessie O'Shea, Dan Young, Josef Locke with Sally Barnes, Sonny Burke, Joanne Bracewell, Effie Mackintosh, Peter Lilley, Rita Varian, Rita Young, Danny Young, Bert Tracey, Patrina Bowman
Archive Status: Held with Blakeley's Films
Blakeley's holds 35 mm print of 95min version. NWFA have digibeta of this for access.

Somewhere in Politics – 1948
Offered to the BBFC for classification at a running time of 110m
The classification of '**A**' granted on 13th October was achieved with no cuts to the film.
Length on release: 9700ft. 108mins.
Production Company: Film Studios (Manchester) Ltd
Distribution: The Mancunian Film Corporation
Studio: Film Studios Manchester
Marconi Visatone Sound System
Producer: John E. Blakeley.
Director: John E. Blakeley.

Story: Harry Jackson, Arthur Mertz, Frank Randle
Cinematographer: Ernest Palmer, Ben Hart
Editor: Dorothy Stimson
Art Dir: Joseph Gomersall
Musical Arrangements: Fred Harris and Fred Bonelli
Cast: Frank Randle, Tessie O'Shea, Josef Locke, Syd & Max Harrison, Sally Barnes, Jimmy Clitheroe, Bunty Meadows, Sonny Burke, Anthony Oakley, Effie Macintosh, Kay Compston, Bernard Graham, Fred Simister, George Little.
Archive Status: Lost (see 'shorts' section – 'Full House')

School for Randle - 1949
Offered to the BBFC for classification at a running time of 89m 13s
The classification of '**U**' granted on 4th November was achieved with no cuts to the film
Production Company: Film Studios (Manchester) Ltd
Distribution: The Mancunian Film Corporation
Studio: Film Studios Manchester
Sound System: British Acoustic Film System
Producer: John E. Blakeley
Director: John E. Blakeley
Story: Anthony Toner
Screen Adaptation: Harry Jackson
Cinematographer: Ernest Palmer
Sound: Michael Hobbs
Editor: Dorothy Stimson
Continuity: Doris Martin
Art Director: Joseph Gomersall
Make-up: Harry Webber
Musical Director: Billy Butler
Assistant Director: Tom Blakeley

Studio Manager: Bernard Kelly

Cast: Frank Randle, John Singer, Elsa Tee, Frederick Bradshaw, Dan Young, Alec Pleon, Maudie Edwards, Hilda Bayley, Ian Fleming, Jimmy Clitheroe, Joan Henley, *Gus Aubrey*
Archive Status: Held with Blakeley's Films/NWFA
Blakeley's have 35mm film version. NWFA have digibeta for access.

It's a Grand Life – 1953
Offered to the BBFC for classification at a running time of 106m 40s
The classification of '**U**' granted on 8th October was only achievable through cuts to the film.
Length on release: 102mins

Production Company: Film Studios (Manchester) Ltd
Distribution: The Mancunian Film Corporation
Studio: Film Studios Manchester
Sound System: Gaumont British Kalee
Producer: John E. Blakeley
Director: John E. Blakeley
Story: H. F. Maltby
Cinematographer: Ernest Palmer
Sound: David Howells
Editor: Dorothy Stimson
Continuity: Gladys Goldsmith
Art Dir: Alec Gray
Assistant Dir: Bert Marotta
Make-up: Gerry Fairbank
Production Manager: Tom Blakeley
Cast: Frank Randle, Diana Dors, Dan Young, Michael Brennan, Jennifer Jayne, John Blythe, Anthony Hulme, Charles Peters, Arthur White, Leslie Gould, Kevin Peters, Ian Fleming, Ruth Taylor. Appearances by championship wrestlers: Jack Pye, Bill Garnon, Cab Cashford, Carl Van Wurden. Special Guest Artiste Winifred Atwell

Archive Status: Held with NWFA/Blakeley's Films
Two 35 prints held by NWFA and digibeta for access. NFTVA hold 16mm extract.
DVD Released September 2006 by Odeon Entertainment Ltd

Shorts
With the following films the title that appears in brackets is the film from which the under mentioned 'shorts' were extracted. The dates used are those on which the BBFC granted certification.
(Home Sweet Home)
Randle and All That – 7th December 1945
Cert: **'A'** (with cuts)
Archive Status: Held by the BBC/NWFA
NWFA hold 16mm print and digibeta for access. BBC have 35mm print

(Holidays with Pay)
Tonight's The Nite – 2nd June 1960
1672ft. Cert **'U'** (uncut).
Seaside Frolics – 2nd June1960
1700ft. 18mins. Cert **U** (uncut).
Archive Status: Held at the NWFA.
NWFA holds 35 prints and digibeta for access. Also one-reel extract (title unknown) held at Huntley Film Archive

(Somewhere in Politics)
Full House – 2nd June 1960
1700ft. 18mins Cert **'U'** (uncut).
Archive Status: Held at the NWFA.
NWFA holds 35 prints and digibeta for access.

(School for Randle)
Teacher's Pest – 4th February 1960
4200ft. 46mins. Cert U (uncut)
The Three Who-Flungs – 4th February 1950
1200ft. Cert **'U'** (uncut).
Bella's Birthday – 29th August 1950
1387ft. 15mins. Cert **'U'** (with cuts)
Archive Status: Held at the NWFA.
NWFA holds 35 prints and digibeta for access. Also one-reel extract
(title unknown) held at Huntley Film Archive

(It's a Grand Life)
As You Were – 31st May 1960
1700ft. 18mins. Cert **'U'** (uncut)
Archive Status: Held at the NWFA.
NWFA holds 35 print and digibeta for access.
Rhythm and Atwell – Cert **'U'**
Archive Status: Held at the NFTVA/Huntley Film Archive

Hooray for Jollywood
The Life of John E. Blakeley & The Mancunian Film Corporation

Originally published in 2001 this republication has been eagerly awaited by many. With slightly expanded text and amendments plus the inclusion of many more photos and illustrations this book is a must for any British cinema history buff.

John E. Blakeley was a rare breed in the annals of British film history for all the films he made were produced solely for northern audiences. Indeed, it's probably fair to say that they were despised in the south of the country. Through necessity, his films were initially shot in London, although they were planned and conceived in his home city of Manchester. Made on a shoestring budget and usually bereft of a storyline his stock company of popular northern music hall eccentrics made them extremely popular with the Lancashire working-classes. His stars included George Formby, Nat Jackley, Norman Evans, Duggie Wakefield, Jewel & Warriss, Josef Locke and of course the inimitable Frank Randle.

In 1947 at a time when the film industry was virtually on its knees, Blakeley did the unthinkable and opened his own studio in Manchester. At a cost of £70,000, Film Studios (Manchester) was equipped and housed in an old Wesleyan Church, on Dickenson Road, Rusholme. Known locally as the 'Fun Factory' or 'Jollywood' the studio carried on turning out the popular comedies.

This book tells the story of John E. Blakeley his lifetime in the film industry and of a devoted family man. It also looks behind the scenes of film making both in London and Manchester. Many stories are told of the stars that worked at 'Jollywood' and many are featured in this book.

"The book is a splendid evocation of a golden era of Mancunian and Lancastrian humour...a book I could happily read over and over again". **Manchester Evening News.**

"...a must for all movie buffs". **Tameside Reporter.**

"This book is a 'must-have' for anybody interested in the subject matter contained here. I cannot think of any other work which so comprehensively tells us about this much-missed man and the films he made". **Peter Pollard - George Formby Society**

**Order NOW from your local bookshop priced £15.99
or contact address on page iv for discounted price.**

Published by History on your Doorstep
ISBN 0 9518012 9 5
(Use this number after January 2007 ISBN 978 0 9518012 9 1)

Printed in the United Kingdom
by Lightning Source UK Ltd.
115347UKS00002B/64-309